BOOK 2 – ECONOMICS

READINGS AND
LEARNING OUTCOME STATEMENTS

READINGS

The following material is a review of the Economics principles designed to address the learning outcome statements set forth by CFA Institute.

STUDY SESSION 4

Reading Assignments
Economics, Michael Parkin (Addison Wesley, 2005)

STUDY SESSION 5

Reading Assignments
Economics, Michael Parkin (Addison Wesley, 2005)

STUDY SESSION 6

Reading Assignments
Economics, Michael Parkin (Addison Wesley, 2005)

International Investments, 5th edition, Bruno Solnik and Dennis McLeavey (Addison Wesley, 2004)

LEARNING OUTCOME STATEMENTS (LOS)

STUDY SESSION 4

The topical coverage corresponds with the following CFA Institute assigned reading:
13.   **Elasticity**
      The candidate should be able to:
      a.   define and calculate price elasticity of demand, explain the difference between inelastic and elastic demand, and discuss the different factors that influence the elasticity of demand. (page 10)
      b.   explain and calculate other elasticities of demand. (page 12)
      c.   define and calculate elasticity of supply, and discuss the different factors that influence the elasticity of supply. (page 14)

The topical coverage corresponds with the following CFA Institute assigned reading:
14.   **Efficiency and Equity**
      The candidate should be able to:
      a.   distinguish between marginal benefit and marginal cost, calculate the efficient quantity, and discuss the associated efficiency and inefficiency. (page 20)
      b.   explain consumer surplus and marginal benefit, and how the value of a good or service is calculated. (page 21)
      c.   explain the relationship between marginal (or opportunity) cost and the minimum supply price, and define producer surplus. (page 22)
      d.   discuss the relationship between consumer surplus, producer surplus and equilibrium. (page 23)
      e.   explain how resources move to the most efficient allocation, the obstacles to achieve efficiency, and whether or not competitive markets use resources efficiently. (page 24)
      f.   explain the two groups of ideas about the fairness principle in light of the competitive market, and discuss the draw-backs of utilitarianism, and the symmetry principle. (page 25)

The topical coverage corresponds with the following CFA Institute assigned reading:
15.   **Markets in Action**
      The candidate should be able to:
      a.   discuss the impact of price ceilings on equilibrium in the short and in the long run, and supply and demand, and the impact of a price ceiling on the existence of a black market. (page 31)
      b.   explain the effects of a minimum wage and the effects when it is set either above or below the equilibrium wage level. (page 32)
      c.   discuss the impact of tax, subsidies, quotas, and markets for illegal goods on demand, supply and the market equilibrium. (page 33)

The topical coverage corresponds with the following CFA Institute assigned reading:
16.   **Organizing Production**
      The candidate should be able to:
      a.   explain the different types of opportunity cost and the relationship to economic profit, and calculate economic profit. (page 42)
      b.   discuss the firm's constraints and their impact on maximum profit. (page 43)
      c.   distinguish between technological and economic efficiency, and discuss under which circumstances a firm is technological or economically efficient. (page 43)
      d.   discuss the different ways a firm can organize production, how the principal-agent problem occurs, and which measures a firm can take to reduce the impact of the principal-agent problem. (page 45)
      e.   distinguish between the different types of business organization, discuss the advantages and disadvantages of each of the systems.both individually and relative to each other. (page 46)

f.   identify the different market types, and describe the conditions that characterize them. (page 46)

g.   explain the different ways in which concentration can be measured, and discuss the limitations of concentration measures. (page 47)

h.   discuss the two ways in which economic activity can be coordinated, and the different ways in which firms are often more efficient than markets. (page 48)

The topical coverage corresponds with the following CFA Institute assigned reading:

17.   **Output and Costs**

The candidate should be able to:

a.   explain why technology is a constraint on the increase of output in the short-term, how a firm can change output in the short run using the concepts of total, marginal, and average product, and the implication on short-run cost using the concepts of total, marginal, and average cost. (page 53)

b.   explain the shape of the marginal cost curve and the average total cost curve, and explain the relationships between the different cost curves. (page 57)

c.   discuss the concepts of diminishing returns and diminishing marginal product of capital. (page 58)

d.   explain the relationship between the long-run and short-run costs, and the different economies and diseconomies of scale. (page 59)

The topical coverage corresponds with the following CFA Institute assigned reading:

18.   **Perfect Competition**

The candidate should be able to:

a.   explain why firms in perfect competition are price takers, and discuss the relationship between demand, price and revenue. (page 64)

b.   discuss how the firm maximizes profit in perfect competition, analyze the marginal costs and revenue, and the concepts of economic profit and loss. (page 65)

c.   distinguish between the firm's and the industry's short-run supply curve, and explain the relationship between the two. (page 67)

d.   explain the relationship between the firm's marginal cost, marginal revenue, and price when a firm in perfect competition produces the quantity that maximizes profit. (page 67)

e.   discuss the impact of changes in demand, long-run adjustments, entry and exit, and changes in plant size on the long-run equilibrium. (page 67)

f.   discuss how a permanent change of demand or changes in technology impact price, output, and economic profit. (page 68)

The topical coverage corresponds with the following CFA Institute assigned reading:

19.   **Monopoly**

The candidate should be able to:

a.   discuss the characteristics of a monopoly, how they arise, the key features, and monopoly price strategies. (page 74)

b.   explain the relationship between price, marginal revenue, and marginal cost for a monopoly. (page 75)

c.   distinguish between monopoly and perfect competition, explain why a monopoly can set a higher price, and why a monopoly is considered inefficient. (page 75)

d.   explain the concepts of price discrimination. (page 76)

e.   discuss the reasons why a monopoly exists, how economies of scope and economies of scale can be achieved, and discuss the issues surrounding regulation of a natural monopoly. (page 77)

The topical coverage corresponds with the following CFA Institute assigned reading:

20. **Monopolistic Competition and Oligopoly**

The candidate should be able to:

a. discuss the characteristics of monopolistic competition, economic profit and loss in the short-run, output and price in the long-run, and discuss whether or not monopolistic competition is efficient. (page 82)

b. explain the differences in product development and marketing in monopolistic competition, the impact of advertising costs on the costs curves, and discuss whether or not advertising and branding is efficient in monopolistic competition. (page 84)

c. discuss the characteristics of an oligopoly, and the traditional oligopoly models. (page 85)

d. explain the prisoners' dilemma, how it can be applied to oligopoly price fixing, and the impact on cost, price, demand, and profits. (page 86)

STUDY SESSION 5

The topical coverage corresponds with the following CFA Institute assigned reading:

21. **Demand and Supply in Factor Markets**

The candidate should be able to:

a. explain the difference between marginal revenue and marginal revenue product. (page 93)

b. discuss how the labor demand curve is derived from the marginal revenue product curve, the conditions of profit maximization, the factors determining the demand and for labor, elasticity of the demand for labor, and labor market equilibrium. (page 93)

c. explain the difference between physical and financial capital, and how the demand for physical and financial capital are related to each other. (page 95)

d. discuss how a firm compares the future marginal revenue product of capital with the current price of capital, and the relationship between the quantity of financial capital demanded and the interest rate. (page 95)

e. discuss the main influences on demand and supply of capital, and capital market equilibrium. (page 95)

f. distinguish between the supply of renewable and non-renewable natural resources, and explain how equilibrium in a natural resource market is achieved. (page 96)

g. explain how differences occur between large and small incomes. (page 97)

h. distinguish between economic rent and opportunity costs. (page 97)

The topical coverage corresponds with the following CFA Institute assigned reading:

22. **Monitoring Cycles, Jobs, and the Price Level**

The candidate should be able to:

a. discuss the phases of the business cycle, how the start and end of a recession can be identified, and interpret the main labor market indicators and the relationship of the labor market indicators with the business cycle. (page 103)

b. discuss the concepts of aggregate hours and real wage rates, and how they relate to GDP. (page 104)

c. discuss the types of unemployment, full employment, and the relationship between unemployment and real GDP. (page 105)

d. explain the construction of the CPI, calculate CPI, discuss the relationship between CPI and the inflation rate, and discuss the problems associated with CPI bias. (page 105)

©2007 Schweser

The topical coverage corresponds with the following CFA Institute assigned reading:

23. **Aggregate Supply and Aggregate Demand**

The candidate should be able to:

a. explain the fundamentals of aggregate supply in the long run and in the short run, and discuss different reasons for changes in aggregate supply and the associated movements along the LAS and SAS curves. (page 112)

b. explain the effects that cause the aggregate demand curve to slope downwards, the main factors influencing aggregate demand, and how changes in these factors influence aggregate demand and the aggregate demand curve. (page 114)

c. discuss the difference between short-run and long-run macroeconomic equilibrium, and explain how the relationship between economic growth, inflation and changes in aggregate demand and aggregate supply influence short- and long-run macroeconomic equilibrium. (page 115)

d. compare and contrast the main schools of macroeconomic thought in relation to aggregate demand and aggregate supply. (page 117)

The topical coverage corresponds with the following CFA Institute assigned reading:

24. **Money, Banks, and the Federal Reserve**

The candidate should be able to:

a. discuss the functions of money, and the problems that arise when using commodities as money. (page 122)

b. compare and contrast the different depository institutions, their economic function, and the impact of financial regulation, deregulation, and innovation. (page 122)

c. explain how banks create money, and calculate the amount of loans a bank can generate, given a certain amount of deposits. (page 124)

d. discuss the goals and targets of the U.S. Fed, the balance sheet, and compare and contrast the policy tools. (page 124)

The topical coverage corresponds with the following CFA Institute assigned reading:

25. **Money, Interest, Real GDP, and the Price Level**

The candidate should be able to:

a. discuss the factors determining the demand for money, define the demand for money curve, and the effects of changes in real GDP and financial innovation on the demand for money curve. (page 128)

b. explain how interest rates are determined, the influence on the money market equilibrium, and the interaction between interest rate changes and the money supply. (page 129)

c. discuss the short-run and long-run effects of money on real GDP. (page 130)

d. explain the quantity theory of money. (page 131)

The topical coverage corresponds with the following CFA Institute assigned reading:

26. **Inflation**

The candidate should be able to:

a. discuss the difference between inflation and price-level, and calculate the inflation rate. (page 135)

b. distinguish between the factors resulting in demand-pull and cost-push inflation, and the impact on price levels, and aggregate demand and supply. (page 135)

c. discuss the effects of unanticipated inflation on the labor market and the market for financial capital. (page 137)

d. distinguish between anticipated and unanticipated inflation, and discuss the adverse effects of anticipated inflation. (page 137)

e. discuss the impact of inflation on unemployment, define the short-run and long-run Phillips curve, and discuss changes in the natural rate of unemployment. (page 138)

f. explain the impact of inflation on the nominal interest rate, and discuss how this is related to the money supply discussed in the previous reading. (page 139)

The topical coverage corresponds with the following CFA Institute assigned reading:
27. **Fiscal Policy**
    The candidate should be able to:
    a. interpret potential GDP, and the effects of income tax and tax on expenditure on potential GDP. (page 144)
    b. discuss the sources of investment sources, and the influence of fiscal policy on capital markets. (page 145)
    c. define the generational effects of fiscal policy. (page 146)
    d. compare and contrast how the government purchases multiplier, the tax multiplier, the balanced budget multiplier, and discretionary fiscal policy can assist in stabilizing the business cycle. (page 146)
    e. discuss the limitations of discretionary stabilizers, and distinguish between discretionary fiscal policy and automatic stabilizers. (page 147)

The topical coverage corresponds with the following CFA Institute assigned reading:
28. **Monetary Policy**
    The candidate should be able to:
    a. distinguish between price level stability, and sustainable real GDP growth. (page 152)
    b. compare and contrast the policies that can be implemented to achieve price level stability. (page 152)
    c. discuss policy credibility in relation to aggregate demand and aggregate supply, and the Phillips curve. (page 153)
    d. compare and contrast the new Monetarist and new Keynesian feedback rules. (page 156)

STUDY SESSION 6

The topical coverage corresponds with the following CFA Institute assigned reading:
29. **Trading with the World**
    The candidate should be able to:
    a. discuss opportunity cost associated with trade, how countries can gain from international trade, how countries determine whether to import, export or produce goods and services, and explain the gains of trade for all parties. (page 160)
    b. compare and contrast tariffs, non-tariff barriers, quotas and VERs with respect to international trade. (page 162)
    c. discuss the advantages and disadvantages of protection for each party, and explain the main reasons for trade restriction. (page 164)

The topical coverage corresponds with the following CFA Institute assigned reading:
30. **International Finance**
    The candidate should be able to:
    a. explain the different components of the Balance of Payments Accounts, the transactions recorded for import and export on the different accounts, and how the three sector balances are related. (page 168)
    b. explain the law of demand and the law of supply for foreign exchange, and how changes in demand and supply occur. (page 169)
    c. discuss the influence of supply and demand on the exchange rate, and why exchange rates can be volatile. (page 171)
    d. distinguish between purchasing power and interest rate parity. (page 172)

e. discuss how and why intervention by a central bank in the exchange market may be required. (page 172)

The topical coverage corresponds with the following CFA Institute assigned reading:

31. **Foreign Exchange**
The candidate should be able to:
a. define direct and indirect methods of foreign exchange quotations and convert direct (indirect) foreign exchange quotations into indirect (direct) foreign exchange quotations. (page 178)
b. calculate and interpret the spread on a foreign currency quotation and explain how spreads on foreign currency quotations can differ as a result of market conditions, bank/dealer positions, and trading volume. (page 195)
c. calculate and interpret currency cross rates, given two spot exchange quotations involving three currencies. (page 179)
d. distinguish between the spot and forward markets for foreign exchange. (page 181)
e. calculate and interpret the spread on a forward foreign currency quotation and explain how spreads on forward foreign currency quotations can differ as a result of market conditions, bank/dealer positions, trading volume, and maturity/length of contract. (page 197)
f. calculate and interpret a forward discount or premium and express it as an annualized rate. (page 198)
g. explain interest rate parity and illustrate covered interest arbitrage. (page 198)

The topical coverage corresponds with the following CFA Institute assigned reading:

32. **Foreign Exchange Parity Relations**
The candidate should be able to:
a. explain how exchange rates are determined in a flexible or floating exchange rate system. (page 195)
b. explain the role of each component of the balance-of-payments accounts. (page 195)
c. explain how current account deficits or surpluses and financial account deficits or surpluses affect an economy. (page 196)
d. describe the factors that cause a nation's currency to appreciate or depreciate. (page 196)
e. explain how monetary and fiscal policies affect the exchange rate and balance-of-payments components. (page 197)
f. describe a fixed exchange rate and a pegged exchange rate system. (page 198)
g. discuss absolute purchasing power parity and relative purchasing power parity. (page 198)

ELASTICITY

EXAM FOCUS

Elasticity is a measure of the ratio of the percentage change in one variable to the percentage change in another variable. It is commonly used as a measure of how sensitive the quantity demanded is to changes in the price of a good. After learning all about price elasticity of demand, learn how to apply this concept to calculate and interpret the cross elasticity of demand, the income elasticity of demand, and the elasticity of supply. You must also gain a good understanding of the factors that influence a good's elasticity of demand and elasticity of supply.

LOS 13.a: Define and calculare price elasticity of demand, explain the difference berween inelastic and ecastic demand, and disuss the different factors that influence the elasticity of demand.

The **price elasticity of demand** measures the change in the quantity demanded in response to a change in market price (i.e., a movement along a demand curve).

The formula used to calculate the price elasticity of demand is:

$$\text{price elasticity of demand} = \frac{\text{percent change in quantity demanded}}{\text{percent change in price}} = \frac{\%\Delta Q}{\%\Delta P}$$

$$\text{where: percent change} = \frac{\text{change in value}}{\text{average value}} = \frac{\text{ending value} - \text{beginning value}}{\left(\dfrac{\text{ending value} + \text{beginning value}}{2}\right)}$$

Professor's Note: It is customary to use average values when calculating percentage changes used in elasticity computations. This way a change from 8 to 10 and a change from 10 to 8 both result in the same percentage change of 2/9 = 22.2%. Use this method on the exam!

Figure 1 illustrates the general categories of price elasticity of demand. A discussion of each is presented below:

- If a *small* percentage price change results in a *large* percentage change in quantity demanded, the demand for that good is said to be *highly elastic*. Apples are an example of an elastic good. The absolute value of price elasticity is greater than one, meaning that the percentage change in Q is greater than the percentage change in P.
- If a *large* percentage price change results in a *small* percentage change in quantity demanded, demand is *relatively inelastic*. Gasoline is an example of a relatively inelastic good. The absolute value of price elasticity is less than one, meaning that the percentage change in Q is less than the percentage change in P.
- A *perfectly elastic* demand curve is horizontal, and its elasticity is infinite. If the price increases, quantity demanded goes to zero.
- A *perfectly inelastic* demand curve is vertical, and elasticity is zero. If the price changes, there will be no change in the quantity demanded.

Figure 1: Price Elasticity of Demand

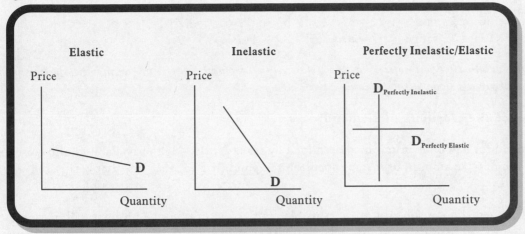

Example: Price elasticity

If the price of product A is increased from $1.00 per unit to $1.10 per unit, the demand will decrease from 5.0 million units to 4.8 million units. Calculate the price elasticity of demand for product A and determine if demand for product A is elastic or inelastic.

Answer:

The percentage change in quantity = [(4.8 – 5.0)] / [(5.0 + 4.8) / 2] = –0.2 / 4.9 = –0.041 = –4.1%. The percentage change in price = [(1.10 – 1.00)] / [(1.10 + 1.00) / 2] = 0.10 / 1.05 = 0.095 = 9.5%. So, the price elasticity of demand for product A is –4.1% / 9.5% = –0.43. Since the absolute value of the price elasticity of demand is less than 1.0, demand for product A is *inelastic*.

Price elasticity of demand is different at different points along a demand curve. Consider the demand curve presented in Figure 2.

Figure 2: Price Elasticity of Demand vs. Location on the Demand Curve

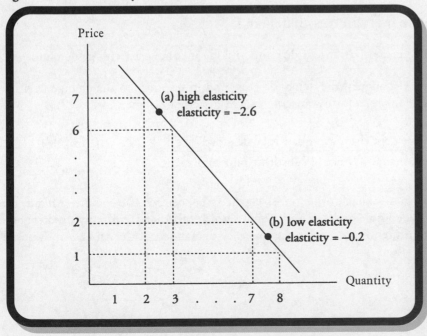

- At point (a), in a higher price range, the price elasticity of the good is greater than at point (b) in a lower price range.
- Price elasticity in the $6 to $7 range is [(2 – 3) / 2.5] / [(7 – 6) / 6.5] = –2.6.
- Price elasticity in the $1 to $2 range is [(7 – 8) / 7.5] / [(2 – 1) / 1.5] = –0.2

Professor's Note: It is important that you notice that price elasticity of demand changes as you move along the demand curve. Elasticity is not simply the slope of the demand curve!

Factors That Influence the Elasticity of Demand

Price elasticity of demand for a good is primarily determined by three factors: (1) the availability and closeness of substitute goods, (2) the relative amount of income spent on the good, and (3) the time that has passed since the price change of the good.

- *Availability of substitutes.* If good substitutes are available, a price increase in one product will induce consumers to switch to a substitute good. As such, elasticity of demand is determined, in part, by the availability of good substitutes. For example, the demand for gasoline is inelastic (less than one) because it has no practical substitutes, at least in the short run. On the other hand, the price elasticity for beef is high because there are many suitable substitutes, such as fish or chicken.
- *Relative amount of income spent on the good.* When the portion of consumer budgets spent on a particular good is relatively small, demand for that good will tend to be relatively *inelastic*. For example, consider toothpaste versus automobiles. Since people spend a relatively small amount of their incomes on toothpaste, a 10% increase in the price of toothpaste is not likely to change their consumption significantly, if at all. On the other hand, since the cost of an automobile is typically a significant proportion of a person's budget, a 10% increase in car prices may cause annual demand for cars to decrease significantly. Consumers can drive less and do more repairs to keep existing vehicles longer, or they can switch to alternative forms of transportation.
- *Time since the price change.* The price elasticity of demand for most products is greater in the long run than in the short run. Consider the situation in the 1970s when oil and gas prices rose significantly from historical levels. The short-run response was that people simply drove less (picking a closer vacation spot, taking the bus to work, or carpooling) and/or kept their homes at a slightly lower temperature in the winter. Over time, however, other substitutions were made. People bought smaller cars, chose to live closer to work, installed more home insulation, and installed wood burning stoves as an alternative source of heat.

LOS 13.b: Explain and calculate other elasticities of demand.

Two other elasticities of demand are (1) cross elasticity of demand and (2) income elasticity of demand.

Cross elasticity of demand measures the change in the demand for a good in response to the change in price of a substitute or complementary good. The formula for calculating cross elasticity of demand is:

$$\text{cross elasticity of demand} = \frac{\text{percent change in quantity demanded}}{\text{percent change in price of substitute or complement}}$$

When two goods are reasonable substitutes for each other, cross elasticity is positive. On the other hand, cross elasticity is negative when two goods are complements. Complements are goods that are usually used together, so that an increase in the price of one would tend to decrease the quantity demanded of the other. An example would be automobiles and gasoline.

Example: Cross elasticity of demand (substitutes)

Suppose that the price of ice cream at your local ice cream parlor is $1.50 per scoop and 600 scoops per day are sold. Now, assume that at the same parlor, the price of frozen yogurt increases $1.25 to $1.75 per scoop. While nothing else has changed that could affect customers' buying patterns, the sale of ice cream increased from 600 to 750 scoops per day. Calculate the cross elasticity of demand of ice cream relative to frozen yogurt.

Answer:

The average quantity of ice cream demanded is (750 + 600) / 2 = 675 scoops, so the percentage change in the quantity of ice cream demanded is (750 – 600) / 675 = +22.2%. The average price for frozen yogurt is ($1.25 + $1.75) / 2 = $1.50 per scoop, so the percentage change in the price of frozen yogurt is ($1.75 – $1.25) / $1.50 = +33.3%. The cross elasticity of demand for ice cream relative to the price of yogurt is 22.2 / 33.3 = +0.67.

Professor's Note: For many people, ice cream and frozen yogurt are substitutes, so the cross elasticity of ice cream relative to the price of frozen yogurt is positive.

Example: Cross elasticity of demand (complements)

Suppose that the price of donuts is $0.50 and the local donut shop serves 800 donuts per day. At the same donut shop, the price of coffee is increased from $0.75 to $1.25 per cup. No other changes have occurred and the number of donuts sold decreases to 600 per day. Calculate the cross elasticity of demand for donuts relative to the price of coffee.

Answer:

The average quantity of donuts demanded is (800 + 600) / 2 = 700, so the percentage change in the quantity of donuts demanded is = (600 – 800) / 700 = –28.6%. The average price for a cup of coffee is ($0.75 + $1.25) / 2 = $1.00 per cup, so the percentage change in the price of coffee is ($1.25 – $0.75) / $1.00 = 50%. The cross elasticity of demand for ice cream relative to yogurt is –28.6 / 50 = –0.57.

Professor's Note: Coffee and donuts are complements, so the cross elasticity of donuts relative to the price of coffee is negative.

The **income elasticity of demand** measures the sensitivity of the quantity of a good or service demanded to a change in a consumer's income. The formula for income elasticity of demand is:

$$\text{income elasticity of demand} = \frac{\text{percent change in quantity demanded}}{\text{percent change in income}}$$

Income elasticity of demand is related to the type of good being evaluated. An **inferior good** has negative income elasticity. As income increases (decreases), quantity demanded decreases (increases). Inferior goods include things like bus travel and generic margarine. In contrast, a **normal good** has positive income elasticity, which means that as income increases (decreases), demand for the good increases (decreases). Bread and tobacco are generally considered normal goods. Normal goods that have relatively low income elasticities (between 0 and +1) are considered *necessities,* while normal goods with high income elasticities (values greater than 1) are generally considered *luxury goods.*

Example: Income elasticity

Suppose that your income has risen by $10,000 from an initial rate of $50,000. Further, your consumption of bread has increased from 100 loaves per year to 110 loaves per year. Given this information, determine whether bread is a necessity or a luxury good.

Answer:

Your average income is ($50,000 + $60,000) / 2 = $55,000, so the percentage change in income is ($60,000 – $50,000) / $55,000 = 18.2%. Similarly, the average quantity of bread demanded is (100 + 110) / 2 = 105 loaves, so the percentage change in the quantity of bread demanded is (110 – 100) / 105 = 9.5%. Thus, the income elasticity of bread is 9.5/18.2 = 0.52. Since its income elasticity of demand is less than 1.0, bread must be a necessity.

LOS 13.c: Define and calculate elasticity of supply, and discuss the diffrent factors that influence the elasticity of supply.

The **price elasticity of supply** is similar to the price elasticity of demand. It is a measure of the responsiveness of the quantity supplied to changes in price. That is:

$$\text{price elasticity of supply} = \frac{\text{percent change in quantity supplied}}{\text{percent change in price}} = \frac{\%\Delta Q}{\%\Delta P}$$

As shown in panel (a) of Figure 3 below, a perfectly inelastic (vertical) supply curve has an elasticity of supply of zero. Panel (b) illustrates a perfectly elastic (horizontal) supply curve with an elasticity of supply equal to infinity. For most goods and services, however, the elasticity of supply falls somewhere between these two extremes.

Figure 3: Inelastic and Elastic Supply

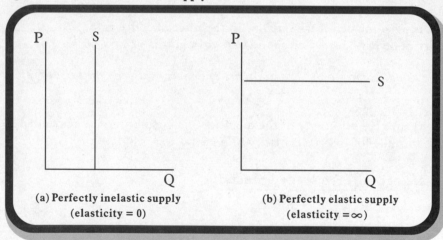

(a) Perfectly inelastic supply (elasticity = 0)

(b) Perfectly elastic supply (elasticity = ∞)

Example: Elasticity of supply

Suppose that the demand curve for coffee increases and that the equilibrium price for a pound of coffee increases from $8 to $10 per pound. At the new price, the quantity supplied increases from 100,000 kilograms per month to 120,000 kilograms per month, although the supply curve has not shifted. Calculate the elasticity of supply for coffee.

Answer:

In this situation, the average quantity of coffee supplied is (100,000 + 120,000) / 2 = 110,000 kilograms, and the average price of coffee is ($8 + $10) / 2 = $9 per pound. So, the percentage change in quantity is (120,000 – 100,000) / 110,000 = 18.18% and the percentage change in price is (10 – 8) / 9 = 22.22%. Thus, the elasticity of supply is 18.18 / 22.22 = 0.82.

Factors that influence the elasticity of supply are: (1) the available substitutes for resources (inputs) used to produce the good and (2) the time that has elapsed since the price change.

Available resource substitutions. When a good or service can only be produced using unique or rare inputs, the elasticity of supply will be low. That is, the short-run supply curve may be nearly vertical for these goods. On the other hand, consider agricultural goods such as sugar and rice. These goods can be grown using the same land (resources), and the opportunity cost of substituting one for the other is nearly constant. As such, both of these products have highly elastic (nearly horizontal) supply curves.

Supply decision time frame. Three time-dependent supply curves must be considered when evaluating how the length of time following a price change affects the elasticity of supply: (1) momentary supply, (2) short-term supply, and (3) long-term supply.

1. *Momentary supply* refers to the change in the quantity of a good supplied immediately following the price change. When producers cannot change the output of a good immediately, the momentary supply curve is vertical or nearly vertical, and the good is highly inelastic. Grapes and oranges are examples of goods for which the quantity produced cannot be immediately changed in response to price changes. On the other hand, goods such as electricity have nearly perfectly elastic momentary supply curves. No matter what the demand for electricity, the amount provided can be changed without a significant change in price.

2. *Short-term supply* refers to the shape a supply curve takes on as the sequence of long-term adjustments are made to the production process. For example, manufacturing firms will adjust the amount of labor they use in response to a price change. The resulting increase or decrease in the cost of this input changes the shape of the supply curve. As time passes, additional adjustments may be made, such as technological innovations and training new workers, which will further change the shape of the supply curve, making it more elastic the longer the adjustment period.

3. *Long-term supply* refers to the shape of the supply curve after all of the possible ways of adjusting supply have been employed. This is usually a lengthy process. It may involve building new factories or distribution systems, and training workers to operate them. Typically, long-term supply is more elastic than short-term supply, which is more elastic than momentary supply.

KEY CONCEPTS

1. Price elasticity of demand measures the change in the quantity demanded in response to a change in market price.

$$\text{price elasticity of demand} = \frac{\text{percent change in quantity demanded}}{\text{percent change in price}} = \frac{\%\Delta Q}{\%\Delta P}$$

   where %Δ uses average values

2. Price elasticity of demand for a good is primarily determined by three factors: (1) the relative attractiveness of substitute goods, (2) the relative proportion of income spent on the good, and (3) the time that has passed since the price change occured.

3. Cross elasticity of demand measures the change in the demand for a good in response to a change in the price of another good. The formula for calculating cross elasticity of demand is:

$$\text{cross elasticity of demand} = \frac{\text{percent change in quantity demanded}}{\text{percent change in price of substitute or complement}}$$

4. Cross elasticity of demand is positive for goods that are substitutes for each other, and negative for goods that are complements.

5. Income elasticity of demand measures the sensitivity of the quantity demanded to an increase or decrease in a consumer's income. The formula for income elasticity of demand is:

$$\text{income elasticity of demand} = \frac{\text{percent change in quantity demanded}}{\text{percent change in income}}$$

6. Inferior goods have negative income elasticities and normal goods have positive income elasticities. Normal goods that have income elasticities between 0 and +1 are considered necessities, while normal goods with income elasticities greater than +1 are generally considered luxury goods.

7. The price elasticity of supply is a measure of the responsiveness of the quantity supplied to changes in price.

$$\text{price elasticity of supply} = \frac{\text{percent change in quantity supplied}}{\text{percent change in price}}$$

8. Elasticity of supply is influenced by the time frame within which the supply decision is made and by the ability to make substitutions between productive resources.

CONCEPT CHECKERS: ELASTICITY

1. If the number of ice cream bars demanded increases from 19 to 21 when the price decreases from $1.50 to $0.50, the price elasticity of demand is:
    A. −5.
    B. −0.2.
    C. −0.1.
    D. 1.

2. If quantity demanded increases 20% when the price drops 2%, this good exhibits:
    A. elastic, but not perfectly elastic demand.
    B. inelastic, but not perfectly inelastic demand.
    C. perfectly elastic demand.
    D. perfectly inelastic demand.

3. The primary factors that influence the price elasticity of demand for a product are:
    A. changes in consumers' incomes, the time since the price change occurred, and the availability of substitute goods.
    B. changes in consumers' price expectations, changes in consumers' incomes, and the expected time until the price change will occur.
    C. the proportions of consumers' budgets spent on the product, the size of the shift in the demand curve for a product, and changes in consumers' price expectations.
    D. the availability of substitute goods, the time that has elapsed since the price of the good changed, and the proportions of consumers' budgets spent on the product.

4. If a good has elastic demand, a small percentage price increase will cause:
    A. no change in the quantity demanded.
    B. a smaller percentage increase in the quantity demanded.
    C. a larger percentage decrease in the quantity demanded.
    D. a larger percentage increase in quantity demanded.

5. The cross elasticity of demand for a substitute good and the income elasticity for an inferior good are:

	Cross elasticity	Income elasticity
A.	< 0	> 0, < 1
B.	< 0	< 0
C.	> 0	> 0, < 1
D.	> 0	< 0

6. Income elasticity is defined as the percentage change in:
    A. quantity demanded divided by the percentage change in income.
    B. income divided by the percentage change in the quantity demanded.
    C. quantity demanded divided by the percentage change in the price of the product.
    D. the price of a product divided by the percentage change in the quantity demanded.

7. If quantity demanded for a good rises 20% when incomes rise 2%, the good is a(n):
    A. necessity.
    B. luxury good.
    C. inferior good.
    D. inelastic good.

8. When household incomes go up and the quantity of a product demanded goes down, the product is a(n):
   A. necessity.
   B. luxury good.
   C. inferior good.
   D. normal good.

9. If the price elasticity of demand is −2 and the price of the product decreases by 5%, the quantity demanded will:
   A. decrease 2%.
   B. decrease 10%.
   C. increase 5%.
   D. increase 10%.

10. Which of the following is *most likely* a factor that influences the elasticity of supply for a good?
    A. The price of the productive resources used to produce it.
    B. The proportion of consumers' budgets spent on the good.
    C. The availability of substitute productive resources.
    D. The price elasticity of demand for the good.

ANSWERS – CONCEPT CHECKERS: ELASTICITY

1. C   If the number of widgets demanded changes from 19 to 21 when the price changes from $1.50 to $0.50, the percentage change in quantity is $(21 - 19) / [(21 + 19) / 2] = 10\%$ and the percentage change in price is $(0.50 - 1.50) / [(1.50 + 0.50) / 2] = -100\%$. Thus, price elasticity $= 10\% / -100\% = -0.1$.

2. A   If quantity demanded increases 20% when the price drops 2%, this good exhibits elastic demand. Whenever demand changes by a greater percentage than price, demand is considered to be elastic.

3. D   The three primary factors influencing the price elasticity of demand for a good are the availability of substitute goods, the proportions of consumers' budgets spent on the good, and the time since the price change. If there are good substitutes, when the price of the good goes up, some customers will switch to substitute goods. For goods that represent a relatively small proportion of consumers' budgets, a change in price will have little effect on the quantity demanded. For most goods, the price elasticity of demand is greater in the long run than in the short run.

4. C   If a good has elastic demand, a small price increase will cause a larger decrease in the quantity demanded. Demand is elastic when the percentage change in quantity demanded is larger than the percentage change in price.

5. D   The cross elasticity of substitutes is positive and the income elasticity of an inferior good is negative.

6. A   Income elasticity is defined as the percentage change in quantity demanded divided by the percentage change in income. Normal goods have positive values for income elasticity and inferior goods have negative income elasticity.

7. B   A luxury good is a good for which the percentage increase in quantity demanded is greater than the percentage increase in income. A necessity is a good for which, when income increases by a given percentage, the quantity demanded increases, but by a smaller percentage. Since quantity demanded rose 20% when incomes rose 2%, the good in question is a luxury good.

8. C   When household incomes increase and the quantity demanded of a good decreases, the product is an inferior good. Examples of inferior goods are bus travel and margarine (for some income ranges).

9. D   If the price elasticity of demand is −2, and the price of the product decreases by 5%, the quantity demanded will increase 10%. The value, −2, indicates that the percentage increase in the quantity demanded will be twice the percentage decrease in price.

10. C   The factors that influence the elasticity of supply are the possible resource substitutes and the time frame for the supply decision.

EFFICIENCY AND EQUITY

EXAM FOCUS

The primary focus of this review is the efficient allocation of resources. The concepts of marginal benefit, marginal cost, consumer surplus, and producer surplus are all central to understanding the efficient allocation of productive resources. A basic understanding of the obstacles to the efficient allocation of resources and of the two schools of thought on economic "fairness" should be sufficient.

LOS 14.a: Distinguish between marginal benefit and marginal cost, calculate the efficient quantiry, and discuss the associated efficiency and inefficiency.

Marginal benefit is the benefit an individual gets from consuming an additional unit of a good or service. Marginal benefit is quantified as the maximum price that a consumer is willing to pay for one additional unit of a good or service. In most cases, the marginal benefit of a good or service decreases as the quantity consumed increases. For instance, the amount a consumer is willing to pay for a piece of cheesecake decreases as the number of pieces of cheesecake consumed over a given period increases. This concept is known as the *principle of decreasing marginal benefit* or *diminishing marginal utility*.

Marginal cost is the cost of producing one more unit of output. Marginal cost is referred to as an *opportunity cost* because it represents the value (in their next-highest-valued use) of the resources required to produce an additional unit of output. For example, the cost to a baker of providing an additional cheesecake is the value of whatever is the next most valuable product that could be produced with the ingredients and labor required to make the cheesecake. Perhaps, a cherry pie.

Figure 1 illustrates the marginal cost (MC) and marginal benefit (MB) curves for cheesecakes and three possible situations: (1) the marginal benefit is greater than marginal cost, (2) the marginal benefit is less than marginal cost, and (3) the marginal benefit equals marginal cost. Let's examine each of these situations.

Marginal benefit > marginal cost. Referring to the marginal benefit curve in Figure 1, we can see that when the quantity of cheesecakes produced is 1,000 per day, the marginal benefit is $30, which means that a consumer is willing to pay $30 for the 1,000th cheesecake offered for sale.

From the marginal cost curve in Figure 1, we see that the cost of producing the 1,000th cheesecake is $10, which is $20 less than the marginal benefit of the 1,000th cheesecake. This means that if the 1,000th cheesecake is baked, consumers are willing to pay $20 more than the baker's cost of producing it. In other words, the value of the 1,000th cheesecake to consumers exceeds the value of the goods or services that must be forgone by the baker to produce the 1,000th cheesecake. In this situation, more value is created by using resources to increase the production of cheesecakes and decrease the production of other goods. The efficient quantity of cheesecakes is the output for which the marginal benefit equals the marginal cost. In Figure 1, we see that this occurs at a production level of 2,000 cheesecakes.

Marginal benefit < marginal cost. From the marginal benefit curve in Figure 1, we can see that consumers are willing to pay only $10 for the 3,000th cheesecake; the marginal benefit to society of the 3,000th cheesecake is $10. The marginal cost curve in Figure 1 shows that the cost of producing the 3,000th cheesecake is $30, which is $20 more than its marginal benefit. The value of the goods and services that must be forgone to produce the

3,000th cheesecake is $20 more than what consumers are willing to pay for it. In this situation, more value will be created by reducing the quantity of cheesecakes produced and reallocating the resources to the production of other goods.

Marginal benefit = marginal cost. At the quantity of production where the marginal cost equals marginal benefit, the total value created by producing a good is at a maximum. We refer to this as the optimal quantity of production and say that productive resources are being allocated efficiently. In terms of our simple example, the 2,001st cheesecake will require resources that are more highly valued when used for production of other goods, while the value in other production of the resources required to produce the 1,999th cheesecake is less than their value when used to produce a cheesecake.

Figure 1: The Efficient Quantity of Cheesecake

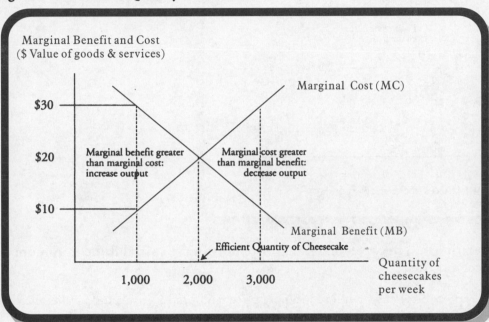

LOS 14.b: Explain consumer surplus and marginal benefit, and how the value of a good or service is calculated.

The value, or marginal benefit, that we derive from a good or service is often greater than the amount we have to pay for it. **Consumer surplus** is the difference between the total value consumers place on the quantity of a good produced and the total amount they must pay for that quantity. For an individual, consumer surplus is defined as the sum of the differences between what that individual is *willing to pay* for each individual unit of a good or service that he or she consumes and the amount that she *actually pays* for each of these units.

Consumer surplus depends on consumers' demand (marginal benefit) curves. For example, at a given market price, the consumer surplus for the third slice of cheesecake to a cheesecake lover will be greater than the consumer surplus for the average cheesecake consumer. This situation is described in Figure 2 where the weekly cheesecake demand (marginal benefit) is depicted for a cheesecake lover named Juan. In Figure 2, we see that the market price for a slice of cheesecake is $5.00 and that Juan is willing to pay $7.00 for one slice per week. This means that Juan's consumer surplus from the first slice of cheesecake is $7.00 − $5.00 = $2.00. Assuming Juan buys five slices of cheesecake in one week, the consumer surplus to Juan is the sum of the consumer surpluses generated by the consumption of each of these five slices. This is represented by the more darkly shaded area in Figure 2. Note that Juan gains no consumer surplus from consuming the fifth piece. He values it at $5.00, an amount just equal to its price. To determine Juan's weekly consumer surplus, we can calculate this area. For Juan, consumer surplus for five slices of cheesecake is:

($7.00 – $5.00) + ($6.50 – $5.00) + ($6.00 – $5.00) + ($5.50 – $5.00) + ($5.00 – $5.00) = $5.00

Figure 2: Juan's Demand for Cheesecake and Consumer Surplus

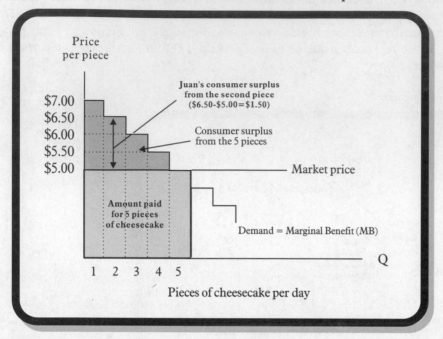

LOS 14.c: Explain the relationship between marginal (or opportunity) cost and the minimum supply price, and define producer surplus.

The concepts of marginal (opportunity) cost, minimum supply price, and producer surplus parallel the concepts of marginal benefit (value), price, and consumer surplus.

For producers of goods and services, marginal cost is the value of the alternatives that producers forego to provide a given good or service, whereas price is what they receive for the good or service when it is sold. Marginal cost is the opportunity cost (value of the foregone opportunity) of producing an additional unit of a good. This is the minimum price, or *minimum supply price*, that producers must receive in order for them to willingly supply an additional unit of a good. It is this minimum acceptable price that determines the quantity that producers supply. Just as the marginal benefit curve is equal to the demand curve for a good or service, the *marginal cost curve for a good or service is the same as the supply curve for that good or service.*

Whenever the market price for a good or service exceeds the marginal cost of producing it, producers realize a producer surplus. **Producer surplus** is formally defined as the sum of the differences between the price received for each unit of good produced and the opportunity cost of each unit for the total units produced.

Producer surplus is illustrated in Figure 3 for a given bakery's supply (marginal cost) curve for cheesecakes. From this cheesecake supply curve, we see that the minimum supply price (marginal cost) for the bakery to produce the 2,000th cheesecake is $20. Note in Figure 3 that the marginal cost of the 1,000th cheesecake is $10 and that the producer surplus from the 1,000th cheesecake is $20 – $10 = $10. Assume that $20 is the equilibrium market price for cheesecakes. So, for this bakery, producer surplus is the sum of the producer surpluses associated with each cheesecake produced up to the 2,000th cheesecake produced. Producer surplus is represented by the shaded triangular area above the supply curve (and below the price of $20) in Figure 3. The area below the supply curve in Figure 3 represents the firm's opportunity cost of producing 2,000 cheesecakes.

Figure 3: Producer Surplus, Supply, and Marginal Cost

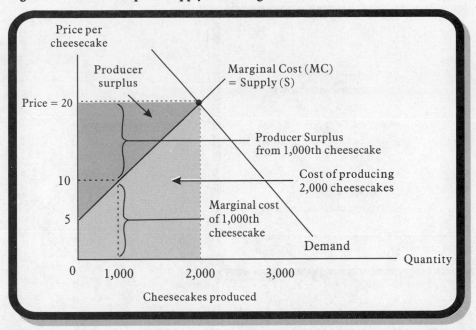

LOS 14.d: Discuss the relationship between consumer surplus, producer surplus and equilibrium.

When the marginal benefit from a good or service is aggregated among all consumers in the market, the resulting marginal benefit curve is called the **marginal social benefit** (MSB) curve and is the market demand curve. Similarly, if the individual marginal cost curves are aggregated among all producers, the resulting marginal cost curve is referred to as the **marginal social cost** (MSC) curve and is the market supply curve.

Given the MSB (market demand) and MSC (market supply) curves for a given product in a competitive market, the equilibrium price and quantity for the product will be determined by the intersection of the MSB and MSC curves. *At this equilibrium price and quantity, the sum of the consumer and producer surpluses is at a maximum.* This is illustrated in Figure 4. The point here is that in competitive markets, when the equilibrium quantity of each good is produced, the economic gains to society are maximized. Resources will be allocated to the production of all goods in such a way as to maximize the total value to society of the economy's production.

Figure 4: Consumer and Producer Surpluses at Equilibrium

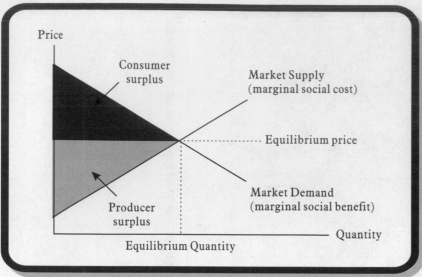

LOS 14.e: Explain how resources move to the most efficient allocation, the obstacles to achieve efficiency, and whether or not competitive markets use resources efficiently.

We can examine how the allocation of resources moves toward their highest-valued use by looking at the example of microwave ovens. Upon their market introduction, microwave ovens were expensive and were primarily sold to restaurants. As technological advances in production reduced the cost of producing microwave ovens, supply increased and prices fell. The (equilibrium) quantity demanded increased, resulting in more resources being devoted to the production of microwave ovens. These resources were removed from the production of other goods and services where the value of what they could produce was less than the value of the microwave ovens that they could produce. Changes in consumer tastes and advances in technology lead to a constant reallocation of productive resources in an economy from one use to another, as the maximum benefit to society can be achieved by the production of a different mix of goods and services.

Adam Smith, considered the father of economics, wrote of the individual in an economy in his 1776 book, *The Wealth of Nations:* "He generally, indeed, neither intends to promote the public interest, nor knows how much he is promoting it. By preferring the support of domestic to that of foreign industry, he intends only his own security; and by directing that industry in such a manner as its produce may be of the greatest value, he intends only his own gain, and he is in this, as in many other cases, *led by an invisible hand to promote an end which was no part of his intention*...By pursuing his own interest he frequently promotes that of the society more effectually than when he really intends to promote it."

Two centuries later, in the 1987 movie *Wall Street*, the character Gordon Gecko famously said, "The point is, ladies and gentleman, that greed—for lack of a better word—is good." While the language is quite different, the sentiment is the same. By pursuing their own self-interests, workers, consumers, and producers produce and consume an amount and mixture of goods and services that maximizes the overall benefit to society of economic production and consumption. When markets are competitive, unconstrained, and well functioning, the resulting mix of goods and services produced is the optimal one, and the allocation of productive resources is efficient. It is as if people were guided by an "invisible hand" to serve society's interests instead of their own.

There are, however, obstacles to this idealized view of the operation of competitive markets. Some of the **obstacles to the efficient allocation of productive resources** are:

- **Price controls**, such as price ceilings and price floors, distort the incentives of supply and demand, leading to levels of production different from those of an unregulated market. Rent control and a minimum wage are examples of a price ceiling and a price floor.

- **Taxes and trade restrictions**, such as subsidies and quotas, also impede the natural process toward the efficient allocation of resources. *Taxes* increase the price that buyers pay and decrease the amount that sellers receive. *Subsidies* are government payments to producers that effectively increase the amount sellers receive and decrease the price buyers pay, leading to production of more than the efficient quantity of the good. *Quotas* are government-imposed production limits, resulting in production of less than the efficient quantity of the good. All three lead markets away from producing the quantity for which marginal cost equals marginal benefit.

- **Monopoly** refers to a situation where there is a single seller of a particular good or service. A single seller will choose a (profit-maximizing) quantity of production that is less than the efficient level of production.

- **External costs** are costs imposed on others by the production of goods, and they are not taken into account in the production decision. An example of an external cost is the cost imposed on fishermen by a firm that pollutes the ocean as part of its production process. The firm does not necessarily consider the resulting decrease in the fish population as part of its cost of production, even though this cost is borne by the fishing industry and society. In this case, the output quantity of the polluting firm is greater than the efficient quantity. The societal costs are greater than the direct costs of production the producer bears. The result is an over-allocation of resources to production by the polluting firm.

- **External benefits** are benefits of consumption enjoyed by people other than the buyers of the good and are not taken into account in buyers' consumption decisions. An example of an external benefit is the development of a tropical garden on the grounds of an industrial complex that is located along a busy thoroughfare. The developer of the grounds only considers the marginal benefit to the firms within the complex when deciding whether to take on the grounds improvement, not the benefit received by the travelers who take pleasure in the view of the garden. External benefits result in demand curves that do not represent the societal benefit of the good or service, so that the equilibrium quantity produced and consumed is less than the efficient quantity.

- **Public goods and common resources.** *Public goods* are goods and services that are consumed by people regardless of whether or not they paid for them. National defense is a public good. If others choose to pay to protect a country from outside attack, all the residents of the country enjoy such protection, whether they have paid for their share of it or not. Competitive markets will produce less than the efficient quantity of public goods because each person can benefit from public goods without paying for their production. This is often referred to as the "free rider" problem. A *common resource* is one which all may use. An example of a common resource is an unrestricted ocean fishery. Each fisherman will fish in the ocean at no cost and will have little incentive to maintain or improve the resource. Since individuals do not have the incentive to fish at the economically efficient (sustainable) level, over-fishing is the result. Left to competitive market forces, common resources are generally over-used and production of related goods or services is greater than the efficient amount.

LOS 14.f: Explain the two groups of ideas about the fairness principle in light of the competitive market, and discuss the draw-backs of utilitarianism, and the symmetry principle.

Two schools of thought regarding the fairness of the efficient allocation of resources in a competitive market focus on whether the results of the allocation of resources are fair and on whether the rules of the economic allocation of resources are fair.

One school of economic thought regarding efficient resource allocation is based on the general idea that it is not fair that individuals have dramatically different incomes. For instance, this school of thought contends that it is not fair that the CEO of a firm earns a significantly higher income than the common laborer. From within this framework, some early economists believed in the idea of utilitarianism—that the value of an economy is maximized when each person owns an equal amount of the resources. This early belief in utilitarianism has been proven wrong, but it warrants a closer look.

Utilitarianism is an idea that proposes that the greatest good occurs to the greatest number of people when wealth is transferred from the rich to the poor to the point where everyone has the same wealth. Proponents of utilitarianism argue that: (1) everyone wants and needs the same things and has the same capacity to enjoy life, and (2) the marginal benefit of a dollar is greater for the poor than the rich, so the gain in marginal benefit to the poor from a transfer of wealth is greater than the loss of marginal benefit to the rich. Since more is gained than lost, the end result after the wealth transfer is that the total combined marginal benefit of the rich and the poor will be greater.

The biggest problem with the utilitarian concept is the trade-off between fairness and efficiency resulting from the cost of executing the utilitarian wealth transfer. The most important criticism of utilitarianism is based on the following argument. Wealth can be transferred from high income earners to low income earners by taxing the high income earners. This will cause the high income earners to work less, resulting in a less-than-efficient quantity of labor being supplied. Further, the taxation of income earned from capital investments will lead to reduced savings and investment. The end result is that the quantities of both labor and capital will decrease, and the economy will shrink in absolute size.

A second source of inefficiency associated with transferring wealth from the rich to the poor through taxation is administrative costs. Taxation involves costs of collecting taxes and auditing returns to enforce compliance. There is significant time and effort devoted to calculating taxes by taxpayers. Welfare agencies have significant administrative costs, which also reduce the amount of the actual transfer. All of the resources and labor used in these activities could be used to produce other goods and services that have value to consumers.

A second school of economic thought is based on the **symmetry principle**. The symmetry principle holds that people in similar situations should be treated similarly. It is basically a moral principle that advocates treating other people the way you prefer to be treated. Economically speaking, this means equality of opportunity.

In *Anarchy, State, and Utopia* (1974), Robert Nozick argues that results are irrelevant to the idea of fair resource allocation—fairness must be based on the fairness of the rules. He suggests that fairness adhere to two rules: (1) governments must recognize and protect private property, and (2) private property must be given from one party to another only when it is voluntarily done. Rule (1) means that everything that is valuable must be owned by individuals, and the government must enforce private property rights. Rule (2) means that the only way an individual can acquire property is through its exchange for something else that he or she owns (including his or her own labor).

Nozick argues that if these uniquely fair rules are followed, the result will be fair. It doesn't matter if the whole economy is shared equally, as long as it is constructed by the same individuals, each of whom provides services on a voluntary basis in exchange for economic benefit. This is what is meant by symmetry—individuals get goods and services from the economy that are equal in value to their contributions to the economy.

KEY CONCEPTS

1. Marginal benefit is the benefit that a consumer gets from the consumption of an additional unit of a good or service.

2. Marginal cost is the cost that a producer incurs to produce one more unit of output. Marginal cost is an opportunity cost because it represents the value of what the productive resources used to produce one more unit of a good could produce in their next highest-valued use.

3. Consumer surplus is the difference between the total value to consumers of the quantity of a good or service consumed and the total amount consumers pay for that production.

4. Minimum supply price is the marginal cost of production.

5. Producer surplus is the difference between the total cost of producing the output of a good or service and the total amount received for that output.

6. The equilibrium quantity produced and consumed in well-functioning unregulated competitive markets is the quantity for which the sum of consumer surplus and producer surplus is maximized.

7. Obstacles to the efficient allocation of resources include price controls, taxes and trade restrictions, monopoly, external costs and benefits, and public goods and common resources.

8. Utilitarianism refers to the idea that the greatest good occurs to the greatest number of people when wealth is transferred from the rich to the poor in order to make everyone's wealth equal.

9. Symmetry is an economic concept based on the idea that what an individual receives from the economy is equal to his contribution and is based on fairness of opportunity, not equality of results.

CONCEPT CHECKERS: EFFICIENCY AND EQUITY

1. If you are willing to pay $20 for a shirt but you only have to pay $16, the $4 difference is:
    A. consumer surplus.
    B. consumer deficit.
    C. producer deficit.
    D. producer surplus.

2. The marginal benefit from consuming the third unit of a product is $12, and the marginal cost to the producer of the third unit is $8. Under these circumstances, which of the following statements is *most accurate*?
    A. Consumer surplus is maximized.
    B. Producer surplus is maximized.
    C. The efficient quantity is less than three.
    D. Producing and selling the third unit will increase efficiency.

3. The idea that a competitive market allocates resources fairly as long as the same rules apply to all participants is suggested by:
    A. utilitarianism.
    B. the fairness principle.
    C. the symmetry principle.
    D. proponents of the equality of outcomes.

4. In an unregulated competitive market, which of the following conditions *most accurately* describes the condition that exists when the efficient quantity of a good or service is produced and consumed?
    A. Producer surplus is maximized.
    B. Consumer surplus is maximized.
    C. Consumer surplus equals producer surplus.
    D. The sum of consumer surplus and producer surplus is maximized.

5. Producer surplus is *best defined* as the:
    A. number of units by which the supply is greater than the quantity demanded by consumers.
    B. the sum of the differences between the price of each unit of a good and its opportunity cost.
    C. difference between the price a consumer pays for a good and the price she is willing to pay for it.
    D. amount by which the price of the next unit of a good exceeds the consumer's marginal benefit from the good.

6. Which of the following statements *most accurately* describes what will occur in an unrestricted economy when tastes change so that marginal benefit exceeds marginal cost at the current quantity produced and sold of a good or service?
    A. The quantity consumed will decrease.
    B. The quantity of the good or service produced will increase.
    C. The quantity of other goods and services produced will increase.
    D. Both the quantity produced and the quantity consumed will remain unchanged.

7. All of the following are obstacles to the efficient allocation of resources EXCEPT:
    A. price deregulation.
    B. monopoly producers.
    C. taxes, quotas and subsidies.
    D. public goods and common resources.

8.   As the demand (marginal benefit) curve becomes less elastic, if the equilibrium price and quantity remain unchanged, consumer surplus:
        A. decreases.
        B. increases.
        C. remains unchanged.
        D. it is not possible to determine with the information provided.

ANSWERS – CONCEPT CHECKERS: EFFICIENCY AND EQUITY

1. A   If you are willing to pay $20 for a shirt but you only pay $16 for the shirt, the $4 difference is consumer surplus. The consumer surplus plus the market price equals the total value of the product to the consumer.

2. D   When marginal benefit exceeds marginal cost, increasing the quantity of the good produced improves allocative efficiency.

3. C   The symmetry principle holds that people in similar situations should be treated similarly. It implies that the market allocates resources fairly if the rules that markets operate by are equitable.

4. D   When the efficient quantity is produced, the sum of consumer surplus and producer surplus is maximized.

5. B   The sum of the differences between price and opportunity cost is producer surplus.

6. B   In an unrestricted economy, the efficient quantity is the one for which the marginal benefit equals the marginal cost. When marginal benefit is greater than marginal cost at a given quantity, producers will produce more since consumers are willing to pay more than the cost of production.

7. A   Price deregulation removes an obstacle to the efficient allocation of resources.

8. B   Refer to Figure 4. You can see that the area of the triangle that represents consumer surplus increases as the steepness of the demand (marginal benefit) curve increases at a given equilibrium price and quantity.

MARKETS IN ACTION

EXAM FOCUS

This review examines how market equilibrium is affected by price ceilings, minimum wages, taxes, subsidies, quotas, and trade in illegal goods. For each of these you should know how supply, demand, and the resulting market equilibrium price and quantity are affected. Understand why economists believe that, in general, interference with market forces causes economic inefficiency (an inefficient allocation of resources).

LOS 15.a: Discuss the impact of price ceilings on equilibrium in the short and in the long run, and supply and demand, and the impact of a price ceiling on the existence of a black market.

A **price ceiling** is an upper limit on the price which a seller can charge. If the ceiling is above the equilibrium price, it will have no effect. As illustrated in Figure 1, if the ceiling is below the equilibrium price, the result will be a shortage (excess demand) at the ceiling price. The quantity demanded, Q_d, exceeds the quantity supplied, Q_s. Consumers are willing to pay P_{ws} (price with search costs) for the Q_s quantity suppliers are willing to sell at the ceiling price, P_c. Consumers are willing to expend effort with a value of $P_{ws} - P_c$ in search activity to find the scarce good. The reduction in quantity exchanged due to the price ceiling leads to a deadweight loss in efficiency as noted in Figure 1.

Figure 1: Price Ceiling

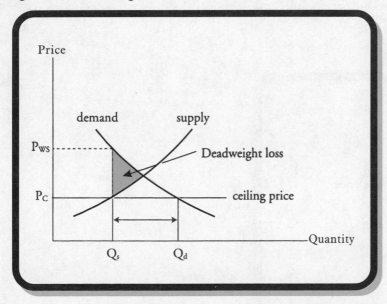

With an effective price ceiling, price is no longer an effective means of rationing the good or service. In the long run, price ceilings lead to the following:

- Consumers may have to wait in long lines to make purchases. They pay a price (an opportunity cost) in terms of the time they spend in line.

- Suppliers may engage in discrimination, such as selling to friends and relatives first.
- Suppliers "officially" sell at the ceiling price, but take bribes to do so.
- Suppliers may also reduce the quality of the goods produced to a level commensurate with the ceiling price.

In the housing market, price ceilings are appropriately called **rent ceilings** or rent control. Rent ceilings are a good example of how a price ceiling can distort a market. Renters must wait for units to become available. Renters may have to bribe landlords to rent at the ceiling price. The quality of the apartments will fall. Other inefficiencies can develop. For instance, a renter might be reluctant to take a new job across town because it means giving up a rent-controlled apartment and risking not finding another (rent-controlled) apartment near the new place of work.

A **black market** refers to economic activity that takes place illegally. This includes selling goods at prices that exceed legally imposed price ceilings. Bribing a landlord to get a rent-controlled apartment is an example of black market activity. Another way for a landlord to charge rent that exceeds the rent ceiling is to "officially" rent at the ceiling, then charge excessive fees for items such as mailboxes, keys and locks, or window treatments.

A black market is generally inefficient because:

- Contracts are not as enforceable.
- The risk of prosecution increases the prices required by suppliers.
- Quality control deteriorates, which leads to more defective products.

LOS 15.b: Explain the effects of a minimum wage and the effects when it is set either above or below the equilibrium wage level.

A **price floor** is a minimum price that a buyer can offer for a good, service, or resource. If the price floor is below the equilibrium price, it will have no effect on equilibrium price and quantity. Figure 2 illustrates a price floor that is set above the equilibrium price. The result will be a surplus (excess supply) at the floor price, since the quantity supplied, Q_s, exceeds the quantity demanded, Q_d, at the floor price. There is a loss of efficiency (DWL) because the quantity actually transacted with the price floor, Q_d, is less than the unrestricted equilibrium quantity, Q_e.

Figure 2: Impact of a Price Floor

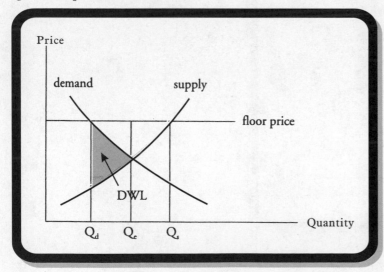

©2007 Schweser

In the long run, price floors lead to inefficiencies:

- Suppliers will divert resources to the production of the good with the anticipation of selling the good at the floor price, but then will not be able to sell all they produce.
- Consumers will buy less of a product if the floor is above the equilibrium price and substitute other, less expensive consumption goods for the good subject to the price floor.

The **minimum wage** in the United States is an example of a price floor. At a minimum wage above the equilibrium wage, there will be an excess supply of workers, since firms cannot employ all the workers who want to work at that wage. Since firms must pay at least the minimum wage for the workers, firms substitute other productive resources for labor and use more than the economically efficient amount of capital. The result is increased unemployment because even when there is a large number of unemployed low-skilled workers willing to work at a wage lower than the minimum, firms cannot legally hire them. Furthermore, firms may decrease the quality or quantity of the nonmonetary benefits they previously offered to workers, such as pleasant, safe working conditions and on-the-job training.

LOS 15.c: Discuss the impact of tax, subsidies, quotas, and markets for illegal goods on demand, supply and the market equilibrium.

The Incidence of a Tax

A tax on a good or service will increase its equilibrium price and decrease its equilibrium quantity. Figure 3 illustrates the effects of a *tax on producers* and of a *tax on buyers* (e.g., a sales tax). In panel (a) the points indicated by P_E and Q_E describe the equilibrium prior to the tax. As a result of this tax, the supply curve shifts from S to S_{tax}, where the quantity Q_{tax} is demanded at the price P_{tax}.

The tax is the difference between what buyers pay and what sellers ultimately earn per unit. This is illustrated by the vertical distance between supply curve "S" and supply curve "S_{tax}." At the new quantity, Q_{tax}, buyers pay P_{tax}, but net of the tax, suppliers only receive P_S. The triangular area is a **deadweight loss** (DWL). This is the loss of gains from production and trade that results from the tax (i.e., because less than the efficient amount is produced and consumed).

Figure 3: Incidence of a Tax on Producers and a Tax on Buyers

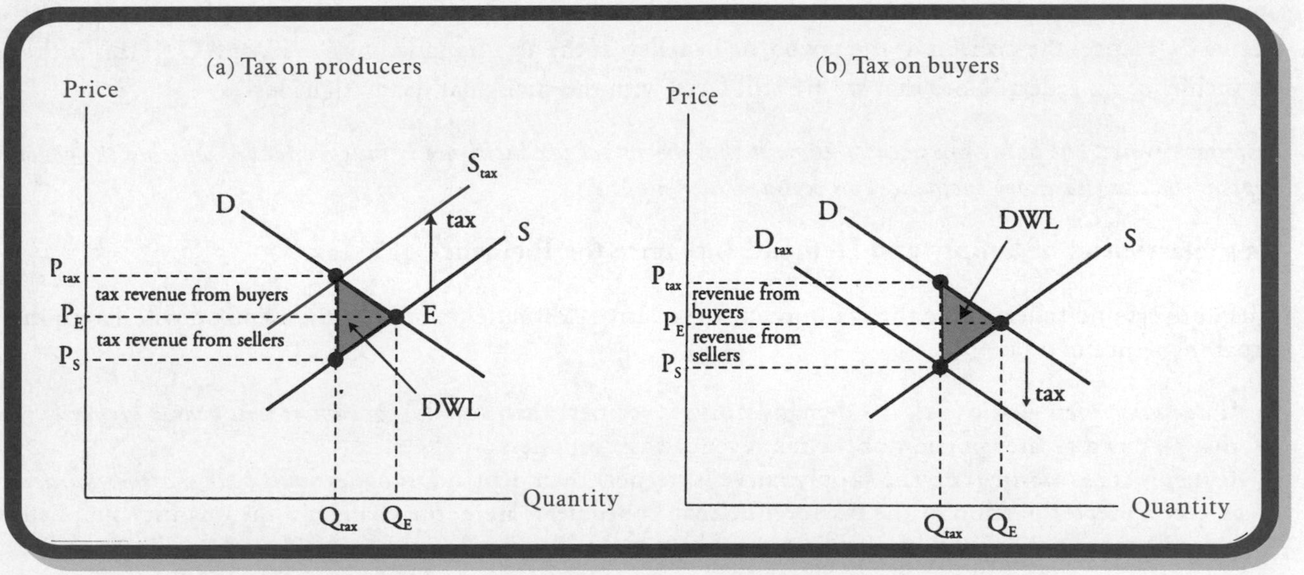

Note that in panel (b), although the statutory incidence of the tax is on buyers, the actual incidence of the tax, the reduction in output, and the consequent deadweight loss are all the same as in panel (a), where the tax is imposed on sellers.

The **tax revenue** is the amount of the tax times the new equilibrium quantity, Q_{tax}. Economic agents (buyers and sellers) in the market share the burden of the tax revenue. The **incidence of a tax** is allocation of this tax between buyers and sellers. The rectangle denoted "revenue from buyers" represents the portion of the *tax revenue* that the buyers effectively pay. "Revenue from sellers" illustrates the portion of the tax that the suppliers effectively pay.

Actual and Statutory Incidence of a Tax

Statutory incidence refers to who is legally responsible for paying the tax. The **actual incidence of a tax** refers to who actually bears the cost of the tax through an increase in the price paid (buyers) or decrease in the price received (sellers). In Figure 3(a), we illustrated the effect of a tax on the *sellers* of the good as opposed to the *buyers* of the good (note that the price is higher over all levels of production—the supply curve shifts up). Thus, the *statutory incidence* in Figure 3(a) is on the supplier. The result is an increase in price at each possible quantity supplied.

Statutory incidence on the *buyer* causes a downward shift of the demand curve by the amount of the tax. As indicated in Figure 3(b), prior to the imposition of a tax on buyers, the equilibrium price and quantity are at the point of intersection of the supply and demand curves (i.e., P_E, Q_E). The imposition of the tax forces suppliers to reduce output to the point Q_{tax} (a movement along the supply curve). At the new equilibrium, price and quantity are denoted by P_{tax} and Q_{tax}, respectively.

The tax that we are analyzing in Figure 3(b) could be a sales tax that is added to the price of the good at the time of sale. So, instead of paying P_E, buyers are now forced to pay P_{tax}, (i.e., tax = $P_{tax} - P_E$). The *buyer* pays the entire tax (the statutory incidence). Since, prior to the imposition of the tax, their reference point was P_E, the *buyer* only sees the price rise from P_E to P_{tax} (the buyer's tax burden). Hence, the portion of the tax borne by buyers is the area bounded by P_E, P_{tax}, and Q_{tax}; this is the actual tax incidence on buyers.

Note that the supply curve in Figure 3(b) does not move as a result of a tax on buyers, and that given the original demand curve, D, suppliers would have supplied the equilibrium quantity Q_E at price P_E. The result is that suppliers are penalized because they would have produced at the Q_E, P_E point, but instead produce at Q_{tax} and receive P_s. Hence, the portion of the tax borne by sellers is the area bounded by P_E, P_s, and Q_{tax}; this is the actual tax incidence on sellers. Note that we are still faced with the triangular deadweight loss.

Professor's Note: The point you need to know is that the actual tax incidence is independent of whether the government imposes the tax (statutory incidence) on consumers or suppliers.

How Elasticities of Supply and Demand Influence the Incidence of a Tax

When buyers and sellers share the tax burden, the relative elasticities of supply and demand will determine the actual incidence of a tax.

- If *demand is less elastic* (i.e., the demand curve is steeper) than supply, *consumers will bear a higher burden*, that is, pay a greater portion of the tax revenue than suppliers.
- If *supply is less elastic* (i.e., the supply curve is steeper) than demand, *suppliers will bear a higher burden*, that is, pay a greater portion of the tax revenue than consumers. Here, the change in the quantity supplied for a given change in price will be small—buyers have more "leverage" in this type of market. The party with the more elastic curve will be able to react more to the changes imposed by the tax. Hence, they can avoid more of the burden.

Panels (a) and (b) in Figure 4 are the same in all respects, except that the supply curve in panel (b) is significantly steeper—it is less elastic. Comparing panel (a) with panel (b), we can see that the portion of tax revenue borne by the seller is much greater than that borne by the buyer as the supply curve becomes less elastic. When demand is more elastic relative to supply, buyers "pay" a lower portion of the tax because they have the greater ability to substitute away from the good to a substitute.

Notice that as the elasticity of either demand or supply decreases, the deadweight loss is also reduced. This is because fewer trading opportunities are eliminated by the imposition of the tax, meaning that it is more difficult for either demanders or suppliers to substitute away from the good. With less effect on equilibrium quantity, the allocation of resources is less affected and efficiency is reduced less.

Figure 4: Elasticity of Supply and Tax Incidence

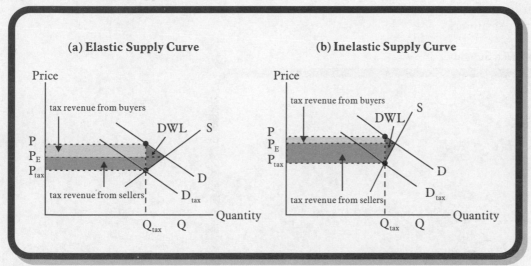

In Figure 5, we illustrate the result for differences in the elasticity of demand. In panel (b) demand is relatively more inelastic, and we see that the size of the deadweight loss (and the decrease in equilibrium output) is smaller when demand is more inelastic. We can also see that the actual incidence of the tax imposed on suppliers falls more heavily on buyers when demand is more inelastic.

Figure 5: Elasticity of Demand and Tax Incidence

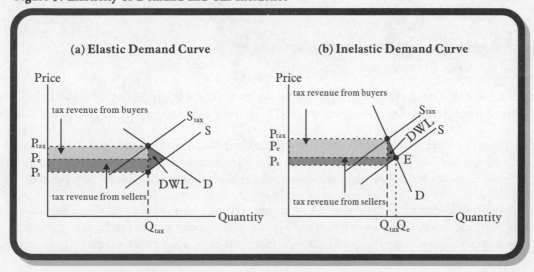

Subsidies and Quotas

Subsidies are payments made by governments to producers, often farmers. The effects of a subsidy are illustrated in Figure 6, where we use the market for soybeans as an example. Note here that with no subsidies, equilibrium quantity in the market for soybeans is 60 tons annually at a price of $60 per ton. A subsidy of $30 per ton causes a downward shift in the supply curve from S to (S – subsidy), which results in an increase in the equilibrium quantity to 90 million tons per year and a decrease in the equilibrium price (paid by buyers) to $45 per ton. At the new equilibrium, farmers receive $75 per ton (the market price of $45, plus the $30 subsidy).

Recognizing that the (unsubsidized) supply curve represents the marginal cost and that the demand curve represents the marginal benefit, the marginal cost is greater than the marginal benefit at the new equilibrium with the subsidy. This leads to a deadweight loss from overproduction. The resources used to produce the additional 30 million tons of soybeans have a value in some other use that is greater than the value of these additional soybeans to consumers.

Figure 6: Soybean Price Subsidy

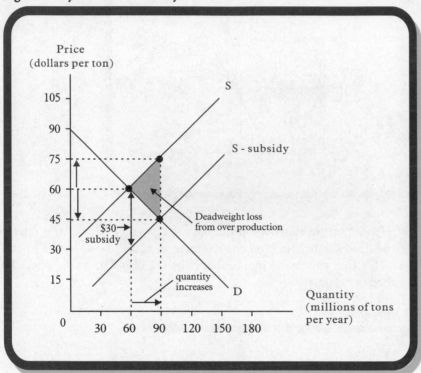

Production quotas are used to regulate markets by imposing an upper limit on the quantity of a good that may be produced over a specified time period. Quotas are often used by governments to regulate agricultural markets.

Continuing with our soybean example, let's suppose the government imposes a production quota on soybeans of 60 million tons per year. In Figure 7, we see that in the absence of a quota, soybean production is 90 million tons per year at a price of $45 per ton. With a 60 million ton quota, the equilibrium price rises to $75 per ton.

The reduction in the quantity of soybeans produced due to the quota leads to an inefficient allocation of resources. The quota not only increases the market price, it lowers the marginal cost of producing the quota quantity. At the quota amount, marginal benefit (price) exceeds marginal cost. This explains why producers often seek the imposition of quotas.

Note that if a quota is greater than the equilibrium quantity of 90 million tons, nothing will change because farmers are already producing less than the maximum production allowed under the quota.

Figure 7: Soybean Production Quota

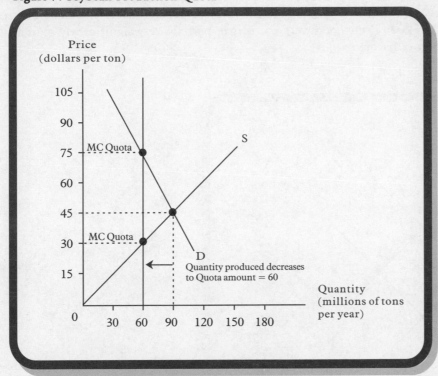

Illegal Goods

When people get caught buying or selling illegal goods, such as drugs or guns, they must pay penalties, including fines, imprisonment, or both. As the severity of the penalty or the likelihood of getting caught increases, the total costs of illegal trade increase. To see how the penalties from breaking the law affect the equilibrium quantity of an illegal good, consider the U.S. market for Cuban cigars illustrated in Figure 8. Here, the supply curve, S, represents the minimum prices that sellers would accept if Cuban cigars were legal, and the demand curve, D, represents the maximum prices that buyers would pay for Cuban cigars without any laws restricting their purchase. The equilibrium price and quantity under legal trade are at point L, where the equilibrium quantity is Q_L at a price of P_L. Because selling Cuban cigars is illegal in the U.S., the compensation for the *expected penalty* for selling cigars, EP_S, is added to the sellers' minimum prices, shifting the supply curve in Figure 8 up to $S + EP_S$. If only sellers are penalized, the new equilibrium is represented by point M.

In the U.S. it is also illegal to purchase and possess Cuban cigars, so the cost of the expected penalties for buyers must be subtracted from the maximum price that buyers are willing to pay. This causes the demand curve to shift downward to $D - EP_D$. If only buyers were subject to the penalty, the Cuban cigar market would move from point L to N.

When both buyers and sellers of illegal Cuban cigars must pay a penalty, the new equilibrium price and quantity are represented by point O in Figure 8. As we have drawn it, the expected penalties for sellers and buyers are equal ($EP_S = EP_D$), so the new market price remains at the original market price, P_L, but the quantity purchased declines to Q^*. Effectively, buyers pay P_B, which is P_L plus an added cost equal to the value of the expected penalty for buying and possessing Cuban cigars, and sellers effectively receive P_S, which is P_L minus the amount to compensate for the expected penalty for selling Cuban cigars. Note that buyers pay, and sellers receive, a cash price equal to P_L in this example.

The decrease in supply or demand for an illegal good increases as the value of the penalty increases. If the penalty is larger for the seller, the supply curve will shift by a greater amount than the demand curve and the cash market price will rise above what it would have been if the good were not illegal, perhaps very significantly so. The opposite is true when penalties are higher for buyers.

Figure 8: Market for Illegal Cigars

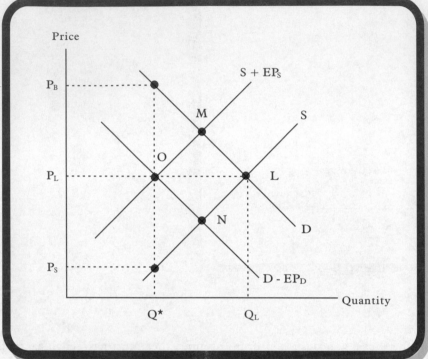

KEY CONCEPTS

1. Price ceilings set below the equilibrium price lead to shortages, waiting in line, bribes, a decrease in quality, and black markets.
2. A black market operates outside the legal system, selling goods that are illegal or under price controls.
3. A minimum wage above the equilibrium wage leads to unemployment and lengthy job searches.
4. The actual incidence of a tax refers to the extent to which buyers and sellers actually bear the cost of a tax. The statutory incidence of the tax refers to who must legally pay the tax. The actual incidence of a tax is independent of the statutory incidence of the tax and depends on the relative elasticities of supply and demand.
5. Subsidies increase equilibrium quantities and lead to deadweight losses from overproduction.
6. Production quotas decrease equilibrium quantities and lead to deadweight losses from underproduction.
7. The expected penalties for trading in illegal goods cause both demand and supply curves to shift to the left, decreasing the equilibrium quantities compared to equilibrium quantities if the goods were legal.

CONCEPT CHECKERS: MARKETS IN ACTION

1. A market that operates outside the legal system, having prices that exceed legally imposed price ceilings, is a/an:
    A. black market.
    B. incident market.
    C. subsidized market.
    D. quota controlled market.

2. Rent control is an example of a:
    A. quota.
    B. subsidy.
    C. price floor.
    D. price ceiling.

3. A minimum wage is an example of a:
    A. quota.
    B. subsidy.
    C. price floor.
    D. price ceiling.

4. Quotas placed above the equilibrium quantity:
    A. increase marginal cost.
    B. result in overproduction.
    C. have no effect on output.
    D. result in underproduction.

5. A subsidy:
    A. shifts the supply curve down.
    B. has no effect on output.
    C. increases marginal benefit.
    D. leads to underproduction.

6. As a result of a production quota set below the equilibrium quantity:
    A. marginal benefit will exceed marginal cost.
    B. marginal cost will exceed marginal benefit.
    C. marginal benefit and marginal cost will decline.
    D. marginal benefit will be forced into equality with marginal cost.

7. Assume a good becomes illegal to buy or sell, and the expected penalty for selling the good is greater than that for buying the good. Relative to when the good was legal:
    A. price and quantity will rise.
    B. price and quantity will decline.
    C. price will rise and quantity will decline.
    D. price will remain the same, but quantity will fall.

8. A price ceiling is only effective if it:
    A. is set above the equilibrium price.
    B. is set below the equilibrium price.
    C. has been in effect over a long time.
    D. has been in effect in over a relatively short time.

9. An example of a price floor is:
    A. rent controls.
    B. a tax on ceramic tile.
    C. a subsidy for wheat production.
    D. a minimum price for milk.

10. The government imposes a tax on a good. The relative amounts that each economic unit in the market pays of the tax is called the:
    A. statutory tax.
    B. tax incidence.
    C. tax imposition.
    D. deadweight loss.

ANSWERS – CONCEPT CHECKERS: MARKETS IN ACTION

1. **A**   A black market is a market where trades of goods prohibited by law or trades at prices prohibited by law are made.

2. **D**   Rent controls are price ceilings and have the effect of reducing supply.

3. **C**   A minimum wage is a price floor and will likely increase unemployment.

4. **C**   A quota that is less than the equilibrium output quantity leads to a decrease in production and a deadweight loss from an inefficient allocation of resources. Quotas above the equilibrium quantity have no effect on output quantity.

5. **A**   A subsidy effectively shifts the supply curve down. The resulting new equilibrium will be at a quantity where marginal cost is greater than marginal benefit so that there is an economic loss from production of more than the optimal amount of the subsidized good.

6. **A**   If output is forced to be below the equilibrium quantity, the marginal benefit will exceed the marginal cost and a deadweight loss comes about from underproduction.

7. **C**   If the expected penalty to sellers of illegal goods is greater than that to the buyers, the supply curve will shift up more than the demand curve will shift downward. The result is that price will rise and quantity will decline.

8. **B**   A price ceiling is only effective if it is lower than the equilibrium price without the ceiling. This leads to a shortage as consumers wish to purchase a quantity of the good at the ceiling price which is greater than the quantity supplied at that price.

9. **D**   A price floor is a minimum on the price that suppliers can charge. Such floors were once common in agricultural markets.

10. **B**   This is the definition of the incidence of a tax. It is determined by the shape of the supply and demand curves, not upon whom the tax is imposed legally (the statutory incidence of the tax).

ORGANIZING PRODUCTION

EXAM FOCUS

Make sure you can calculate economic profit, which requires that you identify relevant opportunity costs. Also, you should understand the different types of market competition and the issues surrounding the concentration measures of the degree of competition.

The pros and cons of the different forms of business organization are another likely exam topic. You should also be able to differentiate between technological and economic efficiency. A basic understanding of what the principal-agent problem will be sufficient here.

LOS 16.a: Explain the different types of opportunity cost and the relationship to economic profit, and calculate economic profit.

Opportunity cost is the return that a firm's resources could have earned elsewhere in its next most valuable use. Opportunity cost includes both explicit and implicit costs.

Explicit costs are observable, measurable expenses such as the dollar cost of production inputs and the interest cost of renting (borrowing) capital.

Implicit costs are not explicitly observable and fall into two categories: (1) the opportunity cost to a firm of using its own capital and (2) the opportunity cost of the time and financial resources of the firm's owners.

- The *implied rental rate* is the term used to describe the opportunity cost to a firm for using its own capital. It represents what the firm could have earned if it had rented its capital (money and/or physical assets) to another firm. The implied rental rate is the sum of: (1) *economic depreciation*, which is the decrease in the value of a firm's assets over time, and (2) *foregone interest*.
- *Normal profit* is the opportunity cost of owners' entrepreneurial expertise. It represents what owners could have earned if they used their organizational, decision-making, and other entrepreneurial skills in another activity, such as running another business.

Economic profit considers both explicit and implicit costs. When the firm's revenues are just equal to its opportunity costs (explicit and implicit costs, including a normal profit), economic profits are zero. The computation of economic profit is illustrated in Figure 1.

Figure 1: Calculating Economic Profit for Patrick's Surfboard Company

Account		*Amount*
Total revenue		**$340,000**
Opportunity costs		
Fiberglass	$100,000	
Electricity	30,000	
Employee wages paid	55,000	
Interest paid on borrowed funds	5,000	
Total explicit costs		$190,000
Patrick's foregone wages	35,000	
Patrick's foregone interest	10,000	
Economic depreciation on buildings	5,000	
Normal profit	60,000	
Total implicit costs		$110,000
Total cost		**$300,000**
Economic profit		**$40,000**

Professor's Note: Accounting profit only recognizes explicit costs, so it is greater than economic profit.

LOS 16.b: Discuss the firm's constraints and their impact on maximum profit.

Constrained profit maximization. Firms face three primary constraints as they endeavor to maximize profits: (1) technological, (2) information, and (3) market constraints.

Technology constraints. For our current purposes, technology may be defined simply as the means of producing a good or service. Technological developments are continuous. At any given point in time, a firm has the opportunity to increase output, and ultimately revenue, by employing additional technological resources. But to do so often means that the firm must incur additional costs. The additional profit from any increased output and revenue is limited by the cost of adopting new technology.

Information constraints. Profit maximization is constrained by the lack of information on which to base decisions. Many times, more information is available, but the cost of obtaining it may exceed its value (to increase firm profits). As with any productive resource, the firm will expend resources to acquire additional information only up to the point where the increase in total revenue from additional information is greater than the cost of the information.

Market constraints. Profits are also constrained by how much consumers are willing to pay for a firm's product or service and by the prices and marketing activities of its competitors. Resource markets also place constraints on profit maximization. The prices and availability of the resources that a firm uses and the willingness of people to invest in the firm present constraints on the firm's growth.

LOS 16.c: Distinguish between technological and economic efficiency, and discuss under which circumstances a firm is technological or economically efficient.

Technological efficiency refers to using the least amount of specific inputs to produce a given output.

Economic efficiency refers to producing a given output at the lowest possible cost.

The difference between technological and economic efficiency is illustrated in the following example. Consider the four methods of producing a microwave oven illustrated in Figure 2.

Figure 2: Methods for Manufacturing 100 Microwave Ovens Per Day

Method*	Input Quantities	
	Capital (machine-day equivalent)	Labor (worker-days)
Robotic manufacturing (RM)	5,000	5
Assembly line manufacturing (ALM)	50	50
Work station manufacturing (WSM)	50	500
Hand crafted manufacturing (HCM)	5	5,000

*Method descriptions:
- RM requires one worker to monitor a completely robotic process.
- ALM requires the microwave assembly to be automatically moved from one work station to the next, where the worker at that station performs a specific, repetitive operation.
- WSM requires the workers to move from station to station to perform the same operation.
- HCM requires one worker to build an entire microwave oven using specialized tools.

An examination of the microwave oven manufacturing methods described in Figure 2 reveals that robotic manufacturing (RM) uses the most capital and least labor, whereas hand crafted manufacturing (HCM) uses the most labor and least capital. Assembly line manufacturing (ALM) and work station manufacturing (WSM) fall between these two extremes. WSM uses 50 units of capital and 500 units of labor to produce 100 ovens per day; ALM can also produce 100 ovens using 50 units of capital, but requires only 50 units of labor. ALM is more *technologically efficient* than the WSM method because it uses absolutely less inputs to produce the same output.

Both the RM and HCM methods are technologically efficient because compared to ALM, RM uses less labor (but more capital), and HCM uses less capital (but more labor).

Economic efficiency is achieved when a given level of output is achieved at the least possible cost. Let's assume for our example that labor costs $75 per worker-day and capital costs $250 per machine-day. The costs of the four different methods are shown in Figure 3. ALM has the lowest cost per oven. Even though RM requires the least amount of labor, it requires more capital. On the other hand, while the HCM method requires the least amount of capital, it uses much more labor.

Recall that WSM is not technologically efficient. This fact ensures that WSM is not economically efficient either. WSM uses the same capital input ($12,500) as ALM, but requires much more labor ($37,500 versus $3,750).

The total costs in Figure 3 will be different if the costs of labor and capital are different. Firms must routinely re-evaluate economic efficiency as the costs of inputs change.

Figure 3: The Cost of Four Methods of Manufacturing 100 Microwave Ovens Per Day

Method	Capital Cost $250/unit	Labor Cost $75/unit	Total Cost	Cost Per Oven
RM	$1,250,000	$375	1,250,375	$12,503.75
ALM	12,500	3,750	16,250	162.50
WSM	12,500	37,500	50,000	500.00
HCM	1,250	375,000.	376,250	3,762.50

LOS 16.d: Discuss the different ways a firm can organize production, how the principal-agent problem occurs, and which measures a firm can take to reduce the impact of the principal-agent problem.

Firms can organize production in two different ways: (1) command systems and (2) incentive systems.

Command systems organize production according to a managerial chain of command. In a command system, managers spend much of their time processing information about the performance of the people who report to them, about what steps to take, and the best way to implement those steps. The U.S. military is an example of a command system; the President is at the top of the hierarchy. For a corporation using a command system of organizing production, the Chief Executive Officer is at the top of the system.

An **incentive system** is a means of organizing production whereby senior management creates a system of rewards intended to motivate workers to perform in such a way as to maximize profits. It is an effective system for organizing the production of a large sales force, where sales people may be paid a base salary that is relatively small, and also rewarded for sales volume. CEOs are often subject to incentive systems, which provide them with compensation based on their firm's profit, sales, or stock price performance.

Command systems and incentive systems are often mixed within the same organization. Command systems are used when it is easy to monitor the performance of employees, as in the case of production workers. Incentive systems are usually most effective for organizing the production of employees whose activities are difficult or costly to monitor, like those of the firm's CEO and senior officers or outside sales people.

The **principal-agent problem** refers to the problems that arise when the incentives and motivations of managers and workers (agents) are not the same as the incentives and motivations of their firm's owners (principals). In many corporations, agents have their own goals, which may be different than those of the principals. For workers, there is often an incentive to shirk, which is to work below their normal level of productivity. At the managerial level, managers may work to maximize their own income and benefits rather than to maximize the value of the firm to its owners. The essence of the problem is that it is difficult or costly for the principals to monitor the actions of the agents.

Three methods are commonly used to reduce the principal-agent problem by better aligning the motivations of agents with those of principals: (1) ownership, (2) incentive pay, and (3) long-term contracts.

- When managers or workers have an *ownership* interest in the firm, it may motivate them to perform in a manner that maximizes the firm's profits or value. Ownership arrangements are commonly used with senior management, but less so for workers.
- *Incentive pay* is pay that is based on performance and is quite common in many industries. Incentive pay may be based on profits, sales, production quotas, or stock prices. Promotions may also be used as a form of incentive pay to align the interests of a firm's agents and principals.
- *Long-term contracts* for employment are often assigned to firms' CEOs to encourage them to develop strategies that will maximize profits over a relatively long period.

LOS 16.e: Distinguish between the different types of business organization, discuss the advantages and dissdvantages of each of the systems both individually and relative to each other.

Types of business organization. The three main forms of business organization are: (1) proprietorships, (2) partnerships, and (3) corporations. Each form has its own advantages and disadvantages.

A **proprietorship** is a form of business organization with a single owner who has unlimited liability for the firm's debts and other legal obligations. Income flows through to the proprietor (owner) who pays taxes on it as personal income.

- *Advantages*: Easy to establish, simple decision making process, and profits are only taxed once.
- *Disadvantages*: Decisions are not checked by a group consensus, the owner's entire wealth is exposed to risk, the business may cease to exist when the owner dies, and raising capital can be difficult and relatively expensive.

A **partnership** form of business organization involves two or more owners who both have unlimited liability for the debts and other legal obligations of the partnership. A partnership's taxable income is allocated (as personal income) to the partners based on their proportional ownership of the partnership.

- *Advantages*: Easy to establish, decision making is diversified among partners, may survive even if a partner leaves or dies, and profits are only taxed once.
- *Disadvantages*: It can be difficult to achieve consensus decisions, owners' entire wealth is exposed to risk, and there may be a capital shortfall when a partner dies or leaves for other reasons. Since each partner may bring capital to the firm, capital is generally more readily available than for a proprietorship, but there are still significant limitations on the ability to raise large amounts of capital.

A **corporation** is owned by its stockholders, and their liability is legally limited to the amount of money they have invested in the firm. The firm is a legal entity that pays (corporate) income taxes. Corporations account for the largest share of revenue by far among the three types of business organization.

- *Advantages*: Owners have limited liability, large amounts of relatively inexpensive capital are available, management expertise is not limited to that of the owners, a corporation's life is not limited to that of the owners, and long-term labor contracts can be used to reduce costs.
- *Disadvantages*: Relatively complex management structure may make the decision-making process slow and costly, and double taxation—corporate earnings are taxed when earned and again when distributed to owners as dividends.

Professor's Note: The most commonly cited advantages of the corporate form of business over proprietorships and partnerships is its unlimited access to relatively cheap capital and its limited liability to the owners. The biggest disadvantage of the corporate form over the other two forms is the double taxation of distributed profits.

LOS 16.f: Identify the different market types, and describe the conditions that characterize them.

The four types of economic markets are: (1) perfect competition, (2) monopolistic competition, (3) oligopoly, and (4) monopoly.

Perfect competition exists when all the firms in the market produce identical products. There is a large number of independent firms, each seller is small relative to the total market, and there are no barriers to entry or exit. Furthermore, each of the many buyers and sellers knows the prices of the competing products in the market.

Monopolistic competition is the term used to describe markets where a large number of competitors produce (slightly) differentiated products. *Product differentiation* gives a degree of market power to firms under monopolistic competition because each firm produces a slightly different product. Laundry detergent and canned spaghetti sauce are examples of products that are sold under monopolistic competition.

Oligopoly is a market structure characterized by a small number of producers selling products that may be similar or differentiated. There is interdependence among competitors in that the decisions made by one firm affect the demand, price, and profit of others in the industry. Also, significant barriers to entry exist which often include large economies of scale. The U.S. auto and soft drink industries are examples of oligopoly markets.

Monopoly markets are characterized by a single seller of a specific, well-defined product that has no good substitutes. Barriers to entry are high in monopoly markets. Whether a monopoly exits often depends on how we define the product. Microsoft Corp. certainly has a monopoly of sorts on the Windows® operating system and related software. If we define the market more broadly, there are other operating systems, word processing programs, spreadsheet programs, and so forth.

LOS 16.g: Explain the different ways in which concentration can be measured, and discuss the limitations of concentration measures.

The concentration of a market refers to the distribution of firms' market shares. Markets with a few large firms are more concentrated than markets with many smaller firms. There are two primary measures of market concentration, the four-firm concentration ratio and the Herfindahl-Hirschman Index.

Professor's Note: You will see the concentration ratio and the Herfindahl index again in Study Session 14.

The **four-firm concentration ratio** is the percentage of total industry sales made by the four largest firms in an industry. A highly competitive industry may have a four-firm concentration ratio near zero, while the ratio is 100% for a monopoly. A four-firm concentration ratio below 40% is considered an indication of a competitive market, and a four-firm ratio greater than 60% indicates an oligopoly.

The **Herfindahl-Hirschman Index** (HHI) is calculated by summing the squared percentage market shares of the 50 largest firms in an industry (or all of the firms in the industry if there are less than 50). The HHI is very low in a highly competitive industry and increases to 10,000 (= 100^2) for an industry with only one firm. An HHI between 1,000 and 1,800 is considered moderately competitive, while an HHI greater than 1,800 indicates a market that is not competitive.

The usefulness of concentration measures as indicators of the degree of competition in a market is limited because they do not properly account for: (1) the geographical scope of the market, (2) barriers to entry and firm turnover in a market, and (3) the relationship between a market and an industry.

The *geographical scope of the market* refers to the fact that products may be marketed in regional, local, or global markets. For example, concentration measures for newspapers in the global market are low, indicating a highly competitive market. But the concentration of newspapers in any given city is usually quite high, indicating relatively low competition at the local market level.

Barriers to entry and firm turnover in a market are not captured in concentration measures. While a small town may have few appliance stores, indicating a lack of competition, there is no barrier to opening a new appliance store, which increases the competitiveness of the market.

The *relationship between a market and an industry* is not always close, even though concentration measures assume that each firm fits neatly within one specific industry. There are three reasons why firms do not always fit neatly in a given industry. First, markets are often narrower than an industry. Companies may be in the same industry but sell specific products that do not compete with each other. Second, most large firms produce many different products, each facing different levels of competition. Concentration ratios, however, assume one market for the firm as a whole. Finally, firms may switch from one market to another in order to maximize profit. The ability to easily enter and exit a market increases the competition in that market.

LOS 16.h: Discuss the two ways in which economic activity can be coordinated, and the different ways in which firms are often more efficient than markets.

Economic activity can be produced through market coordination or through firm coordination.

Market coordination is best described through an example. Consider the production of a heavyweight boxing match. The fight promoter hires an arena, a boxing ring, broadcast specialists, concession services, some boxers, a publicity agency, and a ticket agent. These are all market transactions. The promoter then sells tickets to the event through the ticket agent, along with broadcasting rights to a television network. So, the fight is produced through the coordination of markets.

Another example of market coordination is outsourcing. With outsourcing, a manufacturer of a product buys some or all of the product's components from other firms. The manufacturer then assembles all of the outsourced components to produce the final product. Outsourcing is a common practice in the automobile and personal computer industries.

Firm coordination occurs when firms can coordinate economic activity more efficiently than markets can. This is possible because firms can often achieve lower transaction costs, economies of scale, economies of scope, and economies of team production.

- *Transaction costs* refer to the costs associated with the negotiations that must take place when attempting to coordinate markets. Firms can often reduce transaction costs by reducing the number of individual transactions that must take place.
- *Economies of scale* exist when the average unit cost of producing a good decreases as output increases.
- *Economies of scope* occur when a firm can use its specialized resources to produce a range of goods and services. For example, a publisher hires editors, typists, reporters, marketing experts, and media distribution specialists and uses their skills across all of the firm's published products. This is less expensive to the publisher than it would be for an individual who attempted to hire these services individually in the markets.
- *Economies of team production* occur when a team of a firm's employees becomes highly efficient at a given task. It is usually less expensive for a firm with a well-honed team to produce a good or service than for an individual who has to hire the individual members of a team in the markets.

KEY CONCEPTS

1. Opportunity cost for a firm is the value of the resources it owns in their next highest valued productive use.

2. Explicit costs are measurable expenses. Implicit costs include the opportunity cost to a firm from the use of its own capital, and the opportunity cost associated with the use of the owners' resources.

3. Implied rental rate is the opportunity cost to a firm for using its own capital and includes economic depreciation and foregone interest. Normal profit is the opportunity cost of owners' time, resources, and entrepreneurial expertise.

4. Economic profit is total revenue minus both explicit and implicit costs, including normal profits.

5. The three primary constraints on profit maximization are the level of technology, the amount of information, and the characteristics of the markets for the firm's output and for the resources it employs.

6. Technological efficiency is achieved when the least amount of inputs is used to produce a given output. Economic efficiency is achieved when a given output is produced at the lowest possible cost.

7. Command systems organize production according to a chain of command. Incentive systems organize production through a system of rewards.

8. The principal-agent problem exists because agents (managers and workers) do not have the same motivations and incentives as the firm's principals (owners). Ownership interests, incentive pay, and long-term employment contracts are used to reduce the effects of the principal-agent problem.

9. A proprietorship, a business with one owner, is easy to start, has a simple decision process, and its profits are only taxed once; however, there are no decision reviews, the owner's entire wealth is at risk, the business may cease to exist if its proprietor dies, and its ability to raise capital is quite limited.

10. A partnership, a business with two or more owners, is easy to start, its decisions are reviewed by partners, it can survive if a partner leaves or dies, and its profits are only taxed once; however, it may be difficult to reach consensus decisions, each partner's entire wealth is at risk, there may be a capital shortfall if a partner leaves, and access to capital is limited compared to a corporate structure.

11. A corporation is a legal entity owned by its stockholders who each have limited liability. A corporation can raise large amounts of capital, has managerial expertise that is not limited to that of the owners, and has an unlimited life; however, corporations are burdened by complex management structures and double taxation of profits that are distributed to shareholders.

12. Perfect competition exists when many firms exist, all the firms sell the same identical product, each firm is small relative to the total market, and there are no barriers to entry or exit.

13. Monopolistic competition refers to a market in which a large number of competitors produce slightly differentiated products.

14. Oligopoly refers to a market in which a small number of firms sell products that may or may not be differentiated and decisions made by one firm affect the demand, price, and profit of its competitors.

15. Monopoly markets have one seller of a specific, well-defined product that has no good substitutes and high barriers to entry.

16. Market concentration measures indicate the degree of competition. The four-firm concentration ratio is the sum of the percentage market shares of the four largest firms in an industry. The Herfindahl-Hirschman Index is the sum of the squared percentage market shares of the 50 largest firms in an industry. The usefulness of concentration measures is limited because they do not reflect the geographical scope of the market, barriers to entry and firm turnover, or the relationship between markets and industries.

17. Outsourcing is an example of market coordination, production by coordinating the activities of several other producers.

18. Firm coordination occurs when firms can coordinate economic activity more efficiently than markets by reducing transaction costs and by achieving economies of scale, scope, and team production.

CONCEPT CHECKERS: ORGANIZING PRODUCTION

1. Economic profits are zero if:
   A. implicit costs equal explicit costs.
   B. economic depreciation equals zero.
   C. total revenue equals the sum of all opportunity costs.
   D. the implied rental rate equals forgone interest.

2. Assume that a firm had total revenue of $50 million and used $30 million in labor and materials to generate that revenue. Other costs included $100,000 in foregone interest, economic depreciation of $20,000, and normal profit is $65,000. Using this information, calculate the economic profit to the firm.
   A. $19,803,000.
   B. $19,815,000.
   C. $19,856,000.
   D. $20,000,000.

3. Which of the following statements regarding technological and economic efficiency is *most accurate*?
   A. Whenever an activity is technologically efficient, it must be economically efficient.
   B. It is not possible for an economic activity to be both economically and technologically efficient.
   C. For a given output, a technologically efficient method uses the least amount of inputs and an economically efficient method has lowest possible cost.
   D. For a given output, a technologically efficient method uses the least amount of labor and an economically efficient method uses the least amount of capital.

4. Consider two markets: one has a Herfindahl-Hirschman Index (HHI) of 500, while the other has a four-firm ratio concentration ratio equal to 2%. Which of the following statements *most accurately* describes these two markets?
   A. Both markets are highly competitive.
   B. Both of these markets are monopolies.
   C. The market with the HHI equal to 500 is very competitive, while the other market has a low degree of competition.
   D. The market with the HHI equal to 500 has a low degree of competition, while the other market is highly competitive.

5. The implied rental rate includes:
   A. normal profit and explicit costs.
   B. foregone interest and normal profit.
   C. economic depreciation and normal profit.
   D. economic depreciation and foregone interest.

6. An industry with a Herfindahl-Hirschman Index (HHI) of 2,800 and a four-firm concentration ratio of 75% is *most likely* competing in which type of market?
   A. Oligopoly.
   B. Monopoly.
   C. Perfect competition.
   D. Monopolistic competition.

7. Which of the following is *least likely* to be used to reduce the principal-agent problem in corporations?
    A. Use of a company jet.
    B. An ownership incentive.
    C. An incentive-pay system.
    D. Long-term employment contracts.

8. Which of the following statements *least accurately* describes why firms can sometimes coordinate economic activity more efficiently than markets? Firms can achieve economies of:
    A. scale.
    B. scope.
    C. cost.
    D. team production.

9. Consider two manufacturing processes that can be used to produce the same quantity of a given product. Process A uses 10 units of labor and 50 units of physical capital. Process B uses 10 units of labor and 500 units of capital. Which of the following *most accurately* describes these two processes?
    A. Process A is economically efficient and technologically efficient.
    B. Process B is technologically inefficient and economically efficient.
    C. Process A is technologically efficient and either may be economically efficient.
    D. Process B is technologically inefficient and either may be economically efficient.

ANSWERS – CONCEPT CHECKERS: ORGANIZING PRODUCTION

1. C   Economic profit considers both explicit and implicit opportunity costs. When total revenues are just equal to opportunity costs (explicit and implicit, including normal profit), economic profits are zero.

2. B   Economic profit = total revenue – opportunity costs = total revenue – (explicit + implicit costs). In this case, the labor and material cost of $30 million is the explicit cost. Implicit costs include the $100,000 in foregone interest, economic depreciation of $20,000, and normal profit of $65,000. So, total implicit costs equal $100,000 + $20,000 + $65,000 = $185,000. Thus, economic profit is $50,000,000 – $30,000,000 – $185,000 = $19,815,000.

3. C   Technological efficiency is achieved by using the least amount of inputs to produce a given output. Economic efficiency is achieved by producing a given output at the lowest possible cost.

4. A   An HHI of 500 is low, indicating a high degree of competition. A four-firm concentration ratio of 2% indicates a high level of competition. The higher (lower) the concentration measure, the lower (greater) the degree of competition.

5. D   The implied rental rate includes economic depreciation and foregone interest. When discussing economic profit, economic depreciation is the decrease in the value of an asset while that asset is being used to produce a product.

6. A   A monopoly market has a Herfindahl-Hirschman Index of 10,000 and a four-firm concentration ratio of 100%. An HHI index greater than 1,800 indicates an uncompetitive market and a four-firm ratio greater than 60% indicates an oligopoly market. Therefore, the firms in the industry described are most likely in an oligopoly market.

7. A   A company jet could be a symptom of a principal-agent problem and does not address a divergence of incentives. The other three are common methods to reduce the principal-agent problem.

8. C   Firms can often coordinate economic activity more efficiently than markets because firms can reduce the costs of market transactions, and they can achieve economies of scale, scope, and team production. Economies of cost is a made-up term.

9. A   Process A is technologically efficient because for the same 10 units of labor, it can produce the given output with less capital. For any prices of capital and labor, Process A must have a lower cost, so it is also the economically efficient process.

The following is a review of the Economics principles designed to address the learning outcome statements set forth by CFA Institute®. This topic is also covered in:

OUTPUT AND COSTS

Study Session 4

EXAM FOCUS

This review is primarily focused on the relationship between short-run costs and output. You should know how total, marginal, and average product relate to the components of total cost. Be able to describe diminishing returns to labor and capital, and understand the long-run conditions that lead to economies of scale.

LOS 17.a: Explain why technology is a constraint on the increase of output in the short-term, how a firm can change output in the short run using the concepts of total, marginal, and average product, and the implication on short-run cost using the concepts of total, marginal, and average cost.

The ***short term*** (short run) is defined as a time period for which quantities of some resources are fixed. A firm has chosen its production methods and, if it is a manufacturer, the machinery it will use to produce its products.

So the technology of production is fixed in the short run and is a constraint on a firm's ability to increase production. Typically, economists treat labor and raw materials as variable in the short run, holding plant size, capital equipment, and technology constant.

In what follows, we will examine output in the short run, allowing only the quantity of labor employed to vary.

The table in Figure 1 contains output information for a hypothetical maker of shirts, Sam's Shirts. The first column of the table lists different quantities of workers per day that can be employed. The second column lists the total number of shirts per day that Sam's can produce with different numbers of workers, holding plant and equipment constant. This total output of shirts is called the **total product**. The third column has the number of additional shirts per day from adding each successive worker. This is the **marginal product** of labor, the additional output from adding one more unit (in this case one worker-day) of labor. The fourth column lists the average number of shirts per worker that are produced for each quantity of workers. This is the **average product** of labor. Note that the units of total, marginal, and average product are units of the good produced per unit of the input under consideration, in this case, shirts per worker day.

Figure 1: Short-Run Output as a Function of Labor Employed

Workers	*Total Product*	*Marginal Product*	*Average Product*
1	8	8	8
2	20	12	10
3	26	6	8.7
4	30	4	7.5
5	32	2	6.4
6	33	1	5.5

Panel (a) and panel (b) of Figure 2 show the total product curve and marginal product curve, respectively, for Sam's Shirts. The total and marginal product curves in Figure 2 have been "smoothed" to account for fractional worker days.

Note that the marginal product curve shown in panel (b) of Figure 2 initially increases, reaches a peak, and then begins to decline. This behavior is typical. The marginal product curve for an input typically shows increasing marginal returns initially, and diminishing marginal returns at some point. **Diminishing marginal returns** describes a situation where the marginal product of an input decreases as additional units of that input are employed.

Figure 2: Total Product and Marginal Product

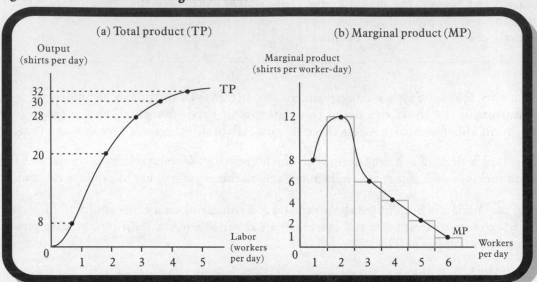

Figure 3 shows the relation between the average product curve for Sam's Shirts and the marginal product curve. Note in Figure 3 that average product is at its maximum at the point where the marginal product curve intersects it from above. For Sam's Shirts, this intersection occurs between two and three workers per day. Note that for the second worker, MP is greater than AP, but with three workers, MP is less than AP. This relationship is not unique to Sam's Shirts. Typically, marginal product exceeds average product up to some input quantity where they are equal. Beyond that point, marginal product is less than average product.

Figure 3: Average Product and Marginal Product of Labor

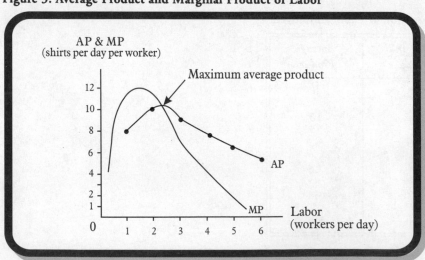

Short-Run Cost

To increase output in the short run, firms must use more labor, which increases cost. The relationship between output and cost may be explained in terms of three cost concepts: (1) total cost, (2) marginal cost, and (3) average cost.

Total cost, TC, is the sum of all costs associated with the generation of output. Total cost is made up of total *fixed* cost and total *variable* cost.

Total fixed cost, TFC, is the cost of fixed inputs, such as property, plant, and equipment, plus *normal profit,* i.e., the value of the entrepreneurial ability of the firm's owners or managers. Total fixed cost is independent of the level of the firm's output in the short run.

Total variable cost, TVC, is the cost of all variable production inputs. Total variable cost increases as output increases. The single biggest variable cost for most firms is the cost of labor (and raw materials for manufacturing firms).

total cost = total fixed cost + total variable cost

Figure 4 illustrates the components of total cost for Sam's Shirts at different output levels. We will assume that Sam's fixed cost is $20 per day to rent one sewing machine. This amount will not change regardless of the quantity of shirts produced. So, the TFC curve is a horizontal line at $20 per day.

For simplicity, assume that labor is the only variable cost, and that Sam pays his workers $20 per day. So total variable cost will increase by $20 as each additional worker is required to increase output. Notice in Figure 4 that the vertical distance between the TVC and the TC curves is total fixed cost. It is also important to note that both TVC and TC are increasing. This is because TVC increases as output increases. Total cost at various levels of output for Sam's Shirts is tabulated in Figure 5.

Figure 4: Total Cost Curves

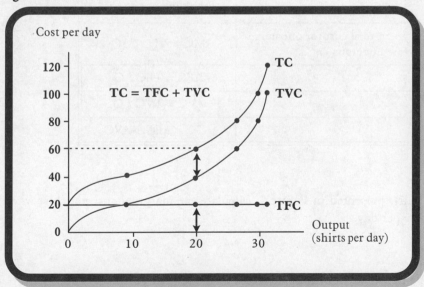

Notice that the TC and TVC curves in Figure 4 increase at an increasing rate. This behavior can be explained through a discussion of the concept of marginal cost.

Marginal cost, MC, is the increase in total cost for one additional unit of output. Since the addition of each worker results in multiple additional shirts, we divide the change in total cost by the increase in output to get the marginal cost amounts in Figure 5. That is:

$$\text{marginal cost} = \frac{\text{change in total cost}}{\text{change in output}}, \text{ or } MC = \frac{\Delta TC}{\Delta Q}$$

For Sam's Shirts, MC has been calculated and tabulated in Figure 5.

Figure 5: Total, Marginal, and Average Costs for Sam's Shirts

Output (Shirts)	Labor (workers/day)	TFC ($/day)	TVC	TC	MC ($/additional shirt)	AFC ($/shirt)	AVC	ATC
0	0	20	0	20	-----2.50-----			
8	1	20	20	40	----1.67-----	2.50	2.50	5.00
20	2	20	40	60	-----3.33-----	1.00	2.00	3.00
26	3	20	60	80	-----5.00-----	0.77	2.31	3.08
30	4	20	80	100	-----10.00-----	0.67	2.67	3.33
32	5	20	100	120		0.63	3.13	3.75

TFC = Total fixed cost	cost of fixed inputs; independent of output	
TVC = Total variable cost	cost of variable inputs; changes with output	
TC = Total cost		TC = TFC + TVC
MC = Marginal cost	change in total cost for one unit increase in output	MC = ΔTC / ΔQ
AFC = Average fixed cost		AFC = TFC / Q
AVC = Average variable cost		AVC = TVC / Q
ATC = Average total cost		ATC = AFC + AVC

Example: Marginal cost

Using the information for Sam's Shirts presented in Figure 5, calculate the marginal cost per shirt when output increases from 8 to 20 shirts per day.

Answer:

In Figure 5, we see that the change in TC when output increases from eight to 20 shirts is $60 − $40 = $20. Since the change in output is 20 − 8 = 12 shirts, the marginal cost can be calculated as:

MC = $20 / 12 shirts = $1.67 per shirt

Average cost is the average cost per unit of output at a given level of output. Since there are three types of costs, there are three corresponding average costs. These are:

- **Average fixed cost**, AFC, total fixed cost per unit of output.
- **Average variable cost**, AVC, total variable cost per unit of output.
- **Average total cost**, ATC, total cost per unit of output.

The individual average costs are calculated by dividing the total costs at a given level of output, Q, by that level of output. Mathematically, we have:

$$\frac{TC}{Q} = \frac{TFC}{Q} + \frac{TVC}{Q}, \text{ or ATC} = \text{AFC} + \text{AVC}$$

Average costs at the various output levels for Sam's have been calculated and tabulated in Figure 5. The marginal cost (MC) and average cost (ATC, AVC, and AFC) curves for Sam's Shirts are in Figure 6.

Figure 6: Average and Marginal Costs

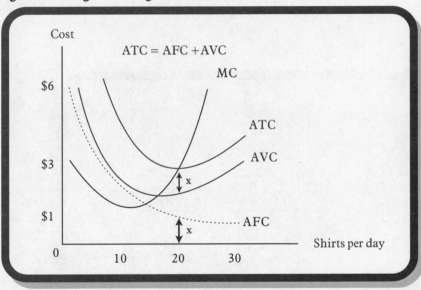

LOS 17.b: Explain the shape of the marginal cost curve and the average total cost curve, and explain the relationships between the different cost curves.

Important relationships among the marginal and average cost curves in Figure 6 are:

- *AFC slopes downward*. This is because fixed costs are constant, but are distributed over a larger and larger number of products as output quantity increases.
- *The vertical distance between the ATC and AVC curves is equal to AFC*. This is indicated by the arrows marked "x" at an output of 20 shirts per day.
- *MC declines initially, then increases*. At low output quantities, efficiencies are realized from the specialization of labor. However, as more and more labor is added, marginal cost increases. This is due to *diminishing returns*, which means that at some point, each added worker contributes less to total output than the previously added worker.
- *MC intersects AVC and ATC at their minimum points*. The intersection comes from below, which implies that when MC is less than ATC or AVC, respectively, ATC or AVC are decreasing, This also implies that when MC exceeds ATC or AVC, respectively, ATC or AVC are increasing.
- *ATC and AVC are U-shaped*. AVC decreases initially, but as output increases, the effect of diminishing returns sets in and AVC eventually slopes upward, giving the curve its U-shape. However, since fixed costs are spread out over a larger and larger quantity of output, AFC decreases as output increases, and eventually flattens out. ATC gets its U-shape because as output increases we are adding a curve that goes from downward

sloping to flat (AFC) to a U-shaped curve (AVC), which results in a U-shaped ATC curve. Remember, ATC = AVC + AFC.

The relationship between product curves and cost curves is illustrated in Figure 7, where average and marginal product curves for a firm are presented in panel (a), and marginal and average cost curves are presented in panel (b). Figure 7 illustrates the following important links between a firm's product curves (technology) and its cost curves.

- Over the initial increase in labor from zero to L_1 in panel (a), MP and AP increase and MP reaches its maximum. Over the corresponding output range in panel (b), MC and AVC decrease to output quantity Q_1 where MC is at a minimum. Note that L_1 is the labor required to produce Q_1.
- As labor increases from L_1 to L_2, and output increases from Q_1 to Q_2, AP continues to increase to a maximum at L_2 and AVC continues to fall to its minimum at Q_2. Over this same production range, MP is declining and MC is rising.
- As labor increases beyond L_2 and output increases beyond Q_2, MP and AP both decrease, and MC and AVC both increase.

Figure 7: Product and Cost Curves

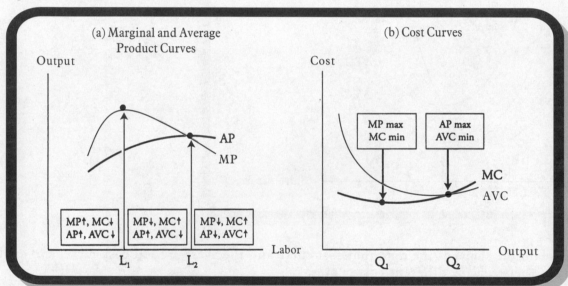

LOS 17.c: Discuss the concepts of diminishing returns and diminishing marginal product of capital.

The **law of diminishing returns** states that at some point, as more and more of one resource (e.g., labor) is added to the production process, holding the quantity of other inputs constant, the output continues to increase, but at a decreasing rate. For example, if an acre of corn needs to be picked, the addition of a second and third worker is highly productive. If you already have 300 workers in the field, the additional output from adding the 301st worker is lower than that of the second worker.

The *marginal product of capital* is the increase in output from using one additional unit of capital, holding the quantity of labor constant. **Diminishing marginal product of capital** means that at a constant level of labor, output increases as capital is added, but at some point, the increase in output from adding one more unit of capital begins to decrease.

LOS 17.d: Explain the relationship between the long-run and short-run costs, and the different economies and diseconomies of scale.

Short-run cost curves apply to a plant of a given size. In the long run, everything is variable, including technology, plant size, and equipment. Long-run cost curves are known as *planning curves*. There is often a trade-off between the size of the firm and unit costs in the long run.

Three reasons unit cost may decline as output or plant size increase are:

- Savings due to mass production.
- Specialization of labor and machinery.
- Experience.

The downward sloping segment of the long-run average total cost curve presented in Figure 8 indicates that **economies of scale** are present. In this range increasing the scale (size) of the firm results in lower average unit costs. The upward sloping segment of this long-run average total cost curve indicates that **diseconomies of scale** are present when average unit costs rise as the scale of the business increases. The flat portion of the long-run average total costs curve in Figure 8 represents *constant returns to scale*. As shown, the optimal firm size (the one that will minimize average unit costs) is one which will produce Q* units of output.

Figure 8: Long-Run Average Total Cost

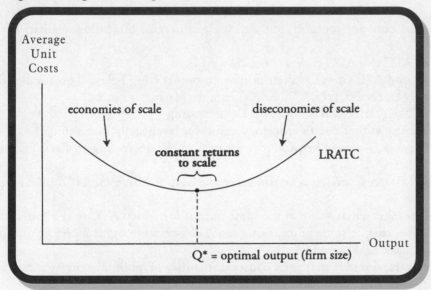

Diseconomies of scale may result as the increasing bureaucracy of larger firms leads to inefficiency, as well as from problems of motivating a larger work force, greater barriers to innovation and entrepreneurial activity, and increased principal-agent problems.

KEY CONCEPTS

1. Technology constraints arise from production capital and methods that cannot be changed in the short run.
2. Total product is the total output of goods.
3. Marginal product is the increase in total product from using one additional unit of input.
4. Average product is total output divided by the units of a variable input. The average product curve is at its maximum at the point where the marginal product curve intersects it from above.
5. Total cost is the sum of total fixed and total variable costs.
6. Total fixed cost is the cost of fixed inputs, such as property, plant, and equipment and it is independent of output. Total variable cost is the cost of all variable production inputs (e.g., labor) and it increases as output increases.
7. Marginal cost is the increase in total cost for a one unit increase in output.
8. As labor is added, marginal cost decreases at first, but eventually increases due to diminishing returns (diminishing marginal product).
9. There are three average costs:
    - Average fixed cost (AFC) is total fixed cost per unit of output.
    - Average variable cost (AVC) is total variable cost per unit of output.
    - Average total cost (ATC) is total cost per unit of output.

$$\frac{TC}{Q} = \frac{TFC}{Q} + \frac{TVC}{Q}, \text{ or ATC} = \text{AFC} + \text{AVC}$$

10. AFC slopes downward because fixed costs are constant, but are averaged over an increasing quantity of output.
11. The vertical distance between the ATC and AVC curves is equal to AFC.
12. The MC curve intersects the AVC and ATC curves at their minimum points from below. This implies that:
    - when MC is less than ATC or AVC, respectively, ATC or AVC are decreasing.
    - when MC exceeds ATC or AVC, respectively, ATC or AVC are increasing.
13. The AVC curve is U-shaped, declining at first due to efficiency gains, but eventually increasing due to diminishing returns. The ATC curve is U-shaped because it is the sum of the decreasing-to-flat AFC curve and the U-shaped AVC curve.
14. As labor and output increase, the MP curve reaches a maximum at the output where the MC curve is at its minimum.
15. As labor and output increase, AP reaches a maximum at the same output for which AVC is at a minimum.
16. The law of diminishing returns states that, at some point, using more of a variable input increases output at a decreasing rate when other inputs are held constant.
17. Diminishing marginal product of capital means that for a constant quantity of labor, output increases at a decreasing rate as more capital is employed.
18. Short-run cost curves are plant-size specific, whereas long-run cost curves show minimum average unit costs for different firm sizes (scale of operations).
19. Economies of scale are present when unit costs fall as plant size increases.
20. Diseconomies of scale are present when costs rise as plant size increases, often arising from the bureaucratic inefficiencies that occur with larger firms.

CONCEPT CHECKERS: OUTPUT AND COSTS

1. Which of the following *most accurately* describes the relationship between marginal product (MP) and average product (AP) of labor in the short run?
    A. AP is always less than MP.
    B. Initially, AP = MP, then AP > MP.
    C. Initially, AP < MP, then AP = MP, then AP > MP.
    D. Initially, AP > MP, then AP = MP, then AP < MP.

2. When marginal product is at a maximum:
    A. marginal cost is at a minimum.
    B. average product is at a minimum.
    C. average variable cost is increasing.
    D. average variable cost is at a minimum.

3. As a result of increasing labor from 100 to 110 workers, output increased from 1,250 to 1,550 units per day. The marginal product of an additional worker is *closest* to:
    A. 30 units per day.
    B. 1.55 units per day.
    C. 1.25 units per day.
    D. 300 units per day.

4. If both average product (AP) and marginal product (MP) are equal to 4 when 10 workers are employed, what can we *most likely* conclude about AP and MP when 15 workers are employed?
    A. AP = MP = 5.
    B. AP = 5 and MP = 6.
    C. AP = 4 and MP = 6.
    D. AP = 7 and MP = 5.

5. Which of the following *most accurately* describes the shapes of the average variable cost (AVC) curve and average total cost (ATC) curve?
    A. The AVC curve and the ATC curve are both U-shaped.
    B. The AVC and ATC curves both decrease initially, then flatten.
    C. The AVC curve is U-shaped; the ATC curve declines initially then flattens.
    D. The AVC curve declines initially then flattens; the ATC curve is U-shaped.

6. The vertical distance between the average total cost (ATC) curve and average variable cost (AVC) curve:
    A. increases as output increases.
    B. decreases as output increases.
    C. remains constant as output increases.
    D. increases and then decreases as output increases.

7. Which of the following *most accurately* describes the shape of the average fixed cost curve?
    A. It becomes relatively flat at large output levels.
    B. It is always below the average variable cost curve.
    C. It has the same shape as the average total cost curve.
    D. It intersects the marginal cost curve at its minimum.

8.   Economies of scale:
        A. increase at a decreasing rate.
        B. are dependent on short-run average costs.
        C. occur when average unit costs fall with larger firm size.
        D. occur when the long-run average cost curve is sloping upward.

9.   For a fixed level of capital, output increases as the quantity of labor increases, but at a decreasing rate. This phenomenon is *most accurately* described by the law of diminishing:
        A. returns to labor.
        B. costs to labor.
        C. returns to capital.
        D. returns to technology.

10.   When average product is at a maximum:
        A. marginal cost is at a minimum.
        B. marginal product is increasing.
        C. marginal product is at a minimum.
        D. average variable cost is at a minimum.

ANSWERS – CONCEPT CHECKERS: OUTPUT AND COSTS

1. C MP intersects the AP minimum from above. MP is initially greater than AP, and then MP and AP intersect. Beyond this intersection, MP is less than AP. (Hint: draw the curves.)

2. A Marginal product is at a maximum when marginal cost is at a minimum. At the corresponding labor and output levels, average variable cost is decreasing and average product is increasing.

3. A Marginal product is the change in output divided by the change in input (labor). Since output changed by 300 units and labor changed by 10 workers, the marginal product is 300 / 10 = 30 units per day.

4. D For most production processes, as the quantity of labor increases, marginal product is initially greater than average product. Then at some level of labor input, the two curves intersect. Then beyond this intersection, marginal product is less than average product. So, beyond AP = MP = 4, MP must be less than AP. (Hint: draw the curves.)

5. A The AVC curve is U-shaped, declining at first due to efficiency, but eventually increasing due to diminishing returns. The AFC curve decreases as output increases, and eventually flattens out. The ATC is U-shaped because it is the sum of the decreasing-to-flat AFC curve plus the U-shaped AVC curve. ATC = AFC + AVC.

6. B The vertical distance between the average total cost curve and average variable cost curve is average fixed cost, which decreases as output increases because more output is averaged over the same cost.

7. A Average fixed cost initially declines rapidly, but as output increases it flattens out, because fixed cost is being averaged over more and more units of output.

8. C Economies of scale occur when the percentage increase in output is greater than the percentage increase in cost of all inputs. They occur when the long-run average cost curve slopes downward.

9. A The law of diminishing returns states that at some point, as more and more of a resource (e.g., labor) is devoted to a production process, holding the quantity of other inputs constant, the output increases, but at a decreasing rate.

10. D When average product is at a maximum, average variable cost is at a minimum. At the corresponding labor and output level, marginal product is decreasing and marginal cost is increasing.

The following is a review of the Economics principles designed to address the learning outcome statements set forth by CFA Institute®. This topic is also covered in:

PERFECT COMPETITION

EXAM FOCUS

You should be able to explain what a price-taker market is and how price and output are determined in the short run and the long run. Pay special attention to the relationship between marginal cost, marginal revenue, price, and output for a perfectly competitive firm. Know how the concept of economic profit applies to perfect competition. Finally, you should be able to explain the adjustments that take place in response to changes in industry demand. A good understanding of the case of perfect competition is important because this is the model of economically efficient markets to which we will compare other market structures in the reviews that follow.

LOS 18.a: Explain why firms in perfect competition are price takers, and discuss the relationship between demand, price and revenue.

Price takers are firms that face horizontal (perfectly elastic) demand curves. They can sell all of their output at the prevailing market price, but if they set their output price higher than the market price, they would sell nothing. They are price takers because they take the market price as given and do not have to devote any resources to discovering the best price at which to sell their product. A "price-taker market" is equivalent to a perfectly competitive market.

Perfect competition assumes the following:

- All the firms in the market produce identical products.
- There is a large number of independent firms.
- Each seller is small relative to the size of the total market.
- There are no barriers to entry or exit.

Producer firms in perfect competition have no influence over market price. Market supply and demand determine price. As illustrated in Figure 1, *the individual firm's* demand schedule is *perfectly elastic* (horizontal).

Figure 1: Price-Taker Demand

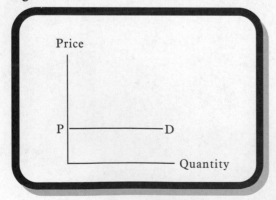

In a perfectly competitive market a firm will continue to expand production until marginal revenue, MR, equals marginal cost, MC. Marginal revenue is the increase in total revenue from selling one more unit of a good or service. For a price taker, marginal revenue is simply price because all additional units are assumed to be sold at the same (market) price. In *pure competition*, a firm's marginal revenue is equal to the market price and a firm's MR curve, presented in Figure 2, is identical to the demand curve.

Figure 2: Marginal Revenue Curve

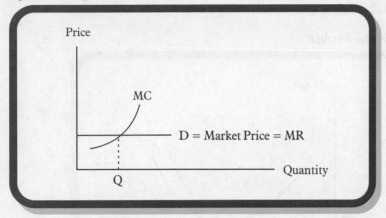

LOS 18.b: Discuss how the firm maximizes profit in perfect competition, analyze the marginal costs and revenue, and the concepts of economic profit and loss.

All firms maximize (economic) profit by producing and selling the quantity for which marginal revenue equals marginal cost. For a price taker in a perfectly competitive market, this is the same as producing and selling the output for which marginal revenue equals (market) price. Economic profit equals total revenues less the opportunity cost of production, which includes the cost of a normal return to all factors of production, including invested capital.

Figure 3(a) illustrates that in the *short run*, economic profit is maximized when marginal revenue = marginal cost = price, or MR = MC = P. As shown in Figure 3(b), profit maximization also occurs when total revenue exceeds total cost by the maximum amount.

An *economic loss* occurs if marginal revenue is less than marginal cost. The firm will be generating losses on its marginal production and will reduce output to where MR = MC.

Figure 3: Short-Run Profit Maximization

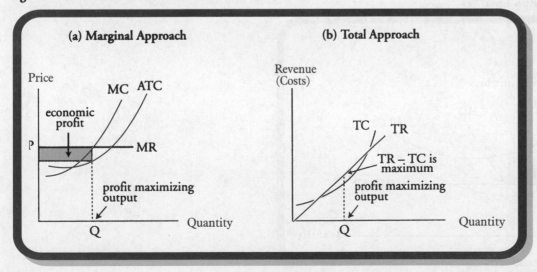

In a perfectly competitive market, a firm will not earn economic profits for any significant period of time. The assumption is that new firms (with average and marginal cost curves identical to those of existing firms) will enter the industry to earn profits, increasing market supply and eventually reducing market price so that it just equals a firm's average total cost (ATC). In equilibrium, each firm is producing the quantity for which P = MR = MC = ATC, so that no firm earns economic profits and each firm is producing the quantity for which ATC is a minimum (the quantity for which ATC = MC). This is illustrated in Figure 4.

Figure 4: Equilibrium in a Perfectly Competitive Market

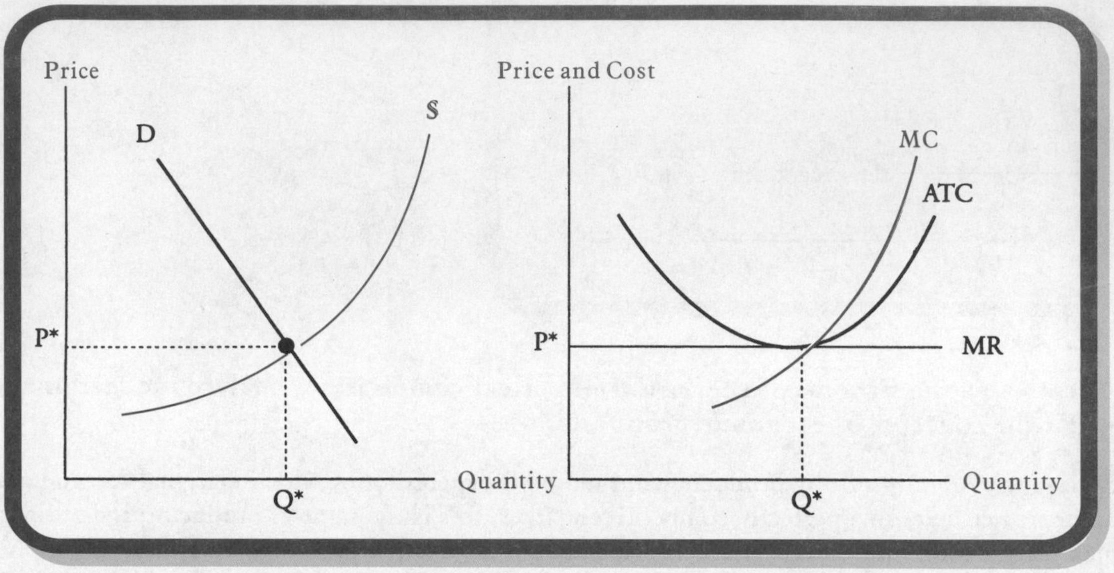

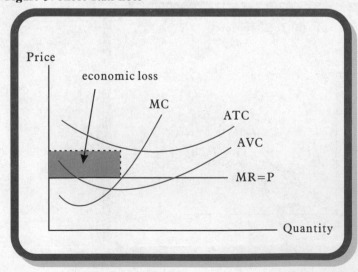

Figure 5 illustrates that firms will experience economic losses when price is below average total cost (P < ATC). In this case, the firm must decide whether to continue operating. A firm will minimize its losses in the short run by continuing to operate when P < ATC but P > AVC. As long as the firm is covering its variable costs and some of its fixed costs, its loss will be less than its fixed (in the short run) costs. If the firm is not covering its variable costs (P < AVC) by continuing to operate, its losses will be greater than its fixed costs. In this case, the firm will shut down (zero output) and lay off its workers. This will limit its losses to its fixed costs (e.g., its building lease and debt payments). If the firm does not believe price will ever exceed ATC in the future, going out of business is the only way to eliminate fixed costs.

Figure 5: Short-Run Loss

The *long-run equilibrium output* level for perfectly competitive firms is where MR = MC = ATC, which is where ATC is at a minimum. At this output, economic profit is zero and only a normal return is realized.

LOS 18.c: Distinguish between the firm's and the industry's short-run supply curve, and explain the relationship between the two.

Recall that price takers should produce where P = MC. Referring to Figure 6(a), a firm will shut down at a price below P_1. Between P_1 and P_2 a firm will continue to operate in the short run. At P_2 the firm is earning a normal profit—economic profit equals zero. At prices above P_2, a firm is making economic profits and will expand its production along the MC line. Thus, the **short-run supply curve for a firm** is its MC line above the average variable cost curve, AVC. The supply curve shown in Figure 6(b) is the **short-run market supply curve**, which is the horizontal sum (add up the quantities from all firms at each price) of the MC curves for all firms in a given industry. Since firms will supply more units at higher prices, the short-run market supply curve slopes upward to the right.

Figure 6: Short-Run Supply Curves

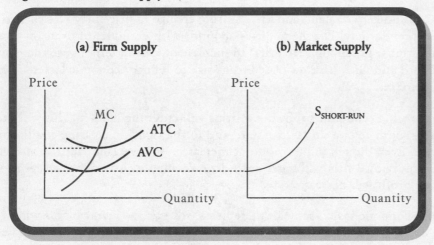

LOS 18.d: Explain the relationship between the firm's marginal cost, marginal revenue, and price when a firm in perfect competition produces the quantity that maximizes profit.

The profit-maximizing output for a competitive firm (price taker) is the output for which marginal revenue equals marginal cost. Since the demand curve faced by each firm in perfect competition is horizontal, marginal revenue is equal to price. For each additional unit the firm sells, its total revenue increases by the price of a unit.

LOS 18.e: Discuss the impact of changes in demand, long-run adjustments, entry and exit, and changes in plant size on the long-run equilibrium.

In the short run, an increase in demand (a shift of the market demand curve to the right) will increase both equilibrium price and quantity, while a decrease in demand will reduce both equilibrium price and quantity. The change in equilibrium price will change the (horizontal) demand curve faced by each individual firm and the profit-maximizing output of a firm. These effects for an increase in demand are illustrated in Figure 7, where we can see that an increase in market demand from D_1 to D_2 increases the short-run equilibrium price from P_1 to P_2 and equilibrium output from Q_1 to Q_2. In Figure 7(b), we see the short-run effect of the increased market price on the output of an individual firm. The higher price leads to a greater profit-maximizing output, Q_{2Firm}. At the higher output level, a firm will earn an economic profit in the short run. So, faced with increased demand, some firms will increase their scale of operations, and new firms will likely enter the industry. On the other hand, when firms are faced with a decrease in demand, the short-run equilibrium price and quantity will fall, and firms will decrease their scale of operations or exit the market.

Figure 7: Short-Run Adjustment to an Increase in Demand Under Perfect Competition

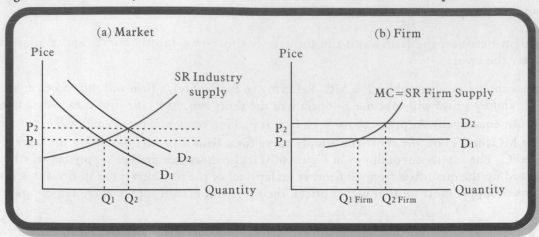

A firm's long-run adjustment to a shift in industry demand and the resulting change in price may be either to alter the size of its plant or leave the market entirely. The marketplace abounds with examples of firms that have increased their plant sizes (or added additional production facilities) to increase output in response to increasing market demand. Other firms, such as Ford and GM, have decreased plant size to reduce economic losses. This strategy is commonly referred to as *downsizing*.

If an industry is characterized by firms earning economic profits, new firms will enter the market. This will cause industry supply to increase (the industry supply curve shifts downward and to the right), increasing equilibrium output and decreasing equilibrium price. Even though industry output increases, however, individual firms will produce less because as price falls, each individual firm will move down its own supply curve. The end result is that a firm's total revenue and economic profit will decrease.

If firms in an industry are experiencing economic losses, some of these firms will exit the market. This will decrease industry supply and increase equilibrium price. Each remaining firm in the industry will move up its individual supply curve and increase production at the higher market price. This will cause total revenues to increase, reducing any economic losses the remaining firms had been experiencing.

LOS 18.f: Discuss how a permanent change of demand or changes in technology impact price, output, and economic profit.

A *permanent change in demand* leads to the entry of firms to or exit of firms from an industry. Let's consider the permanent increase in demand illustrated in Figure 8. The initial long-run industry equilibrium condition shown in Figure 8(a) is at the intersection of demand curve D_0 and supply curve S_0, at price P_0 and quantity Q_0. As indicated in Figure 8(b), at the market price of P_0 each firm will produce q_0. At this price and output, each firm earns a normal profit, and economic profit is zero. That is, MC = MR = P and ATC is at its minimum. Now, suppose industry demand permanently increases such that the industry demand curve in Figure 8(a) shifts to D_1. The new market price will be P_1 and industry output will increase to Q_1. At the new price P_1, existing firms will produce q_1 and realize an economic profit since $P_1 > $ ATC. Positive economic profits will cause new firms to enter the market. As these new firms increase total industry supply, the industry supply curve will gradually shift to S_1, and the market price will decline back to P_0. At the market price of P_0, the industry will now produce Q_2, with an increased number of firms in the industry, each producing at the original quantity, q_0. The individual firms will no longer enjoy an economic profit since ATC = P_0 at q_0.

Figure 8: Effects of a Permanent Increase in Demand

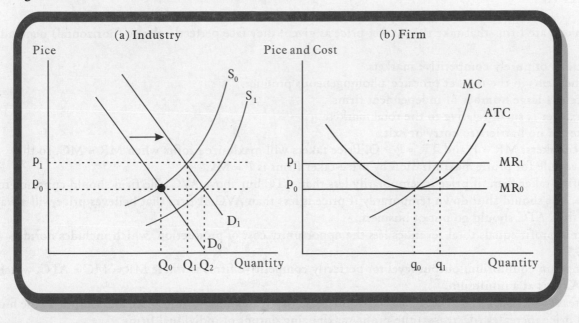

Technological changes, such as a lower-cost production process, usually require firms to invest in additional fixed assets (e.g., plant and equipment). Consequently, technological advances take some time to become common practice throughout an industry. Once individual firms have implemented technological changes, their costs decline and their supply (cost) curve shifts to the right. At the lower costs, firms are willing to supply a given quantity at a reduced price, or provide more of a product at a higher price. In either case, the lower cost structure for the individual firms shifts the industry supply curve to the right. With a given demand, and this repositioned industry supply curve, the industry supplies more of a given product at a lower price.

Firms that are the first to adopt the new cost-reducing technology will earn economic profits. New firms that use the new technology will be attracted to the industry by profits. Existing firms using the older (higher-cost) technology will experience economic losses and be forced to either adopt the new technology or exit the industry. Long-run equilibrium with price equal to minimum average total cost for the new technology will be established after all firms in the industry have adopted the new technology. In long-run equilibrium, firms again will earn zero economic profits as the number of firms in the industry will be the number for which total industry supply makes equilibrium price equal to minimum average total cost (and marginal cost) for each firm.

KEY CONCEPTS

1. Price takers are firms that take the market price as given; they face perfectly elastic (horizontal) demand curves.

2. Conditions of purely competitive markets:
   - All the firms in the market produce a homogeneous product.
   - There is a large number of independent firms.
   - Each seller is small relative to the total market.
   - There are no barriers to entry or exit.

3. For price takers, MR = P and TR = P × Q. Price takers will maximize profits when MR = MC, so the operative rule for profit maximization by price-taker firms is P = MC.

4. For a price-taker firm, if price is temporarily less than ATC but above AVC, the firm should continue to operate, but should shut down temporarily if price is less than AVC. A firm that believes price will always be less than ATC should go out of business.

5. Economic profit equals total revenues less the opportunity cost of production, which includes normal profits.

6. The long-run equilibrium output level for perfectly competitive firms is where MR = MC = ATC, which is where ATC is at a minimum.

7. An increase (decrease) in market demand will increase (decrease) equilibrium price and output as the higher (lower) price increases (decreases) the profit-maximizing output of individual firms.

8. A permanent increase (decrease) in demand leads to an increase (decrease) in the number of firms in the market.

9. Firms that are among the first to adopt new cost-saving technology will expand output and earn economic profits. When all industry firms have adopted the new technology, industry supply will be greater, equilibrium price lower, and equilibrium output higher. Price will again equal MC and minimum ATC for each firm, and economic profit will be zero.

CONCEPT CHECKERS: PERFECT COMPETITION

1. A firm operating under conditions of pure competition will:
    A. be a price-searcher.
    B. face a vertical demand curve.
    C. generate zero economic profit in the long run.
    D. produce a quantity where marginal revenue is less than marginal cost.

2. Under pure competition, a firm will experience economic losses when:
    A. MC is less than ATC.
    B. MR is greater than ATC.
    C. MC = ATC = MR = price.
    D. price is less than ATC.

3. A price-taker firm will increase output as long as:
    A. marginal revenue is positive.
    B. marginal cost is less than average cost.
    C. marginal revenue is greater than marginal cost.
    D. marginal revenue is greater than the average cost.

4. Which of these statements is *most accurate* regarding the characteristics of a perfectly competitive market?
    A. Firms' products are different.
    B. There are more buyers than there are sellers.
    C. The competitors never earn economic profits.
    D. Barriers to entry into the market are nonexistent.

5. Under perfect competition, the long-run equilibrium condition for a firm may be described as:
    A. TC = TR = P.
    B. P = ATC = TR.
    C. MC = TR = TC.
    D. P = MC = ATC.

6. When a firm operates under conditions of pure competition, marginal revenue always equals:
    A. price.
    B. total revenue.
    C. average fixed cost.
    D. average variable cost.

7. A firm is likely to continue production in the short run as long as price is at least equal to:
    A. marginal cost.
    B. average fixed cost.
    C. average total cost.
    D. average variable cost.

8. A purely competitive firm will tend to expand its output so long as:
    A. its marginal revenue is positive.
    B. the marginal revenue is greater than price.
    C. the market price is greater than marginal cost.
    D. the marginal cost is greater than marginal revenue.

9.   The demand for the product of a purely competitive firm is:
     A. perfectly elastic.
     B. perfectly inelastic.
     C. greater than zero but less than one.
     D. dependent upon the availability of substitute products.

10. In a purely competitive market, economic losses indicate that:
     A. collusion is occurring in the market place.
     B. firms need to expand output to reduce costs.
     C. the industry is operating normally and production is at its efficient level.
     D. price is below average total costs.

ANSWERS – CONCEPT CHECKERS: PERFECT COMPETITION

1. C   A firm operating under conditions of pure competition will generate zero economic profit in the long run. In the short run, firms may generate economic profits. However, because of the lack of entry barriers, new competitors will enter the market and prices will adjust downward until economic profits disappear.

2. D   Under pure competition, a firm will experience losses when its selling price is less than average total cost. The other possible answers will not necessarily result in losses.

3. C   A firm will increase output, as long as MR > MC.

    Professor's Note: Don't forget that economic profit is the firm's total revenues less its opportunity cost.

4. D   The only true statement listed in the question is that, under pure competition, there are no barriers to entry into the market. Each of the other possible answers is incorrect. The answer "competitors never earn economic profits" is incorrect because price-taker firms can earn positive economic profits in the short run.

5. D   For a competitive firm, long-run equilibrium is where P = MC = ATC. For price-taker firms, P = MR. Competition eliminates economic profits in the long run so that P = ATC.

6. A   When a firm operates under conditions of pure competition, MR always equals price. This is because, in pure competition, demand is perfectly elastic (a horizontal line) so MR is constant and equal to price.

7. D   If price is greater than average variable cost, a firm will continue to operate in the short run since it is covering at least some of its fixed costs.

8. C   A purely competitive firm will tend to expand its output so long as the market price is greater than MC. In the short term and long term, profit is maximized when P = MC.

9. A   The demand for the product of a purely competitive firm is perfectly elastic. This is true because the market dictates price. If a price taker increases its price above the market price, the firm will sell no units.

10. D   In a purely competitive market, economic losses indicate that firms are overproducing, causing prices to fall below average total costs. This can occur in the short run. In the long run, however, market supply will decrease as firms exit the industry, and prices will rise to the point where economic profits are zero.

MONOPOLY

EXAM FOCUS

Be able to identify the key features of a monopoly and how natural monopolies arise. Know the relationship between price, marginal revenue, average cost, and marginal cost for a monopoly and why monopolies restrict output to an economically inefficient quantity compared to pure competition. Understand the social benefit of regulation imposing average cost pricing and why marginal cost pricing for a natural monopoly requires a subsidy.

LOS 19.a: Discuss the characteristics of a monopoly, how they arise, the key features, and monopoly price strategies.

A **monopoly** is characterized by one seller of a specific, well-defined product that has *no good substitutes*. For a firm to maintain its monopoly position it must be the case that *barriers to entry to the market are high*.

Barriers to entry are factors that make it difficult for competing firms to enter a market. There are two types of barriers to entry that can result in a monopoly, legal barriers and natural barriers.

Legal Barriers

Most legal barriers to entry do not result in actual monopolies. Restrictions on broadcast licenses for radio and television stations granted by the Federal Communications Commission in the U.S. present significant barriers to entry. Within each market, however, several such licenses are granted, so no one station has a monopoly on radio or television broadcasts. Such restrictions also offer an example of how market power of firms protected from competition by legal restrictions can erode over time as substitute products are developed. The introduction of cable television, satellite television, and, most recently, satellite radio have all significantly eroded the protection offered by possessing a local broadcast license.

Patents, copyrights, and government granted franchises are legal barriers to entry that can result in a single, monopoly, producer of a good in a market. U.S. laws give the U.S. Postal System the exclusive right to deliver mail (although substitute products have been introduced) and local laws grant exclusive rights to water, electric and other utilities. Patents give their owners the exclusive right to produce a good for a period of years just as copyright protection is offered to the creators of original material. Pharmaceutical firms, semiconductor firms, and software creators are a few of the types of firms that enjoy such protection from competition.

Natural Barriers

In some industries, the economics of production lead to a single firm supplying the entire market demand for the product. When there are large *economies of scale,* it means that the average cost of production decreases as a single firm produces greater and greater output. An example is an electric utility. The fixed costs of producing electricity and building the power lines and related equipment to deliver it to homes are quite high. The marginal cost of providing electricity to an additional home or of providing more electricity to a home is, however, quite low. The more electricity provided, the lower the average cost per kilowatt hour. When the average cost of production for a single firm is falling throughout the relevant range of consumer demand, we say that the industry is a **natural monopoly**. The entry of another firm into the industry would divide the production between two firms and result in a higher average cost of production than for a single producer. Thus, large economies of scale in an industry present significant barriers to entry.

A monopoly faces a downward sloping demand curve for its product so profit maximization involves a trade-off between price and quantity sold if the firm sells at the same price to all buyers. Assuming a single selling price, a monopoly firm must lower its price in order to sell a greater quantity. Unlike a firm in perfect competition, a firm facing a downward sloping demand curve must determine what price to change, hoping to find the price and output combination that will bring the maximum profit to the firm.

LOS 19.b: Explain the relationship between price, marginal revenue, and marginal cost for a monopoly.

To maximize profit, monopolists will expand output until marginal revenue (MR) equals marginal cost (MC). Due to high entry barriers, monopolist profits do not attract new market entrants. Therefore, long-run positive economic profits can exist. Do monopolists charge the highest possible price? The answer is no, because monopolists want to maximize profits, not price.

Figure 1 shows the revenue-cost structure facing the monopolist. Note that production will expand until MR = MC at optimal output Q*. To find the price at which it will sell Q* units you must go to the demand curve. The demand curve itself does not determine the optimal behavior of the monopolist. Just like the perfect competition model, the profit maximizing output for a monopolist is where MR = MC. To ensure a profit, the demand curve must lie above the firm's average total cost (ATC) curve at the optimal quantity so that price > ATC.

Figure 1: Monopolistic Short-Run Costs and Revenues

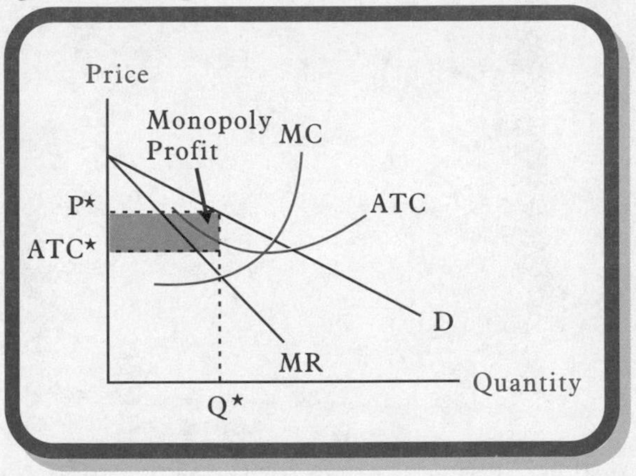

Once again, the *profit maximizing* output for a monopolistic firm is the one for which MR = MC. As shown in Figure 1, the profit maximizing output is Q*, with a price of P*, and an economic profit equal to
(P* – ATC*) × Q*.

Monopolists are *price searchers* and have *imperfect information* regarding market demand. They must experiment with different prices to find the one that maximizes profit.

LOS 19.c: Distinguish between monopoly and perfect competition, explain why a monopoly can set a higher price, and why a monopoly is considered inefficient.

Figure 2 illustrates the difference in allocative efficiency between monopoly and perfect competition. Under *perfect competition*, the industry supply curve, S, is the sum of the supply curves of the many competing firms in the industry. The perfect competition equilibrium price and quantity are at the intersection of the industry supply curve and the market demand curve, D. The quantity produced is Q_{PC} at an equilibrium price P_{PC}. Since each firm is small relative to the industry, there is nothing to be gained by attempting to decrease output in an effort to increase price.

A monopolist facing the same demand curve, and with the same marginal cost curve, MC, will maximize profit by producing Q_{MON} (where MC = MR) and charging a price of P_{MON}.

The important thing to note here is that when compared to a perfectly competitive industry, the monopoly firm will produce less total output and charge a higher price.

Recall from our review of perfect competition that the efficient quantity is the one for which the sum of consumer surplus and producer surplus is maximized. In Figure 2, this quantity is where S = D, or equivalently, where marginal cost (MC) = marginal benefit (MB). *Monopoly is considered to be inefficient* relative to perfect competition because monopolies produce a quantity that does not maximize the sum of consumer surplus and producer surplus.

Figure 2: Perfect Competition Versus Monopoly

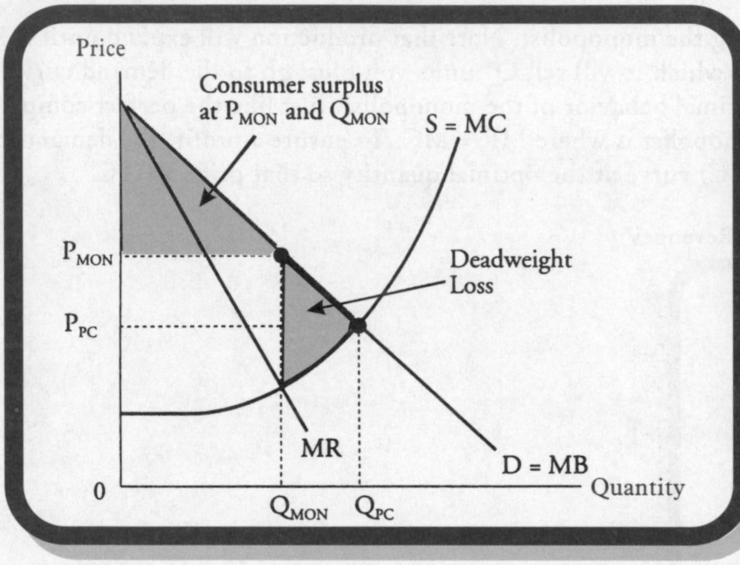

LOS 19.d: Explain the concepts of price discrimination.

Price discrimination is the practice of charging different consumers different prices for the same product or service. Examples are different prices for airline tickets based on whether a Saturday-night stay is involved (separates business travelers and leisure travelers) and different prices for movie tickets based on age.

The motivation for a monopolist is to capture more consumer surplus as economic profit than is possible by charging a single price.

For price discrimination to work, the seller must:

• Face a downward-sloping demand curve.
• Have at least two identifiable groups of customers with *different price elasticities of demand* for the product.
• Be able to prevent the customers paying the lower price from reselling the product to the customers paying the higher price.

As long as these conditions are met, firm profits can be increased through price discrimination.

Figure 3 illustrates how price discrimination can increase the total quantity supplied and increase economic profits. For simplicity, we have assumed no fixed costs and constant variable costs so that MC = ATC. In panel (a) the single profit-maximizing price is $100 at a quantity of 80 (where MC = MR), which generates a profit of $2,400. In panel (b) the firm is able to separate consumers, charges one group $110 and sells them 50 units, and sells an additional 60 units to another group (with more elastic demand) at a price of $90. Total profit is increased to $3,200 and total output is increased from 80 units to 110 units.

Compared to the quantity produced under perfect competition, the quantity produced by a monopolist reduces the sum of consumer and producer surplus by an amount represented by the triangle labeled *deadweight loss* in Figure 2. Consumer surplus is reduced not only by the decrease in quantity but also by the increase in price relative to perfect competition. Monopoly is considered inefficient because the reduction in output compared to perfect competition reduces the sum of consumer and producer surplus. Since marginal benefit is greater than marginal cost, less than the efficient quantity of resources are allocated to the production of the good. Price discrimination reduces this inefficiency by increasing output toward the quantity where marginal benefit equals marginal cost. Note that the deadweight loss (DWL) is smaller in panel (b). The firm gains from those customers with inelastic demand while still providing goods to customers with more elastic demand. This may even cause production to take place when it would not otherwise.

An extreme (and largely theoretical) case of price discrimination is perfect price discrimination. If it were possible for the monopolist to charge each consumer the maximum they are willing to pay for each unit, there would be no deadweight loss, since a monopolist would produce the same quantity as under perfect competition. With perfect price discrimination there would be no consumer surplus. It would all be captured by the monopolist.

Figure 3: Effect of Price Discrimination on Output and Operating Profit

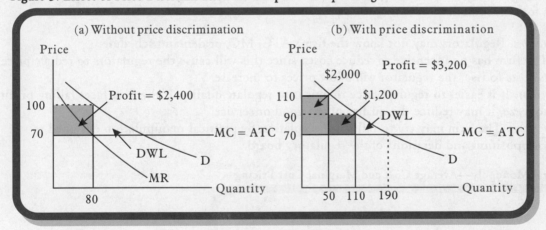

LOS 19.e: Discuss the reasons why a monopoly exists, how economies of scope and economies of scale can be achieved, and discuss the issues surrounding regulation of a natural monopoly.

Recall that a *natural monopoly* is an industry in which economies of scale are so pronounced that the ATC of total industry production is minimized when there is only one firm. Here, average total cost is declining over the entire range of relevant outputs. Fixed costs are high and marginal costs are quite low. We illustrate the case of a natural monopoly in Figure 4. Left unregulated, a single-price monopolist will maximize profits by producing where MR = MC, producing quantity Q_U and charging P_U. Given the economies of scale, having another firm in the market would increase the ATC significantly. Note in Figure 4 that if two firms each produced approximately one-half of output Q_{AC}, average cost for each firm would be much higher than for a single producer producing Q_{AC}.

Economies of scope can also lead to a natural monopoly, especially in an industry where economies of scale also exist. Economies of scope occur when a firm expands the range of goods it produces such that its average total cost is reduced. A firm such as Boeing uses very specialized equipment and computer programs to engineer the many parts that go into an airplane. This means that it can produce these components at a lower average cost than individual suppliers could.

Regulators often attempt to increase competition and efficiency through efforts to reduce artificial barriers to trade, such as licensing requirements, quotas, and tariffs.

Since monopolists produce less than the optimal quantity (do not achieve efficient resource allocation), government regulation may be aimed at improving resource allocation by regulating the prices monopolies may charge. This may be done through **average cost pricing** or **marginal cost pricing**.

Average cost pricing is the most common form of regulation. This would result in a price of P_{AC} and an output of Q_{AC} as illustrated in Figure 4. It forces monopolists to reduce price to where the firm's ATC intersects the market demand curve. This will:

- Increase output and decrease price.
- Increase social welfare (allocative efficiency).
- Ensure the monopolist a *normal* profit since price = ATC.

Marginal cost pricing forces the monopolist to reduce price to the point where the firm's MC curve intersects the market demand curve, which increases output and reduces price but causes the monopolist to incur a loss since price is below ATC, as illustrated in Figure 4. Such a solution requires a government subsidy in order to provide the firm with a normal profit and prevent it from leaving the market entirely.

Regulators sometimes go astray when dealing with the problems associated with markets with high barriers to entry. The reasons for this include:

- *Lack of information.* Regulators may not know the firm's ATC, MC, or demand schedule.
- *Cost shifting.* The firm has no incentive to reduce costs, since this will cause the regulators to reduce price. If the firm allows costs to rise, the regulator will allow prices to increase.
- *Quality regulations.* It is easier to regulate price than it is to regulate quality. If the firm faces falling profits due to a cost squeeze, it may reduce the quality of the good or service.
- *Special interest effect.* The firm may try to influence regulation by political manipulation designed to influence the composition and decisions of the regulatory board.

Figure 4: Natural Monopoly—Average Cost and Marginal Cost Pricing

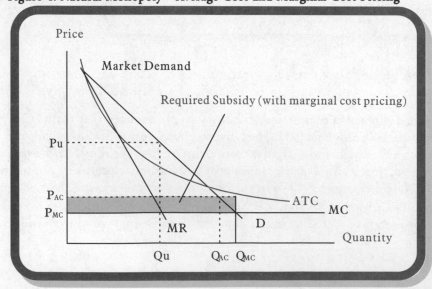

©2007 Schweser

KEY CONCEPTS

1. Monopoly is characterized by one seller of a specific, well-defined product that has no good substitutes and high barriers to entry.

2. Barriers to entry include economies of scale, government licensing and legal barriers, patents or exclusive rights of production, and resource control.

3. Monopolists maximize profit by producing the quantity where MR = MC.

4. Monopolists are price searchers (face downward sloping demand curves) with imperfect information about demand, so they must experiment with different prices to find the profit maximizing price and output quantity.

5. Compared to perfect competition, monopolies produce less total output, charge a higher price, and do not achieve allocative efficiency because the sum of consumer surplus and producer surplus is not maximized.

6. Price discrimination will increase both output and monopoly profits when there are at least two identifiable groups of customers with different price elasticities of demand, and the monopolist can prevent low-price-paying customers from reselling to high-price-paying customers.

7. A natural monopoly exists when economies of scale are so pronounced that ATC is falling (MC < ATC) over the relevant output range so that the cost of total industry production is minimized when there is only one firm in the industry.

8. With average cost pricing, the most common form of regulation, regulators attempt to force monopolists to charge a price equal to ATC where the market demand curve intersects the ATC curve.

9. Marginal cost pricing forces a monopolist to charge a price equal to MC where the firm's MC curve intersects the market demand curve, increasing output and reducing price but requiring a government subsidy since price is then less than ATC.

CONCEPT CHECKERS: MONOPOLY

1. A monopolist will expand production until MR = MC and charge a price determined by the:
    A. marginal cost curve.
    B. marginal revenue curve.
    C. demand curve.
    D. average total cost curve.

2. Which one of the following statements *most accurately* describes a significant difference between a monopoly firm and a perfectly competitive firm? A perfectly competitive firm:
    A. minimizes costs; a monopolistic firm maximizes profit.
    B. maximizes profit; a monopolistic firm maximizes price.
    C. takes price as given; a monopolistic firm must search for the best price.
    D. does not seek to maximize profit because profits are forced to zero in the long run; a monopoly firm will maximize profits.

3. A natural monopoly may exist when:
    A. ATC increases as output increases.
    B. economies of scale are great.
    C. expensive natural resources are used in production.
    D. all production is divided up between just a few firms.

4. A monopolist will maximize profits by:
    A. setting the price as high as possible.
    B. producing at the point where price is equal to MC.
    C. producing at the output level where MR equals ATC and charging a price along the demand curve that corresponds to the output rate.
    D. producing at the output level where MR equals MC and charging a price on the demand curve that corresponds to the output rate.

5. For effective price discrimination to occur, the seller must:
    A. face a downward-sloping demand curve.
    B. have a large advertising budget relative to sales.
    C. be able to ensure resale of the product among customers.
    D. know the demand elasticities of all its customers.

6. A monopoly situation in which the ATC of production steadily declines with increased output is called a:
    A. legal monopoly.
    B. natural monopoly.
    C. structural monopoly.
    D. declining cost monopoly.

7. When a regulatory agency requires a monopolist to use average cost pricing, the intent is to price the product where the:
    A. MR curve intersects the variable cost curve.
    B. MR curve intersects the demand curve.
    C. ATC curve intersects the MR curve.
    D. ATC curve intersects the market demand curve.

ANSWERS – CONCEPT CHECKERS: MONOPOLY

1. **C** A monopolist will expand production until MR = MC, and the price of the product will be determined by the demand curve.

2. **C** Monopolists must search for the profit maximizing price (and output) because they do not have perfect information regarding demand. Firms under perfect competition take the market price as given and only determine the profit maximizing quantity.

3. **B** A natural monopoly may exist when economies of scale are great. The large economies of scale make it inefficient to have multiple producers.

4. **D** A monopolist will maximize profits by producing at the output level where MR equals MC and charging a price on the demand curve that corresponds to the output rate. This will maximize profits. The goal of the monopolist is to maximize profits, not price or revenue.

5. **A** In order for effective price discrimination to occur, the seller must face a downward-sloping demand curve. The seller must also have at least two identifiable groups of customers with different price elasticities of demand for the product, and the seller must be able to *prevent* customers from reselling the product. Knowing the elasticities of demand for *all* its customers is not necessary.

6. **B** A monopoly situation in which the ATC of production continually declines with increased output is called a natural monopoly.

7. **D** When a regulatory agency requires a monopolist to use average cost pricing, the intent is to price the product where the ATC curve intersects the market demand curve. A problem in using this method is actually determining exactly what the ATC is.

The following is a review of the Economics principles designed to address the learning outcome statements set forth by CFA Institute®. This topic is also covered in:

MONOPOLISTIC COMPETITION AND OLIGOPOLY

EXAM FOCUS

Make sure you know the characteristics of both of these types of markets. For monopolistic competition, know the importance of advertising, product differentiation, and product innovation and arguments about the economic efficiency of these activities. Be able to explain how firms in monopolistic competition earn economic profits in the short run, and how output and price are determined in the long run. Understand the incentives of oligopolists to collude and how the Prisoners' Dilemma relates to oligopoly output decisions when two firms enter into a price-fixing agreement.

LOS 20.a: Discuss the characteristics of monopolistic competition, economic profit and loss in the short-run, output and price in the long-run, and discuss whether or not monopolistic competition is efficient.

Monopolistic competition has the following market characteristics:

- *A large number of independent sellers*: (1) Each firm has a relatively small market share, so no individual firm has any significant power over price. (2) Firms need only pay attention to average market price, not the price of individual competitors. (3) There are too many firms in the industry for collusion (price fixing) to be possible.
- Each seller produces a *differentiated product*, so every firm has a product that is slightly different from its competitors (at least in the minds of consumers). The competing products are close substitutes for one another.
- *Firms compete on price, quality, and marketing* as a result of product differentiation. *Quality* is a significant product differentiating characteristic. *Price* and output can be set by firms because they face downward sloping demand curves, but there is usually a strong correlation between quality and the price that firms can charge. *Marketing* is a must in order to inform the market about a product's (differentiating) characteristics.
- *Low barriers to entry* so that firms are free to enter and exit the market. If firms in the industry are earning economic profits, new firms can be expected to enter the industry.

Firms in monopolistic competition face *downward-sloping demand* curves (they are price searchers). Their demand curves are highly *elastic* because competing products are perceived by consumers as close substitutes. Think about the market for toothpaste. All toothpaste is quite similar, but differentiation occurs due to taste preferences, influential advertising, and the reputation of the seller. However, if the price of your favorite brand increased significantly, you would be more likely to try other brands, which you would likely not do if the prices of all brands were similar.

The price/output decision for monopolistic competition is illustrated in Figure 1. Panel (a) of Figure 1 illustrates the short-run price/output characteristics of monopolistic competition for a single firm. As indicated, firms in monopolistic competition maximize economic profits by producing where marginal revenue, MR, equals marginal cost, MC, and by charging the price for that quantity from the demand curve, D. Here the firm earns positive economic profits because price, P^*, exceeds average total cost (ATC^*). Due to low barriers to entry, competitors will enter the market in pursuit of these economic profits.

Panel (b) of Figure 1 illustrates long-run equilibrium for a *representative* firm after new firms have entered the market. As indicated, the entry of new firms shifts the demand curve faced by each individual firm down to the point where price equals average total cost ($P^* = ATC^*$) such that economic profit is zero. At this point, there is no longer an incentive for new firms to enter the market and long-run equilibrium is established. The firm in monopolistic competition continues to produce at the quantity where MR = MC, but no longer earns positive economic profits.

Figure 1: Short-Run and Long-Run Output Under Monopolistic Competition

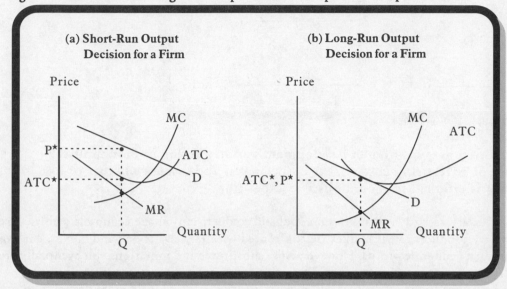

Figure 2 illustrates the differences between long-run equilibrium in markets with monopolistic competition and markets with perfect competition. Note that with monopolistic competition, price is greater than marginal cost (suggesting inefficient allocation of resources), average total cost is not at a minimum for the quantity produced (suggesting inefficient scale of production), and the price is slightly higher than under perfect competition. The point to consider here, however, is that perfect competition is characterized by no product differentiation. The question of the efficiency of monopolistic competition becomes: Is there an economically efficient amount of product differentiation?

In a world with only one brand of toothpaste, clearly average production costs would be lower. That fact alone probably does not mean that a world with only one brand/type of toothpaste would be a better world. While product differentiation has costs, it also has benefits to consumers. As we will see in the next section, additional benefits in terms of greater product innovation and the information about quality that can be conveyed by brand names may also offset the apparent lack of efficiency in markets characterized by monopolistic competition.

Figure 2: Firm Output Under Monopolistic and Perfect Competition

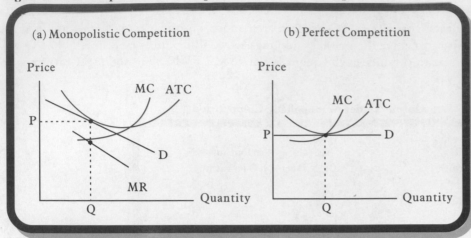

LOS 20.b: Explain the differences in product development and marketing in monopolistic competition, the impact of advertising costs on the costs curves, and discuss whether or not advertising and branding is efficient in monopolistic competition.

Product innovation is a necessary activity as firms in monopolistic competition pursue economic profits. Firms that bring new and innovative products to the market are confronted with less-elastic demand curves, enabling them to increase price and earn economic profits. However, close substitutes and imitations will eventually erode the initial economic profit from an innovative product. Thus, firms in monopolistic competition must continually look for innovative product features that will make their products relatively more desirable to some consumers than those of the competition.

Innovation does not come without costs. The costs of product innovation must be weighed against the extra revenue that it produces. A firm is considered to be spending the optimal amount on innovation when the marginal cost of (additional) innovation just equals the marginal revenue (marginal benefit) of additional innovation.

Advertising expenses are high for firms in monopolistic competition. This is not only because firms need to inform consumers about the unique features of their products, but also to create or increase a perception of differences between products that are actually quite similar. We just note here that advertising costs for firms in monopolistic competition are greater than those for firms in perfect competition and those that are monopolies.

As you might expect, advertising costs increase the average total cost curve for a firm in monopolistic competition. The increase to average total cost attributable to advertising decreases as output increases because more fixed advertising dollars are being averaged over a larger quantity. In fact, if advertising leads to enough of an increase in output (sales), it can actually decrease a firm's average total cost.

Brand names provide information to consumers by providing them with signals about the quality of the branded product. Many firms spend a significant portion of their advertising budget on brand name promotion. Seeing the brand name Toyota on an automobile likely tells a consumer more about the quality of a newly introduced automobile than an inspection of the automobile itself would reveal. At the same time, the reputation Toyota has for high quality is so valuable that the firm has an added incentive not to damage it by producing cars and trucks of low quality.

Efficiency of monopolistic competition is unclear. Consumers definitely benefit from brand name promotion and advertising because they receive information about the nature of a product. This often enables consumers to make better purchasing decisions. Convincing consumers that a particular brand of deodorant will actually increase their confidence in a business meeting or make them more attractive to the opposite sex is not easy or inexpensive. Whether the perception of increased confidence or attractiveness from using a particular product is worth the additional cost of advertising is a question probably better left to consumers of the products. Some would argue that the increased cost of advertising and sales is not justified by the benefits of these activities.

LOS 20.c: Discuss the characteristics of an oligopoly, and the traditional oligopoly models.

Oligopoly is a form of market competition characterized by:

- A small number of sellers.
- Interdependence among competitors (decisions made by one firm affect the demand, price, and profit of others in the industry).
- Significant barriers to entry which often include large economies of scale.
- Products may be similar *or* differentiated.

In contrast to a monopolist, *oligopolists are highly dependent upon the actions of their rivals* when making business decisions. Price determination in the auto industry is a good example. Automakers tend to play "follow the leader" and announce price increases or decreases in close synchronization. They are *not* working explicitly together, but the actions of one producer have a large impact on the others. In addition, the barriers to entry are high in oligopoly markets. The enormous capital investment necessary to start a new auto company or airplane manufacturing firm, because of the large economies of scale in those industries, poses a significant barrier to entry.

One traditional model of oligopoly, the **kinked demand curve model**, is based on the assumption that an increase in a firm's product price will not be followed by its competitors, but a decrease in price will. According to the kinked demand curve model, each firm believes that it faces a demand curve that is more elastic (flatter) above a given price (the kink in the demand curve) than it is below the given price. The kinked demand curve model is illustrated in Figure 3 where the "kink" price is at price P_K where a firm produces Q_K. A firm believes that if it raises its price above P_K its competitors will remain at P_K and it will lose market share because it has the highest price. Above P_K, the demand curve is considered to be relatively elastic, where a small price increase will result in a large decrease in demand. On the other hand, if a firm decreases its price below P_K, other firms will match the price cut, and all firms will experience a relatively small increase in sales.

Figure 3: Kinked Demand Curve Model

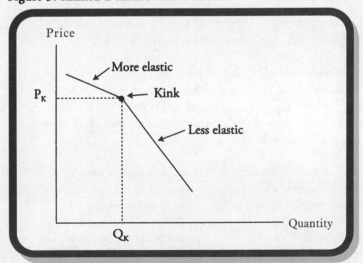

Another traditional oligopoly model, the **dominant firm oligopoly** model, is based on the assumptions that one of the firms in an oligopoly market has a significant cost advantage over its competitors and that this dominant firm produces a relatively large proportion of the industry's output. Under this model, the dominant firm sets the price in the oligopoly market, and the remaining firms are essentially price takers, with little power to set their own prices.

LOS 20.d: Explain the prisoners' dilemma, how it can be applied to oligopoly price fixing, and the impact on cost, price, demand, and profits.

Game theory is used to examine strategic behavior in an oligopoly. **Prisoners' Dilemma** is a simple game that may be used to describe the decisions faced by firms competing under oligopoly conditions. Prisoners' Dilemma may be described as follows:

Two suspects, A and B, are believed to have committed a serious crime. However, the prosecutor does not feel that the police have sufficient evidence for a conviction. The prisoners are separated and offered the following deal:

- If Prisoner A confesses and Prisoner B remains silent, Prisoner A goes free and Prisoner B receives a 10-year prison sentence.
- If Prisoner B confesses and Prisoner A remains silent, Prisoner B goes free and Prisoner A receives a 10-year prison sentence.
- If both prisoners remain silent, each will receive a 6-month sentence.
- If both prisoners confess, each will receive a 2-year sentence.

Each prisoner must choose either to betray the other by confessing, or to remain silent. Neither prisoner, however, knows for sure what the other prisoner will choose to do. The result for each of these four possible outcomes is presented in Figure 4.

Figure 4: Prisoners' Dilemma

	Prisoner B is silent	Prisoner B confesses
Prisoner A is silent	A gets 6 months B gets 6 months	A gets 10 years B goes free
Prisoner A confesses	A goes free B gets 10 years	A gets 2 years B gets 2 years

What should the prisoners do? Well, the *solution to the Prisoners' Dilemma* is to take the best course of action given the action taken by the other prisoner. This means that both prisoners will confess. Why?

Consider Prisoner B's choices. If Prisoner A remains silent, Prisoner B's best option is to confess and go free. If Prisoner A confesses, Prisoner B's best option is to confess and get two years instead of ten. So in either case Prisoner B's best option is to confess. A similar analysis reveals that confessing is Prisoner's A best option as well. The dilemma is that both prisoners know that if they both remain silent, they will only receive a 6-month sentence, but neither has any way of knowing what the other will do.

Oligopoly firms are in a Prisoners' Dilemma type of situation because they can each earn a greater profit if they agree to share a restricted output quantity, but only if neither cheats on the agreement. Oligopolists maximize their total profits by joining together (colluding) and operating as a single seller (monopolist).

Collusion is when firms make an agreement among themselves to avoid various competitive practices, particularly price competition. Figure 5 illustrates a two-firm oligopoly with the potential for collusion.

Figure 5: Cost and Demand for 2-Firm Industry

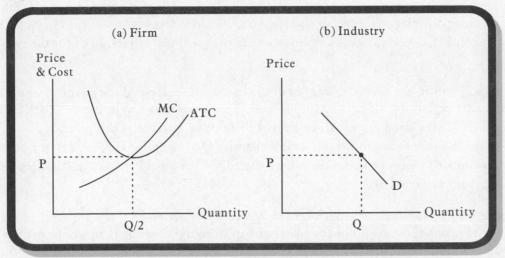

Let's assume that Firm A and Firm B are only two firms in an oligopoly market and they each produce half of the industry's output of an identical product. Figure 5(a) shows that each of these firms produces quantity Q/2 at price P where marginal cost, MC, equals the minimum average total cost, ATC. Figure 5(b) is the industry demand curve, D, where Q is the quantity demanded at price P.

Now, let's assume that Firm A and Firm B have entered into an agreement to reduce output and earn increased profits. As in the Prisoners' Dilemma, these firms have two possible strategies, to honor the agreement or to cheat, so there are four possible outcomes:

• Each firm honors the agreement.
• Both firms cheat.
• Firm A honors the agreement while Firm B cheats.
• Firm B honors the agreement while Firm A cheats.

Let's examine the economic implications of each of these outcomes. Figure 6 illustrates the profit maximizing price and quantity if Firm A and Firm B collude and act jointly as if they were a single monopoly firm.

Figure 6: Price Fixing to Earn Monopoly Profits

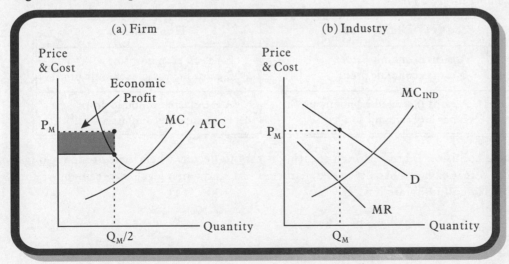

If both firms honor the contract total economic profit will be maximized, and both firms will share it equally. Figure 6(a) shows the marginal cost, MC, and average total cost, ATC, for the each of the firms. Figure 6(b) shows the industry's demand curve, D, marginal cost curve, MC_{IND}, and marginal revenue curve, MR. Note that the industry marginal cost curve, MC_{IND}, is the horizontal sum of the marginal cost curves, MC, for the two firms.

To earn the maximum monopoly profit, the combined output of the two firms must equal the quantity where the marginal revenue for the industry equals the industry's marginal cost. This is quantity Q_M in Figure 6(b). At Q_M, the market price will be P_M. This is the fixed price that the firms will agree to, because at this price, industry demand will be restricted to the monopolistic profit-maximizing quantity Q_M. Assuming that each firm agrees to produce half of the profit maximizing quantity, each firm will produce $Q_M/2$ at price P_M and earn the economic profit indicated in the shaded area in Figure 6(a).

If one firm cheats on the agreement by increasing output above its agreed-upon share, the total economic profit to the industry will be less than that of a monopoly, but the economic profit to the cheating firm will be greater than it would have realized when both firms honored the agreement. On the other hand, the firm that honors the agreement will now be producing the agreed-upon quantity at the same average total cost, but selling at a lower price than expected. This firm may believe that demand has fallen and that the equilibrium price for the agreed-upon total output has fallen. So, the firm that honors the agreement will experience an economic loss. However, the firm that cheated on the agreement by increasing output will realize an increased economic profit by selling more at the lower price, but at a lower average total cost. Total economic profit to the industry will decline.

If both firms cheat by increasing quantity, each firm will increase output to the point where price equals marginal cost and average total cost. The resulting price and output will approach that of a perfectly competitive industry.

Figure 7 below presents the possible outcomes of the collusive agreement between Firm A and Firm B. As in the Prisoners' Dilemma, they will both cheat. Why? Consider the following argument for Firm A.

- *Given that Firm B honors the agreement:* Firm A will earn an economic profit if it honors the agreement, but an even greater economic profit if it cheats. Best Strategy: Firm A should cheat.
- *Given that Firm B cheats:* Firm A will experience an economic loss if it honors the agreement, and zero economic profit if it cheats. Best Strategy: Firm A should cheat.

Therefore, Firm A will cheat. Firm B will cheat as well, based on the same logic.

Figure 7: Prisoners' Dilemma for Two Firms

	Firm B honors	Firm B cheats
Firm A honors	A earns economic profit B earns economic profit	A has an economic loss B earns increased economic profit
Firm A cheats	A earns increased economic profit B has an economic loss	A earns zero economic profit B earns zero economic profit

The probability of successful collusion is greater when cheating is easy to detect, when there are fewer oligopoly firms in a market, when the threat of new entrants to the market is less, and when legal enforcement of anti-collusion laws and penalties for colluding are less.

KEY CONCEPTS

1. Monopolistic competition is characterized by:
   - A large number of independent sellers.
   - Differentiated products.
   - Firms that compete on price, quality, and marketing.
   - Low barriers to entry.
2. Firms in monopolistic competition maximize economic profits (zero may be the maximum in long-run equilibrium) by producing where MR = MC, and by charging the price from the demand curve.
3. Product innovation and large advertising expenditures are necessary for firms in monopolistic competition and the cost of innovation and advertising activity must be weighed against the benefits that they produce.
4. Oligopoly is a market structure characterized by:
   - A small number of sellers.
   - Interdependence among competitors (decisions made by one firm affect the demand, price, and profit of others in the industry).
   - Significant barriers to entry, which often include large economies of scale.
   - Products that may be similar or differentiated.
5. The kinked demand model of oligopoly is based on an assumption that each firm believes that at some specific price, demand is more elastic for a price increase than for a price decrease.
6. The dominant firm model of oligopoly is based on an assumption that one firm dominates the market and the remaining firms are essentially price takers.
7. Prisoners' Dilemma is a game that illustrates that the best course of action for an oligopoly firm, when engaging in collusion with another oligopoly firm, is to cheat.

CONCEPT CHECKERS: MONOPOLISTIC COMPETITION AND OLIGOPOLY

1. A characteristic of monopolistic competition is:
    A. differentiated products.
    B. inelastic demand curves.
    C. high barriers to entry and exit.
    D. a single seller with no competition.

2. The demand for products from monopolistic competitors is elastic due to:
    A. high barriers to entry.
    B. the availability of many close substitutes.
    C. the availability of many complementary goods.
    D. the allocative inefficiency of monopolistic competition.

3. From the prices and outputs for a firm (shown in the table below), determine how many units the firm should produce to maximize profits.

Output	Price	Total Cost
10	4.00	$40
20	3.60	60
30	3.20	80
40	2.60	95

    A. 10.
    B. 20.
    C. 30.
    D. 40.

4. Which of the following *least accurately* describes a feature that monopolistic competition and perfect competition have in common?
    A. Low or no barriers to entry.
    B. Zero economic profits in the long run.
    C. Output occurs where MR = MC.
    D. Extensive advertising to differentiate products.

5. An oligopolistic industry has:
    A. many sellers.
    B. few barriers to entry.
    C. few economies of scale.
    D. a great deal of interdependence among firms.

6. Consider a firm in an oligopoly market that believes the demand curve for its product is more elastic above a certain price than below this price. This belief fits *most closely* to which of the following models?
    A. Dominant firm model.
    B. Kinked demand model.
    C. Variable elasticity model.
    D. Differentiated demand model.

7. Consider an agreement between France and Germany that will restrict wine production so that maximum economic profit can be realized. The possible outcomes of the agreement are presented in the table below.

	Germany complies	Germany defaults
France complies	France gets €8 billion Germany gets €8 billion	France gets €2 billion Germany gets €10 billion
France defaults	France gets €10 billion Germany gets €2 billion	France gets €4 billion Germany gets €4 billion

Based on the game theory framework, the *most likely* strategy followed by the two countries with respect to whether they comply with or default on the agreement will be:
A. both countries will default.
B. both countries will comply.
C. Germany will default; France will comply.
D. Germany will comply; France will default.

ANSWERS – CONCEPT CHECKERS: MONOPOLISTIC COMPETITION AND OLIGOPOLY

1. **A** Differentiated products are a key characteristic of monopolistic competition.

2. **B** The demand for products from firms competing in monopolistic competition is elastic due to the availability of many close substitutes. If a firm increases its product price, it will lose customers to firms selling substitute products at lower prices.

3. **C** profit = total revenue – total cost = TR – TC = P × Q – TC
   At Q = 10, P × Q – TC = $40 – $40 = $0
   At Q = 20, P × Q – TC = $72 – $60 = $12
   At Q = 30, P × Q – TC = $96 – $80 = $16
   At Q = 40, P × Q – TC = $104 – $95 = $9

   The level of output that provides the greatest profit is 30.

4. **D** The only item listed in the question that monopolistic competition and perfect competition do not have in common is the use of advertising to differentiate their products.

5. **D** An oligopolistic industry has a great deal of interdependence among firms. One firm's pricing decisions or advertising activities will affect the other firms.

6. **B.** The kinked demand model assumes that each firm in a market believes that at some price, demand is more elastic for a price increase than for a price decrease.

7. **A** The solution for the game is for each nation is to pursue the strategy that is best, given the strategy that is pursued by the other nation.
   - Given that Germany complies with the agreement: France will get €8 billion if it complies, but €10 billion if it defaults. Therefore France should default.
   - Given that Germany defaults: France will get €2 billion if it complies, but €4 billion if it defaults. Therefore France should default.
   - Because France is better off in either case by defaulting, France will default.
   - Germany will follow the same logic and reach the same conclusion.

DEMAND AND SUPPLY IN FACTOR MARKETS

EXAM FOCUS

Here, you want to gain an understanding of how the demand for inputs to production is determined and which factors influence the elasticity of demand for inputs, especially labor. The second key topic is how the market for financial capital establishes the price (interest rate) for financial capital and the factors that influence the supply of and demand for financial capital. Finally, you should gain an understanding of two components of the payments to productive resources, opportunity cost and economic rent.

LOS 21.a: Explain the difference between marginal revenue and marginal revenue product.

The **marginal product** of a resource is the additional output of a final product produced by using one more unit of a productive input (resource) and holding the quantities of other inputs constant. This is measured in output units and is sometimes called the marginal physical product of the resource. The **marginal revenue** is the addition to total revenue from selling one more unit of output. For a price taker, marginal revenue is equal to price. For a producer facing a downward sloping demand curve, marginal revenue is less than price, since price must be reduced in order to sell additional units of output.

The **marginal revenue product** (MRP) is the addition to total revenue gained by selling the marginal product (additional output) from employing one more unit of a productive resource. The interpretation of MRP is that it is the addition to total revenue from selling the additional output produced by using one more unit of a productive input, holding the quantities of other inputs constant.

LOS 21.b: Discuss how the labor demand curve is derived from the marginal revenue product curve, the conditions of profit maximization, the factors determining the demand and for labor, elasticity of the demand for labor, and labor market equilibrium.

The MRP is downward sloping in any range of output for which diminishing marginal returns are realized from using additional units of a productive resource. This downward-sloping MRP curve is in fact the firm's short-run demand curve for the productive resource or input, as illustrated in Figure 1. This is true of any productive input, of which labor is one.

Figure 1: Marginal Revenue Product (Demand for a Productive Resource)

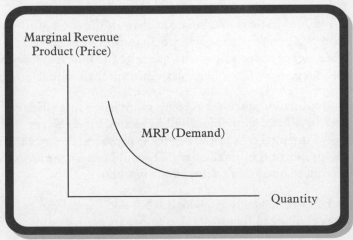

The intuition here is that a profit-maximizing firm will be willing to pay an amount for one more unit of labor (e.g., one more employee day) equal to the addition to total revenue from employing that additional labor in the production process and selling the resulting additional output. The condition for maximizing profits with respect to hiring additional units of labor is to continue to add additional units of labor until

$$MRP_{Labor} = price_{Labor} .$$

Once this condition is met, at any level of production that employed less labor (holding other inputs constant), there would be additional profits to be made. One more unit of labor would cost less than the value of the additional output from hiring an additional unit of labor (the MRP_{Labor}). For additional units of labor beyond the amount that satisfies $MRP_{Labor} = price_{Labor}$, each unit of labor costs more than the additional revenue gained from the output of that unit of labor.

So we can say that a profit-maximizing firm will use additional units of a productive resource as long as its MRP is greater than its price. This supports the conclusion that the MRP curve is a firm's short-run demand curve for a productive resource (short-run, because quantities of other factors are held fixed).

Factors that Determine the Demand for Labor

Now that we understand how a profit-maximizing firm determines the optimal quantity of an input to employ, we can examine the factors that will influence the firm's demand for labor.

An increase (decrease) in the price of the firm's output will increase (decrease) the demand for labor. An increase in the product price will increase the firm's marginal revenue, which increases the MRP of labor, increasing the demand for labor at each wage level, i.e., the demand curve for labor (the MRP curve) shifts upward. A decrease in the price of the firm's output will have the opposite effect, by the same logic.

The effect on the demand for labor of a change in the price of another factor of production will depend on whether that factor is a complement to labor or a substitute for it. The decrease in the price of computers over time has decreased the demand for many types of labor for which a computer is a substitute (e.g., customer service personnel). The demand for IT professionals, however, has increased tremendously, since they are a complement to computers in the production of the final good.

This example also illustrates the effect of technological improvements on the demand for labor. Demand for some types of labor has increased and the demand for other types of labor has decreased. Over time, the effect of technological improvements has been a net increase in the demand for labor. A rising real wage rate (wage rate adjusted for inflation) over time has provided evidence of this.

Elasticity of Demand for Labor

The demand for labor, like other types of demand, is more elastic in the long run than in the short run. This is simply because we define the short run in production as a period over which the quantities of other factors of production are fixed. If the wage rate rises, we will see a greater decrease in the quantity of labor employed when the firm can substitute (demand) other factors of production for labor (e.g., get more automated machinery).

The elasticity of labor will be greater for firms with production processes that are more labor-intensive. A warehouse operation that relies heavily on manpower to fill and ship orders will have a relatively elastic demand for labor because labor represents a large proportion of the total cost of the service it provides. For an airline, on the other hand, labor costs represent a much smaller proportion of total costs. We would expect the airline's demand for pilots to be much less elastic than a warehouse operation's demand for workers.

A third factor affecting the elasticity of demand for labor is the degree to which labor and capital can be substituted. While airplanes may, one day, have the technology to fly themselves, pilots are actually quite difficult to replace with automation (as are flight attendants). In contrast, warehouse operations and manufacturing assembly plants have found many ways to substitute capital for labor through automation and robotics. The elasticity of demand for assembly workers is much more elastic than the demand for airline pilots and flight attendants as a result of this difference in the opportunities to substitute capital for labor in production.

LOS 21.c: Explain the difference between physical and financial capital, and how the demand for physical and financial capital are related to each other.

Physical capital is the physical assets of a firm, including property, plant, and equipment, as well as its inventory of finished goods and goods in process. The greater the demand for physical capital, the greater the demand for the financial capital (money raised through issuing securities) necessary to purchase the physical capital.

LOS 21.d: Discuss how a firm compares the future marginal revenue product of capital with the current price of capital, and the relationship between the quantity of financial capital demanded and the interest rate.

A firm employs physical capital as a factor of production because it is necessary to produce the firm's output and meet customer orders. We can think, in a simple sense, of two primary factors of production: labor and physical capital (people, and machines and goods). In this sense, just as a profit-maximizing firm equates the MRP_{Labor} to the wage rate, it will also equate the $MRP_{Capital}$ to the cost of capital. Since the production of capital assets comes over many periods, the $MRP_{Capital}$ is actually a future MRP. The cost of capital relevant to this decision is the cost of the funds that the firm must raise to buy physical capital. Just think of the $MRP_{Capital}$ as the returns over time (in percentage terms) on the funds necessary to purchase additional physical capital. Viewed in this way, we can say that the future $MRP_{Capital}$ must equal the interest rate the firm must pay to raise the financial capital in order to maximize profits.

Similar to the demand for labor, the demand for capital will be a downward sloping curve derived from its MRP curve. A profit-maximizing firm will employ additional physical capital until its MRP is equal to its cost, the interest rate that the firm must pay on the funds (financial capital) necessary to purchase the physical capital. At higher (lower) interest rates, firms will demand less (more) capital, both physical and financial.

LOS 21.e: Discuss the main influences on demand and supply of capital, and capital market equilibrium.

We need to add one additional point here to account for an important difference between the MRP of capital and the MRP of labor. The additional output from employing an additional unit of labor is produced at the time that the labor is employed. With physical capital—a bulldozer, for example—the additional output will come over many periods into the future. For this reason, it is actually the present value of the future MRP of capital that will determine the return on a current investment in (physical) capital assets. In any event, the demand for financial capital will be a downward sloping function of the interest rate (the cost of financial capital).

Professor's Note: We saw the concept of net present value of an investment in Quantitative Methods and we will see examples of discounting the value of the future output of an asset to evaluate an investment opportunity in Corporate Finance.

Now that we have explained that the demand for financial capital is derived from the present value of MRP of physical capital in production, we can turn our attention to the supply of financial capital. Since the interest rate is the price of capital, the supply curve will be an upward sloping function of interest rates. The suppliers of capital are savers, and they have the choice of consuming now or saving to consume later. Three primary factors influence savings and the supply of financial capital: interest rates, current incomes, and expected future incomes.

- At higher rates of interest, individuals are willing to save more because they will receive greater future amounts. Savers will save more (forego more consumption now) if they can consume 10% more next year than if they are only rewarded with 2% more consumption next year for foregoing consumption now.
- Increases in current income induce individuals to save more (increase the supply of capital), while decreases in current income have the opposite effect.
- If expected future incomes increase, individuals' willingness to trade current consumption for future consumption will decrease. Workers anticipating a decline in their incomes in retirement are motivated to save more now to smooth out their consumption over time. They will save more now (consume less) so that they can consume more in the future when their incomes are lower. College students are in the opposite situation and save little (or go into debt) in anticipation of rising incomes in the future. We can say that, in general, an increase (decrease) in expected future incomes will decrease (increase) the current supply of capital. Changes in current income and expected future income will shift the supply of capital curve; that is, at each interest rate, more or less capital will be supplied.

Equilibrium in the capital market determines interest rates. The interest rate where the quantity of capital supplied equals the quantity of capital demanded is the equilibrium (market) interest rate. Capital market equilibrium is illustrated in Figure 2.

Figure 2: Capital Market Equilibrium

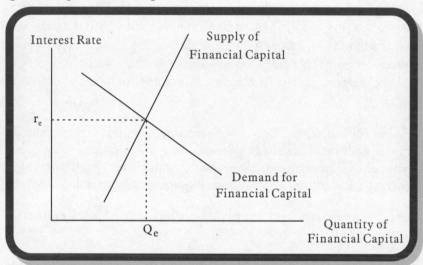

LOS 21.f: Distinguish between the supply of renewable and non-renewable natural resources, and explain how equilibrium in a natural resource market is achieved.

To understand the difference between the supply of renewable and non-renewable resources, assume you own two wells. One well is an oil well and one is a water well. When you take a barrel of oil out of the oil well, it's gone forever—a non-renewable resource. When you take water out of the water well at a sustainable rate, it will be replaced by nature—a renewable resource.

Assuming a competitive market for water, the price will be determined by demand. The supply of renewable resources at a point in time, or per time period, is fixed. Land is also considered a renewable resource—using it now does not mean we cannot use it later, and its quantity is also fixed. The supply of a renewable resource is, therefore, independent of price and is perfectly inelastic.

The quantity of a non-renewable natural resource that has already been discovered is called the **known stock** of the resource. Though the known stock is fixed at any point in time, it tends to increase over time as technological advances make more resources accessible. The rate at which this resource is supplied, also called "flow supply," is perfectly elastic at a price that equals the *present value* of the expected next-period price.

©2007 Schweser

To understand this concept, assume that the price of oil is expected to rise at a rate greater than the interest rate. Oil producing nations would curtail current production and produce more in the next period when the prices are expected to be higher. If the price of oil is expected to rise at a rate lower than the interest rate, oil producing nations are better off increasing their current production and investing the proceeds in a risk-free asset. Based on this principle (the Hotelling Principle), the equilibrium price of oil is expected to rise at a rate equal to the risk-free rate of interest.

Figure 3 illustrates, for a non-renewable resource, that the supply curve is perfectly elastic and the quantity supplied depends only on the demand at that price. For a renewable resource, supply is fixed (perfectly inelastic) and the price is determined by demand.

Figure 3: Equilibrium in Natural Resource Markets

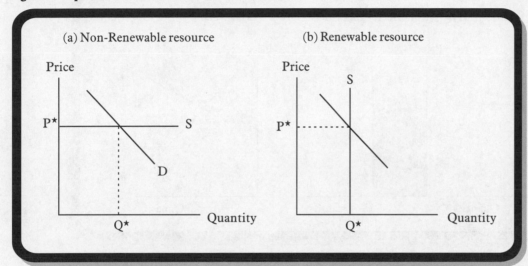

LOS 21.g: Explain how differences occur between large and small incomes.

LOS 21.h: Distinguish between economic rent and opportunity costs.

Differences in incomes are due to differences in workers' marginal revenue products. An actor who can star in a movie and fill theaters has a high marginal revenue product. A worker in a car wash has a low marginal revenue product.

The opportunity cost of an employee is what he could make in his next highest-paying alternative employment. For the worker in the car wash, this may be very close to the wage rate at the car wash. There are many opportunities for employment in low skill/low marginal revenue product jobs.

The difference between what successful actors earn and what they could earn in their next highest-paying alternative may be quite large. This difference between a factor of production's earnings and opportunity cost is called **economic rent**. For many successful actors, a very large part of what they earn is economic rent.

Kesley Grammer (star of the U.S. television show *Frasier*) earned $1.6 million per half-hour episode. Assuming that Grammer's opportunity cost for a week of work (his weekly earnings in his next highest-paying alternative occupation) was considerably less, he would have continued to be a television actor even if the weekly pay were considerably less than $1.6 million. We can think of the opportunity cost as the amount required to induce a person to do particular work or, alternatively, as the amount necessary to bid a factor of production away from its next highest-valued alternative use.

Economic rent is similar to the concept of producer's surplus and depends to a large extent on the shape of the supply curve for the resource. When the supply curve is perfectly elastic, as it is with a non-renewable resource, there is no economic rent. When the supply is perfectly inelastic, as it is with a renewable resource, the entire payment for the factor is economic rent. For an upward sloping supply curve economic rent is part of the total paid for the factor of production. These cases are illustrated in Figure 4.

If the factor of production is relatively easy to create or supply, economic rent is reduced by competition. If a factor of production is very difficult to supply or reproduce (like the skills of a professional athlete or musical performer), *and the factor has a high marginal revenue product*, the factor will receive significant economic rent. Scarcity is not enough. The skill of a top-flight curling player may be in very short supply, but they do not receive anywhere near the rent that a soccer star does.

Figure 4: Economic Rent to Factors of Production

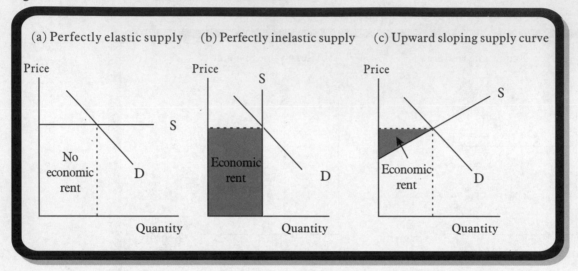

KEY CONCEPTS

1. The marginal revenue product is the addition to total revenue from selling the additional output that results from using one more unit of a productive resource (input), holding the quantities of other inputs constant.

2. Profit is maximized when the cost of the last unit of a productive resource employed is equal to its marginal revenue product.

3. An increase in product price, an increase in the price of a substitute resource, and a decrease in the price of a complementary resource will all increase the demand for labor (or any productive resource in general).

4. The elasticity of demand for labor will be greater the longer the adjustment period, the greater the proportion of labor in the production process, and the greater degree to which other factors of production (capital) can be substituted for labor.

5. As a firm's demand for physical capital to expand production increases, so does its demand for financial capital to fund expansion.

6. A firm will invest in more physical capital when the returns, based on the present value of the future marginal revenue product of additional physical capital, are greater than the cost of the financial capital required to fund the additional physical capital.

7. The equilibrium interest rate in the market for financial capital is determined by the demand for financial capital for funding investment by businesses, and the supply of capital by savers, which depends primarily on interest rates, current incomes, and expected future incomes.

8. For non-renewable natural resources, supply is elastic at the present value of the expected future price, while for renewable natural resources, supply is inelastic at the sustainable quantity of production.

9. Incomes are determined by individuals' marginal revenue products and opportunity costs, but skills in limited supply can also be rewarded with economic rent.

CONCEPT CHECKERS: DEMAND AND SUPPLY IN FACTOR MARKETS

1. The marginal revenue product is *best defined* as the:
    A. price of one more unit of a productive input.
    B. addition to total revenue from selling one more unit of output.
    C. additional output produced by using one more unit of a productive input.
    D. gain in revenue from selling the output produced by using one more unit of an input.

2. For a firm that holds all other resource inputs constant, a curve depicting the marginal revenue product of a resource will be:
    A. the mirror image of the firm's demand curve for the resource.
    B. identical to the firm's supply curve of the final product.
    C. identical to the firm's demand curve for the resource.
    D. the mirror image of the firm's supply curve of the final product.

3. In a given firm, skilled workers currently produce twice as much of its product as unskilled workers do per hour worked. Skilled workers earn $20 per hour, and unskilled workers earn $8 per hour. Based on this information, the firm should:
    A. keep things as they are.
    B. increase the use of skilled workers and/or decrease the use of unskilled workers.
    C. increase the use of unskilled workers and/or decrease the use of skilled workers.
    D. increase the salary of skilled workers to attract more of them.

4. Which of the following is *most likely* to cause an increase in the demand for labor?
    A. An increase in the labor force.
    B. An increase in the demand for final goods or services.
    C. A decrease in the price of substitute technologies.
    D. A decrease in the productivity of labor.

5. Which of the following will be *most likely* to cause a decrease in the demand for a specific type of labor?
    A. A decrease in the number of workers who specialize in that type of labor.
    B. An increase in the demand for the final good or service they produce.
    C. A decrease in the prices of machines that are substitutes in production for that type of labor.
    D. An increase in the productivity of workers who specialize in doing that type of labor.

6. If firms decide to increase their production capacity, what is the *most likely* effect on the demand for physical and financial capital?

	Physical capital	Financial capital
A.	Increase	Increase
B.	Increase	Decrease
C.	Decrease	Increase
D.	Decrease	Decrease

7. A firm will employ physical capital up to the level where the present value of the marginal revenue product of capital is equal to the:
    A. wage rate.
    B. firm's cost of capital.
    C. unit price of the firm's output.
    D. marginal revenue product of labor.

8. The supply of financial capital is *least likely* to be influenced by which of the following?
    A. Interest rates.
    B. MRP of physical capital.
    C. Consumers' current incomes.
    D. Consumers' expected incomes.

9. The supply of a renewable resource is:
    A. the known stock.
    B. perfectly elastic.
    C. perfectly inelastic.
    D. a function of the price.

10. The difference between what a worker earns and what he could earn from his next best alternative employment is called:
    A. productivity.
    B. economic rent.
    C. opportunity cost.
    D. marginal revenue product.

ANSWERS – CONCEPT CHECKERS: DEMAND AND SUPPLY IN FACTOR MARKETS

1. **D**   The marginal revenue product is the addition to total revenue gained by selling the marginal product (additional output) from employing one more unit of a productive resource.

2. **C**   This is true because the firm will maximize profits in this case by employing the variable resource until price equals marginal revenue product. As it increases the use of the resource, marginal revenue product falls. The negative relationship between quantity used and marginal revenue product is identical to the relationship between quantity demanded and price.

3. **C**   The firm should try to equate hourly output with hourly wage for both types of workers. As it is, that ratio is higher for unskilled workers. The firm should substitute away from skilled workers toward unskilled workers. To maximize profits, wage must equal a worker's MRP; skilled workers should not have more than twice the wage of unskilled workers when their MRP is only twice as much.

4. **B**   The demand for labor is a derived demand. When the demand for the final good or service increases, the price of that final good or service increases, which increases the MRP (and demand) for labor.

5. **C**   If the prices of substitutes for a specific type of labor fall, the firm will substitute away from that type of labor. This means the demand for that type of labor will decrease.

6. **A**   If firms are increasing their production capacity, they need to acquire equipment, so the demand for physical capital increases. To buy that equipment they need to raise funds, so the demand for financial capital increases. The greater the demand for physical capital, the greater the demand for the financial capital (money raised through issuing securities) necessary to purchase the physical capital.

7. **B**   A profit-maximizing firm will equate the present value of the $MRP_{Capital}$ to the cost of capital.

8. **B**   The MRP of physical capital determines the demand for financial capital. Interest rates and consumers' current and expected incomes are the primary factors that determine the supply of financial capital.

9. **C**   For a renewable resource, supply is independent of price and is therefore perfectly inelastic. Known stock is the quantity of a non-renewable resource that has been discovered.

10. **B**   Economic rent is what a worker earns above what he could earn from his next best alternative employment. Opportunity cost is what he could earn from his next best alternative employment.

MONITORING CYCLES, JOBS, AND THE PRICE LEVEL

EXAM FOCUS

Nothing too difficult or complex here, but you should learn the terminology related to business cycles, employment statistics and sources of unemployment. Get a good understanding of how the various measures introduced are related to the business cycle.

There is a full topic review devoted to the phenomenon of price inflation, so here you just need to understand how the consumer price index is constructed and used to measure inflation.

LOS 22.a: Discuss the phases of the business cycle, how the start and end of a recession can be identified, and interpret the main labor market indicators and the relationship of the labor market indicators with the business cycle.

The **business cycle** is characterized by fluctuations in economic activity. Real gross domestic product (GDP) and the rate of unemployment are the key variables used to determine the current *phase* of the cycle.

The business cycle has two phases, **expansion** (real GDP is increasing) and **contraction** or **recession** (real GDP is decreasing). The turning points between the phases are called the **peak** and the **trough** of the business cycle. The phases and turning points are illustrated in Figure 1.

Figure 1: Business Cycle

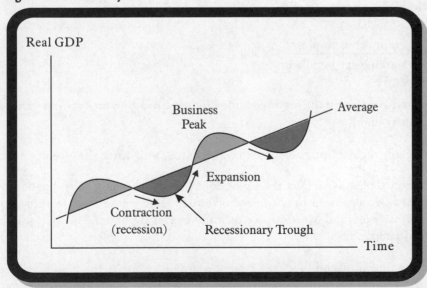

The National Bureau of Economic Research (NBER) is the agency that tracks the phases of the U.S. business cycle. NBER defines a recession as "a significant decline in economic activity spread across the economy, lasting more than a few months, normally visible in real GDP, real income, employment, industrial production, and wholesale-retail sales."[1] The NBER primarily uses measures of employment, industrial production, and personal income to determine whether the economy is expanding or contracting.

Labor Market Indicators

Three important labor market indicators are the unemployment rate, the labor force participation rate, and the employment-to-population ratio.

The **unemployment rate** is the percentage of people in the labor force who are unemployed. The **labor force** includes all people who are either employed or actively seeking employment.

$$\text{unemployment rate} = \frac{\text{number of unemployed}}{\text{labor force}} \times 100$$

The unemployment rate decreases during expansions and increases during recessions.

The **labor-force participation rate** is the percentage of the working-age population who are either employed or actively seeking employment. The **working-age population** is all people 16 years of age or older who are not living in institutions.

$$\text{labor force participation rate} = \frac{\text{labor force}}{\text{working-age population}} \times 100$$

Short-term fluctuations in the labor-force participation rate can occur because of changes in the number of **discouraged workers**, those who are available for work but are neither employed nor actively seeking employment. The labor force participation rate tends to increase when the economy expands and decrease during recessions. Discouraged workers who stopped seeking jobs during a recession are motivated to seek work again once the expansion takes hold and they believe their prospects of finding work are better.

The **employment-to-population ratio** is the percentage of the working-age population who are employed.

$$\text{employment-to-population ratio} = \frac{\text{number of employed}}{\text{working-age population}} \times 100$$

The employment-to-population ratio tends to go up during expansions (when unemployment is low) and down during recessions (when unemployment is high).

LOS 22.b: Discuss the concepts of **aggregate hours** and **real wage rates**, and how they relate to GDP.

The employment indicators we have discussed so far reflect the number of people who have jobs, but to know how much total labor is being performed, we also need to consider how much time workers are working on average. To capture the effects of part-time work and overtime, we measure **aggregate hours**, the total number of hours worked in a year by all employed people.

Aggregate hours have shown a long-term upward trend, but they have not grown as fast as the labor force because the *average workweek* (weekly hours worked per person) has been declining over time. Both aggregate hours and the workweek tend to increase during expansions and decrease during recessions.

---

1. "The NBER's Recession Dating Procedure," October 21, 2003, available from the NBER Web site (www.nber.org/cycles/recessions.html).

Aggregate hours worked is an important measure because it allows us to estimate the *productivity* of labor, the amount of output produced per hour worked. The more productive an hour of labor is, the higher *wage rate* labor can receive. **Real wage rates** are money wage rates adjusted for changes in the overall price level. Real wage rates tell us what an hour's labor is paid in terms of goods and services.

Real wage rates tend to fluctuate with the productivity of labor and are calculated using *total labor compensation*, which includes wages, salaries and employer-paid benefits.

LOS 22.c: Discuss the types of unemployment, full employment, and the relationship between unemployment and real GDP.

There are three types of unemployment:

- **Frictional unemployment** results from constant changes in the economy that prevent *qualified* workers from being matched with existing job openings in a timely manner. Employees spend time and effort seeking work and employers spend time and effort seeking workers. Unemployment resulting from this job search activity, is referred to as frictional unemployment, is always with us as employers expand or contract their businesses and workers move, are fired, or quit to seek other opportunities.
- **Structural unemployment** is caused by (structural) changes in the economy that eliminate some jobs while generating others for which unemployed workers are not qualified. Structural unemployment differs from frictional unemployment in that the unemployed workers do not currently have the skills needed to perform the newly created jobs.
- **Cyclical unemployment** is caused by changes in the general level of economic output. When the economy is operating at less than full capacity, cyclical unemployment is present.

Full employment is the condition that exists when the economy has no *cyclical* unemployment. Note, however, that both structural and frictional unemployment continue to exist even when the economy is at full employment. In other words, some level of unemployment is expected when the economy is at "full employment."

The sum of the frictional and structural unemployment rates is called the **natural rate of unemployment**. **Potential GDP** is the (theoretical) level of output the economy can produce when unemployment is at the natural rate. When real GDP falls below potential GDP, cyclical unemployment increases. When real GDP rises toward and beyond potential GDP, cyclical unemployment decreases. Economists have a range of opinions on what the "natural" rate of unemployment really is, so estimates of potential GDP and cyclical unemployment will differ.

LOS 22.d: Explain the construction of the CPI, calculate CPI, discuss the relationship between CPI and the inflation rate, and discuss the problems associated with CPI bias.

The **consumer price index** (CPI) is the best known indicator of U.S. inflation. The CPI measures the average price for a defined "basket" of goods and services that represents the purchasing patterns of a typical urban household. The Bureau of Labor Statistics (BLS) reports the CPI monthly.

The BLS constructs the CPI in three stages:

1. **Select the CPI basket.** The first step is to determine what goods and services a typical household buys. The BLS surveys a large sample of consumers to find out what percentage of their income they spend on which items. These percentages become the weights for each of the more than 80,000 goods in the overall index. The current weights for the eight major categories in the CPI are shown in Figure 2.

Figure 2: Relative Importance in the CPI as of December 2005*

Category	Percent of Index
Housing	42.4%
Transportation	17.4%
Food and beverages	15.1%
Medical care	6.2%
Recreation	5.6%
Education and communications	6.0%
Apparel	3.8%
Other goods and services	3.5%

*Source: Bureau of Labor Statistics, U.S. Department of Labor

2. **Conduct a monthly price survey.** Every month the BLS records the prices of every item in the CPI in 30 urban areas. The surveyors also record any changes in the individual products, such as package sizes, and adjust prices to make them comparable to past prices.

3. **Calculate the CPI.** This calculation is done in three steps.

    Step 1:   Find the cost of the CPI basket for the base period.

    Step 2:   Find the cost of the CPI basket for the current period.

    Step 3:   Calculate the CPI for both periods. The formula for the index is:

$$\text{CPI} = \frac{\text{cost of basket at current prices}}{\text{cost of basket at base period prices}} \times 100$$

Example: Calculating a consumer price index

The following table shows price information for a simplified basket of goods. Calculate a CPI for this basket in the current period.

Item	Quantity	Price in Base Period	Current Price
Cheeseburgers	200	2.50	3.00
Movie tickets	50	7.00	10.00
Gasoline, gallons	300	1.50	3.00
Digital watches	100	12.00	9.00

©2007 Schweser

Answer:

Base period

Cheeseburgers	200 × 2.50	=	500
Movie tickets	50 × 7.00	=	350
Gasoline	300 × 1.50	=	450
Watches	100 × 12.00	=	1,200
Cost of CPI basket			2,500

Current period

Cheeseburgers	200 × 3.00	=	600
Movie tickets	50 × 10.00	=	500
Gasoline	300 × 3.00	=	900
Watches	100 × 9.00	=	900
Cost of CPI basket			2,900

$$CPI_{current} = \frac{\text{cost of basket in current period}}{\text{cost of basket in base period}} \times 100$$

$$CPI_{current} = \frac{2900}{2500} \times 100 = 116$$

The **inflation rate** is the percentage change in the price level from a year ago. The CPI is one of the primary indicators used to measure the inflation rate. As measured by the CPI, the inflation rate is given by the following formula:

$$\text{inflation rate} = \frac{\text{current CPI} - \text{year-ago CPI}}{\text{year-ago CPI}} \times 100$$

Example: Calculating the inflation rate based on CPI

The CPI for all items was 202.9 in June 2006 and 194.5 in June 2005. The CPI for all items less energy was 203.6 in June 2006 and 198.5 in June 2005. Calculate and interpret the inflation rate based on these two measures.

Answer:

$$\text{all items: } \frac{202.9 - 194.5}{194.5} \times 100 = 4.3\%$$

$$\text{all items ex-energy: } \frac{203.6 - 198.5}{198.5} \times 100 = 2.6\%$$

As measured by the CPI, the inflation rate for goods excluding energy was less than the inflation rate for all items over this 12-month period. This means energy prices must have been increasing faster than the overall price level.

CPI Bias

The CPI is widely believed to overstate the true rate of inflation. The price data the BLS collects reflect long-term structural shifts that should not be included in a measure of the price level. The most significant biases in the CPI data include:

- **New goods.** Older products are often replaced by newer but initially more expensive products. This biases the index because some newly-available goods perform the same function as different lower-priced goods in the base-year market basket.
- **Quality changes.** If the price of a product increases because the product has improved, the price increase is not due to inflation, but still causes an increase in the price index.
- **Commodity substitution.** Even in an inflation-free economy, prices of goods relative to each other change all the time. When two goods are substitutes for each other, consumers increase their purchases of the relatively cheaper good and buy less of the relatively more expensive good. Over time such changes can make the CPI's fixed basket of goods a less accurate measure of typical household spending.
- **Outlet substitution.** When consumers shift their purchases toward discount outlets and away from convenience outlets, they reduce their cost of living in a way the CPI does not capture.

Estimates are that the CPI overstates inflation by about 1% per year. This upward bias in the CPI distorts economic decisions. Many employment contracts with cost-of-living adjustments are based on the rate of increase in the CPI. A substantial portion of government spending, such as entitlement payments, increases automatically with the CPI. The BLS is attempting to reduce the bias by surveying consumers and updating the index weights more frequently.

KEY CONCEPTS

1. The business cycle refers to fluctuations in economic activity and consists of an expansion phase leading to a peak and a recession phase ending at a trough.
2. The primary measures used to determine whether the economy is expanding or contracting are measures of employment, industrial production, and personal income.
3. The main labor market indicators for business cycle analysis are the unemployment rate, the labor force participation rate, and the employment-to-population ratio.
4. The unemployment rate decreases in expansions and increases in recessions, while the employment-to-population ratio and labor force participation rate both tend to increase during expansions and decrease during recessions.
5. Increases in aggregate hours worked and the real wage rate, which is primarily determined by labor productivity, both lead to increases in real GDP and economic expansion.
6. Frictional unemployment results from the time it takes for employers and employees to find each other, structural unemployment results from long-term changes in the economy that require workers to gain new skills to fill new jobs, and cyclical unemployment results from the recession phase of the business cycle.
7. "Full employment" refers to a situation where the economy has reached its potential level of GDP because cyclical unemployment is zero, although both frictional and structural unemployment are always present and positive.
8. The inflation rate is measured as the percentage change in the CPI, which is based on prices of a basket of goods and services that a typical urban consumer purchases.
9. Because of biases that arise from new goods, quality improvements, and consumers' decisions to make substitutions among goods and seek lower-priced shopping outlets, the CPI is believed to overstate the true rate of inflation by about 1% per year.

CONCEPT CHECKERS: MONITORING CYCLES, JOBS, AND THE PRICE LEVEL

1. The phases of the business cycle are:
    A. peak and trough.
    B. inflation and deflation.
    C. expansion and contraction.
    D. employment and unemployment.

2. NBER includes declines in all of the following in its definition of a recession **EXCEPT**:
    A. employment.
    B. industrial production.
    C. wholesale and retail sales.
    D. real GDP for two consecutive quarters.

3. The unemployment rate is defined as the number of unemployed as a percentage of the:
    A. labor force.
    B. number of employed.
    C. working-age population.
    D. civilian noninstitutional population.

4. Which of the following indicators moves inversely with the business cycle?
    A. Aggregate hours.
    B. Unemployment rate.
    C. Labor force participation rate.
    D. Employment-to-population ratio.

5. In which measure(s) of the labor market is a "discouraged worker" included?

	Working age population	Labor force	Number of unemployed
A.	No	No	No
B.	Yes	No	No
C.	Yes	Yes	No
D.	Yes	Yes	Yes

6. Which of the following would be counted as frictional unemployment?
    A. Due to the negative growth of GDP, Smith was laid off.
    B. Johnson was fired from his job after he got into an argument with his foreman, and has not sought a new job.
    C. Although there were jobs available, Jones was unable to find an employer with an opening.
    D. When the plant was modernized, Jones lost her job because she did not have the skill needed to operate the new equipment.

7. Which of the following would be counted as structural unemployment?
    A. Due to the negative growth of GDP, Smith was laid off.
    B. Johnson was fired from his job after he got into an argument with his foreman.
    C. Although there were jobs available, Jones was unable to find an employer with an opening.
    D. When the plant was modernized, Jones lost her job because she did not have the skill needed to operate the new equipment.

Use the following hypothetical information about the conditions in the labor market to answer Question 8.

Employed	177,000
Discouraged workers	2,000
Unemployed	13,000
Household workers	20,000
Students	15,000
Retirees	19,000
Disabled	5,000
Labor force	190,000
Civilian population 16 and over	249,000

8. What is the unemployment rate?
   A. 5.3%.
   B. 6.0%.
   C. 6.8%.
   D. 7.9%.

9. The value of an hour's labor in terms of goods and services is called:
   A. productivity.
   B. the real wage rate.
   C. the nominal wage rate.
   D. total labor compensation.

Use the following table to answer Questions 10 to 12.

CPI data for a recent 12-month period:

Category	Percent of Index	Current Level	Year-ago Level
Commodities	40.0	160	151
Services	60.0	230	223
All items	100.0	?	?

10. The current level of the CPI for all items is *closest to:*
    A. 194.2.
    B. 197.8.
    C. 202.0.
    D. 390.0.

11. The annual inflation rate as measured by CPI was *closest to:*
    A. 3%.
    B. 4%.
    C. 5%.
    D. 6%.

12. Given the bias that is generally believed to exist in the CPI, the true rate of inflation was *most likely:*
    A. 3%.
    B. 4%.
    C. 5%.
    D. 6%.

ANSWERS – CONCEPT CHECKERS: MONITORING CYCLES, JOBS, AND THE PRICE LEVEL

1. **C** The phases of the business cycle are called expansion and contraction (or recession).

2. **D** While popular among analysts, the idea that two consecutive quarters of negative GDP growth constitute a recession is not a part of NBER's definition.

3. **A** The unemployment rate is the number of unemployed as a percentage of the labor force.

4. **B** The unemployment rate increases when GDP decreases, and decreases when GDP increases. The other three indicators move in the same direction as the business cycle.

5. **B** Discouraged workers are not employed and not seeking employment, and are therefore not counted as part of the labor force or among the unemployed. They are, however, included in the working-age population.

6. **C** One of the causes of frictional unemployment is that information regarding prospective employees and employers is costly and sometimes hard to find. The other cause of frictional unemployment is that both employees and employers may spend some time looking for information that will match them up.

7. **D** Structural unemployment exists when changes in the economy eliminate some jobs while generating new job openings for which unemployed workers are not qualified.

8. **C** Unemployment rate = (number of unemployed) / (number in the labor force). In this problem, household workers, students, retirees, and the disabled are not considered unemployed. Thus, the unemployment rate is calculated as: (13,000) / (190,000) = 6.8%.

9. **B** The real wage rate measures the purchasing power of an hour's labor. The nominal wage rate is the money value of an hour's labor. Productivity is output per hour of labor, one of the determinants of the real wage rate. Total labor compensation is one of the measures of the real wage rate.

10. **C** 0.4(160) + 0.6(230) = 202.0

11. **B** current index level = 202.0 (from Question #10)
    year-ago index level = 0.4(151) + 0.6(223) = 194.2

    $$\text{inflation rate} = \frac{202.0 - 194.2}{194.2} \times 100 = 4.0\%$$

12. **A** The CPI calculation is generally believed to add about 1% to the actual inflation rate.

AGGREGATE SUPPLY AND AGGREGATE DEMAND

EXAM FOCUS

The title says it all, but you should spend some quality time here getting the details down. This is the model of equilibrium output and price level for the overall economy and it is used repeatedly for analysis in the topic reviews that follow. Learn it well; no breaks here. Learn the differences between the classical, Keynesian, and monetarist views of economic equilibrium and growth too.

LOS 23.a: Explain the fundamentals of aggregate supply in the long run and in the short run, and discuss different reasons for changes in aggregate supply and the associated movements along the LAS and SAS curves.

Aggregate supply refers to the amount of goods and services produced by an economy. Aggregate supply is a function of the price level. Just as in goods markets, higher prices bring about a greater amount of supply in the short run. Figure 1 illustrates a short run aggregate supply (SAS) curve and a long run aggregate supply (LAS) curve. The overall price level in the economy is on the vertical axis and the real level of output of goods and services (real GDP) is on the horizontal axis.

Figure 1: Aggregate Supply in the Long Run and Short Run

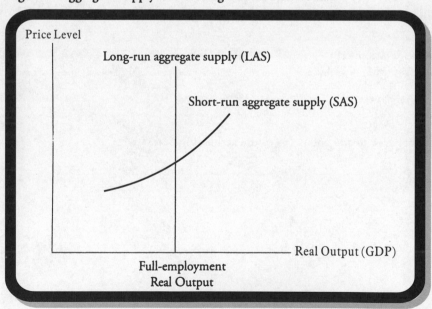

First we will address the questions of why the LAS curve is a vertical line and why the SAS curve is upward sloping. Then we will discuss the factors that cause the curves to shift over time.

LAS is not affected by the price level. LAS is the potential (full-employment) real output of the economy. The potential output of an economy will primarily depend on three factors. Potential output is positively related to:

1. The quantity of labor in the economy.

©2007 Schweser

2. The quantity of capital (productive resources) in the economy.

3. The technology that the economy possesses.

The quantity of labor available at any point in time can vary as unemployment varies. As employees change jobs, businesses expand or fail, and employees decide to enter or leave the work force, the number of people employed and their hours worked will fluctuate. The level of real GDP on the LAS curve is the economy's level of production when the economy is operating at full employment. Full employment does not mean zero unemployment. There will always be some unemployment as workers search for the best available job, employers search for the best available employee, and changes in the economy leave workers from industries with decreasing employment without the necessary skills to work in expanding industries. There is a natural rate of unemployment corresponding to the level of real GDP along the LAS curve. That level of output is referred to as full-employment GDP. As we will see, the economy can operate at less than full employment GDP during a recession when cyclical unemployment is high, and (temporarily) at above full-employment GDP during periods of rapid economic growth.

Over time, the LAS curve may shift as the full-employment quantity of labor changes, as the amount of available capital in the economy changes, or as technology improves the productivity of capital, labor, or both.

In the short run, firms will respond to changes in the prices of goods and services. The key to understanding movements *along* the SAS curve is to understand that we are allowing the prices of final goods and services to vary, while holding the wage rate and the price of other productive resources constant in the short run. When goods and services prices rise (fall), businesses have an incentive to expand (reduce) production, and real GDP will increase (decrease) above (below) the full-employment level shown by the LAS curve. This is why we show real GDP as an upward sloping function of the price level along the SAS curve. Again, in the macroeconomic short run, we are holding the money wage rate, other resource prices, and potential GDP (LAS) constant.

Next we turn our attention to the factors that will shift the SAS curve. Our list begins with those factors that also shift the LAS curve. The SAS and LAS curves will both shift when the full-employment quantity of labor changes, the amount of available capital in the economy changes, or as technology improves the productivity capital, labor, or both.

In Figure 2, we illustrate the effects on LAS and SAS that would result from an increase in full-employment GDP, due to an increase in labor, capital, or an advance in technology. Long-run aggregate supply increases to LAS_2 and short-run aggregate supply increases to SAS_2.

Figure 2: An Increase in Potential GDP

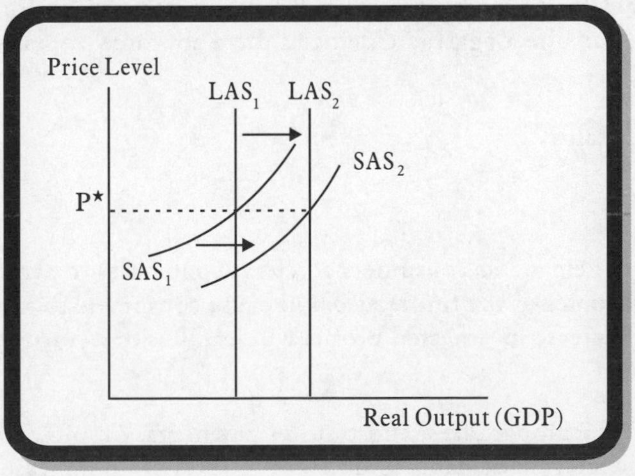

There are some factors that will shift SAS, but not affect LAS. We held the money wage rate and other resource prices constant in constructing the SAS curve. If the wage rate or prices of other productive inputs increase, the SAS curve will shift to the left, a decrease in short-run aggregate supply. When businesses observe a rise in resource prices, they will decrease their output as the profit maximizing level of output declines.

Two important factors influence the change in money wage rates. One is unemployment; when unemployment rises, it puts downward pressure on the money wage rate as there is an excess supply of labor at the current rate. Conversely, if the economy is temporarily operating above full-employment levels, there will be upward pressure on the money wage rate. The second factor that can influence the money wage rate is inflation expectations. An expected increase in inflation will lead to increases in the money wage rate and an expected decrease in inflation will slow the increase of money wages.

LOS 23.b: Explain the effects that cause the aggregate demand curve to slope downwards, the main factors influencing aggregate demand, and how changes in these factors influence aggregate demand and the aggregate demand curve.

We turn our attention now to the **aggregate demand** curve. The aggregate demand curve shows the relation between the price level and the real quantity of final goods and services (real GDP) demanded. The components of aggregate demand are:

- Consumption (C).
- Investment (I).
- Government spending (G).
- Net exports (X), which is exports minus imports.

aggregate demand = C + I + G + X

The aggregate demand curve is downward sloping (a good thing for a demand curve!) because at higher price levels, consumption, business investment, and exports will all likely decrease. There are two effects here to consider. First, when the price level rises, individuals' real wealth decreases. Since they have less accumulated wealth in real terms, individuals will spend less. This is referred to as the "wealth effect." Second, when the price level increases, interest rates will rise. An increase in interest rates decreases business investment (I) as well as consumption (C) as consumers delay or forego purchases of consumer durables such as cars, appliances and home repairs. This is a substitution effect, as consumers substitute consumption later for consumption now because the cost of consuming goods now instead of later (the interest rate) has increased. This is referred to as "intertemporal substitution," substitution between time periods.

So changes in the price level cause changes in (the quantity of) aggregate demand. What factors will shift the aggregate demand curve? Among the many things that can affect aggregate demand there are three primary factors:

- Expectations about future incomes, inflation, and profits.
- Fiscal and monetary policy.
- World economy.

An increase in expected inflation will increase aggregate demand as consumers accelerate purchases to avoid higher prices in the future. An expectation of higher incomes in the future also will cause consumers to increase purchases in anticipation of these higher incomes. An increase in expected profits will lead businesses to increase their investment in plant and equipment.

Fiscal policy refers to government policy with regard to spending, taxes, and transfer payments. An increase in spending increases the government component (G) of aggregate demand. A decrease in taxes or an increase in transfer payments (e.g. social security benefits or unemployment compensation) will increase the amount that consumers have to spend (their disposable income) and increase aggregate demand through an increase in consumption (C).

Monetary policy refers to the central bank's decisions to increase or decrease the money supply. An increase in the money supply will tend to decrease interest rates and increase consumption and investment spending, increasing aggregate demand. We will look at both monetary and fiscal policy effects more closely in subsequent topic reviews.

The state of the world economy will influence aggregate demand through the net exports (X) component. If foreign incomes increase, foreign demand for exports will increase, increasing X. If the country's exchange rate increases (foreign currency buys fewer domestic currency units), its goods are relatively more expensive to foreigners, and exports will decrease. At the same time, imports will be relatively cheaper and the quantity of imported goods demanded will increase. Both effects will decrease net exports (exports minus imports, X) and consequently aggregate demand. As we will examine later in more detail, a decrease in the exchange rate will have the opposite effects on exports, imports, and net exports.

LOS 23.c: Discuss the difference between short-run and long-run macroeconomic equilibrium, and explain how the relationship between economic growth, inflation and changes in aggregate demand and aggregate supply influence short- and long-run macroeconomic equilibrium.

Now we examine **macroeconomic equilibrium** in the short run and in the long run.

In Figure 3, we illustrate long-run equilibrium at the intersection of the LAS curve and the aggregate demand curve. Just as we saw that price was the variable that led us to equilibrium in the goods market in microeconomics, here changes in the price level of final goods and services can move the economy to long-run macroeconomic equilibrium. In Figure 3, equilibrium is at a price level of 110. If we are at a short-run disequilibrium with the price level at 115, there is excess supply; the quantity of real goods and services supplied exceeds the (aggregate) demand for real goods and services. This is sometimes termed a recessionary gap, and there will be downward pressure on prices. Businesses will see a build-up of inventories and will decrease both production and prices in response. This will result in a decrease in the price level, which will move the economy toward long-run equilibrium at a price level of 110. If the price level were 105, there would be excess demand for real goods and services. This is sometimes referred to as an "inflationary gap." Businesses will experience unintended decreases in inventories and respond by increasing output and prices. As the price level increases, the economy moves along the aggregate demand curve toward long-run equilibrium.

Figure 3: Long-Run Equilibrium Real Output

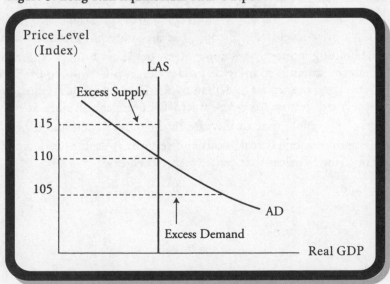

We will now extend this analysis to include shifts in short-run aggregate supply that are part of the process of moving toward the long-run equilibrium output and price level. Recall that in constructing the SAS curve we held money wages and other resource prices constant. If the economy is in short-run equilibrium, but at a level of output above or below full-employment GDP, it is in long-run disequilibrium. In Figure 4, we illustrate two situations where the economy is in short-run equilibrium but not in long-run equilibrium. In panel (a), short-run equilibrium real GDP, GDP_1, is less than full employment GDP (along the LAS curve) and we would interpret this as a recession. As we will detail, this brings downward pressure on money wages and resource prices that will decrease the equilibrium price level from P_1 to P^*. The opposite situation is illustrated in panel (b), where the short-run equilibrium real GDP, GDP_1, is above the full-employment level. This would be the situation in an economic expansion where aggregate demand has grown faster than LAS. The result will be upward pressure on prices that will result in inflation as the general price level increases from P_1 to P^*.

Figure 4: Long-Run Disequilibrium

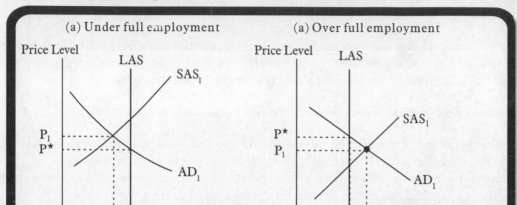

We have essentially described the phases of a business cycle here as deviations of short-run equilibrium real GDP below full-employment GDP (recession) and above full-employment GDP (expansion leading to inflationary pressure). How does this happen? Changes in aggregate demand can drive these business cycles.

Consider the short-run and long-run adjustment to an increase in aggregate demand illustrated in Figure 5. From an initial state of long-run equilibrium at the intersection of AD_0 with LAS, assume that aggregate demand increases to AD_1. The new short-run equilibrium will be at over-full employment with real GDP, GDP_1, above full-employment GDP, GDP^*. The increase in the price level (from P_0 to P_{SR}) at the new equilibrium level means that workers' real wages have decreased (we are holding money wages constant in the short run). At the same time, the increase in demand will cause businesses to attempt to increase production, which will require hiring more workers. These two factors both lead to increased money wage demands. As these demands are met, we get a shift in the SAS curve from SAS_0 to SAS_1, which will restore long-run macroeconomic equilibrium at full-employment real GDP and at a new price level of P_{LR}. Note that an increase in the money wage and other *resource* prices means that business will be willing to supply less real goods and services at each price level (prices of final goods and services). It is the increase in resource prices that causes SAS to decrease.

Figure 5: Adjustment to an Increase in Aggregate Demand

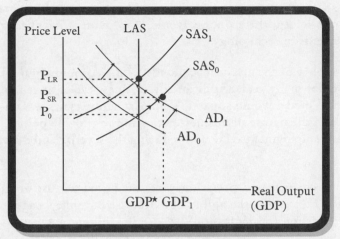

In Figure 6, we illustrate how a decrease in aggregate demand from AD_0 to AD_1 will lead to a new short-run equilibrium with the price level at P_{SR} and real GDP at GDP_1. GDP_1 is less than full-employment GDP (a recession). The resulting excess supply of labor (workers seeking jobs) will put downward pressure on money wage rates and other resource prices. This will lead to a shift in SAS to SAS_1 (an increase in supply), restoring long-run equilibrium at full-employment GDP along the LAS curve and at a new, lower price level of P_{LR}. Remember, a decrease in wages and other input prices increases short-run aggregate supply.

Figure 6: Adjustment to a Decrease in Aggregate Demand

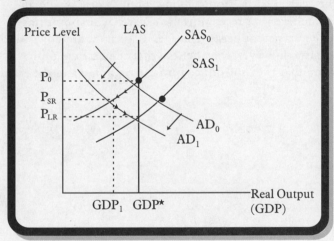

LOS 23.d: Compare and contrast the main schools of macroeconomic thought in relation to aggregate demand and aggregate supply.

While our discussion of the forces leading to short-run and long-run macroeconomic equilibrium gives a basic description of business cycles and the forces that tend to move the economy toward full employment in the long run, there are differences of opinion on how well this process works and the time lags between the short run and the long run.

The **classical economists** believed that shifts in both aggregate demand and aggregate supply were primarily driven by changes in technology over time. Although classical economists did not use the aggregate supply-aggregate demand analysis we have presented, their view of macroeconomic equilibrium is consistent with this analysis. We just need to add the assumption that the long-run adjustment of money wages to restore full-employment equilibrium happens fairly rapidly and that the economy therefore has a strong tendency toward full-employment equilibrium, as either recession or over-full employment lead to decreases or increases in the money wage rate. Their analysis concluded that taxes were the primary impediment to long-run equilibrium and that if the distortions in incentives from taxes were minimized, the economy would grow in an efficient manner with increases in labor and capital and with improvements in technology.

The great depression of the 1930s did not support the view of the classical economists. The economy in the U.S. operated significantly below its full-employment level for many years. Additionally, business cycles in general were more severe and more prolonged than the classical model would suggest. John Maynard Keynes was an economist who attempted to explain the depression and the nature of business cycles and to provide policy recommendations for moving the economy toward full-employment GDP and reducing the severity and duration of business cycles.

Keynes believed that shifts in aggregate demand due to changes in expectations were the primary cause of business cycles and that wages were "downward sticky," decreasing the ability of a decrease in money wages to shift the SAS curve up and move the economy from recession (or depression) back to the full-employment equilibrium level of output. The *New Keynesians* added to this model, asserting that the prices of other productive inputs in addition to labor are also "downward sticky," presenting another barrier to the restoration of full-employment equilibrium.

The policy prescription of **Keynesian economists** was to directly increase aggregate demand through monetary policy (increasing the money supply) or through fiscal policy (increasing government spending, decreasing taxes, or both).

A third view of macroeconomic equilibrium is that held by **monetarists**. Monetarists believe that the main factor leading to business cycles and deviations from full-employment equilibrium is monetary policy. They suggest that to keep aggregate demand stable and growing, the central bank should follow a policy of a steady and predictable increases in the money supply. Monetarists believe that recessions are caused by inappropriate decreases in the money supply and that recessions can be persistent because money wage rates are downward sticky (as do the Keynesians). Like the classical economists, however, they believe that the best tax policy is to keep taxes low to minimize the disruption and distortion that they introduce into the economy and the resulting decrease in full-employment GDP.

KEY CONCEPTS

1. Long-run aggregate supply is vertical at potential (full-employment) real GDP and can change as a result of changes in the labor force, the amount of capital in the economy, or in technology.

2. Short-run aggregate supply is an increasing function of the price level, is affected by the same factors that affect long-run aggregate supply, and is constructed holding the money wage rate constant.

3. Aggregate demand is a decreasing function of the price level. Aggregate demand will increase with increases in incomes, a decrease in a country's exchange rate, or a rise in the expected rate of inflation. Expansionary monetary or fiscal policy can both increase aggregate demand.

4. From an initial long-run equilibrium, an increase (decrease) in aggregate demand will increase (decrease) prices and output in the short run, and the resulting increase (decrease) in money wages will decrease (increase) short-run aggregate supply, resulting in further price increases (decreases) and a return to full-employment long-run equilibrium.

5. The classical economists believed that the adjustment of money wages to restore full-employment equilibrium is rapid and that without the distorting effects of taxes, long-run equilibrium real output would increase with increases in the labor force and accumulated capital, and with improvements in technology.

6. Keynesian economists believe that changes in expectations shift aggregate demand, which causes business cycles, and that because wages are "downward sticky," the economy may not return rapidly from recession to full-employment real GDP. Their policy prescription is to increase aggregate demand directly by expanding the money supply or increasing the government deficit.

7. Monetarists believe that economic cycles are caused by inappropriate monetary policy and that a policy of steady and predictable increases in the money supply, together with low taxes, will lead to stability and maximum growth of real GDP.

CONCEPT CHECKERS: AGGREGATE SUPPLY AND AGGREGATE DEMAND

1. The economy's potential rate of output is *best represented* by:
   A. long-run aggregate supply.
   B. short-run aggregate supply.
   C. long-run aggregate demand.
   D. short-run aggregate demand.

2. Which of these factors is *least likely* to cause a shift in long-run aggregate supply?
   A. Warfare destroys a large number of factories.
   B. Prices of raw materials for production decrease.
   C. An advance in technology increases the rate of productivity.
   D. Older workers retire faster than younger workers enter the labor force.

3. Aggregate demand includes all of the following **EXCEPT**:
   A. investment spending.
   B. government purchases.
   C. consumption expenditures.
   D. foreign trade, exports plus imports.

4. Which of the following factors would *most likely* change the quantity of aggregate demand *without* shifting the AD curve?
   A. The federal deficit expands.
   B. Expected inflation decreases.
   C. Domestic interest rates increase.
   D. Global economic growth accelerates.

5. In short-run equilibrium, if aggregate demand is increasing faster than long-run aggregate supply:
   A. the economy is in recession.
   B. the price level is likely to increase.
   C. downward pressure on wages should ensue.
   D. supply will increase to meet the additional demand.

6. Which school of economic thought holds that unpredictable changes in central bank policy are the primary cause of business cycles?
   A. Classical.
   B. Keynesian.
   C. Monetarist.
   D. Neo-Keynesian.

ANSWERS – CONCEPT CHECKERS: AGGREGATE SUPPLY AND AGGREGATE DEMAND

1. **A** The LRAS curve is vertical at the level of potential GDP.

2. **B** Price changes for productive resources shift the short-run aggregate supply curve but they do not affect long-run aggregate supply. LAS is influenced by changes in the quantity of labor, the quantity of capital, and the level of technology.

3. **D** The foreign trade component of aggregate demand is net exports, or exports minus imports.

4. **C** Increasing interest rates would decrease investment and delay consumption spending, which would be seen as a movement along the AD curve to a lower quantity and a higher price level. Changes in expected inflation, fiscal policy, and world economic growth all shift the AD curve.

5. **B** If AD is increasing faster than LAS, the economy is expanding faster than its full-employment rate of output. This will cause pressure on wages and resource prices and lead to an increase in the price level. The SAS curve will shift to the left—a decrease in supply for any given price level—until the rate of output growth slows to its full-employment potential.

6. **C** Monetarists believe that monetary policy is the main factor leading to business cycles and deviations from full-employment equilibrium.

MONEY, BANKS, AND THE FEDERAL RESERVE

EXAM FOCUS

Not a lot of material here. Know the functions of money, how a fractional reserve banking system creates money, the money expansion multiplier, and the tools that a central bank can use to increase or decrease the money supply.

LOS 24.a: Discuss the functions of money, and the problems that arise when using commodities as money.

Money has three basic functions:

- Money functions as a **medium of exchange** because it is accepted as payment for goods and services. Compare this to a barter economy, where if someone has a goat and wants an ox, they have to find someone willing to trade one for the other (and imagine no eBay). With money, it is possible to sell the goat and buy the ox with the money received.
- Money functions as a **unit of account** because prices of all goods and services are expressed in units of money; dollars, yen, rupees, pesos, and so forth. This allows us to determine how much of any good we are foregoing when consuming another.
- Money functions as a **store of value** because I can work for money now, save it, and use the value of my labor later. Money preserves value better when inflation is low.

LOS 24.b: Compare and contrast the different depository institutions, their economic function, and the impact of financial regulation, deregulation, and innovation.

There are three primary types of depository institutions.

- **Commercial banks** essentially operate as intermediaries between savers and borrowers. Savers make deposits in banks to keep their money safe, but also to earn a return on their savings. Banks take the deposits and put a proportion of those deposits to work by buying short-term securities such as Treasury bills, by investing in longer-term securities such as Treasury and corporate bonds, and by making loans. In a fractional reserve banking system, the bank must hold a specified proportion of deposits in reserve, as cash or (in the U.S.) deposits with the Federal Reserve Bank. This allows the bank to meet customer needs for withdrawals and still earn a return on the deposits not committed to reserves. The bank must manage the risk of its portfolio of loans and other assets to make sufficient interest income to be competitive but, at the same time, not take on risk that its depositors would consider excessive.
- The terms **thrifts** and **thrift institutions** refer to savings banks, credit unions, and savings and loan associations (S&Ls). An S&L offers both checking and savings accounts and makes loans of various types using customer deposits. A **savings bank** is quite similar but does not offer checking accounts and makes primarily home loans for individuals. A **credit union** typically takes savings deposits from, and makes consumer loans to, specific group of individuals, such as a group consisting of the employees of one company. Groups can also be defined more broadly.
- A **money market mutual fund** is technically an investment company. "Money market" usually is used to refer to debt securities with maturities of one year or less. A money market mutual fund manages the pooled funds of many investors, investing it in short-term debt securities to preserve the funds' value and earn returns for

the investors. Investors (depositors) have ready access to their funds, but some funds restrict liquidity by imposing minimum check amounts or a maximum number of withdrawals each month. Offering less liquidity keeps expenses down and consequently increases returns (interest earned).

Depository institutions have four main economic functions:

- They *create liquidity* by using the funds from (short-term) deposits to make (longer-term) loans.
- By acting as *financial intermediaries,* depository institutions lower the cost of funds for borrowers, compared to the cost if borrowers had to seek out lenders on their own.
- Depository institutions are in a better position than individuals would be to *monitor the risk* of loans.
- Institutions *pool the default risks* of individual loans by holding a portfolio of loans.

In the U.S., bank and S&L deposits are insured in the event of failure of the institution to a maximum of $100,000 by the Federal Deposit Insurance Corporation (FDIC). The FDIC imposes restrictions on the institutions to manage the risk of insuring them against failure. Since the existence of deposit insurance significantly reduces the incentive for depositors to monitor the risk of an institution's portfolio, there is significant regulation of banks with respect to their balance sheets in four primary areas:

- A minimum amount of equity (owners') capital must be maintained to give owners strong incentives to manage the risk of their asset portfolio well.
- **Reserve requirements** set a minimum percentage of deposits (different for different types of accounts) that must be retained by the institution, either in cash or as deposits with the (U.S.) Federal Reserve.
- There are restrictions on the types of deposits (e.g. savings deposits versus checking deposits) that the various institutions may accept.
- There are rules about the proportions of various types of loans that the institutions can make. An example would be a restriction on the proportion of, or prohibition of, commercial loans. These restrictions differ by type of institution as well.

During the 1980s and 1990s many of the restrictions that made commercial banks different from savings banks and thrifts were relaxed, allowing the latter to compete more directly with the former, and allowed other institutions to participate in activities which were formerly only permitted to banks and savings institutions. Another area of deregulation was the repeal of earlier laws which restricted banks from opening branches nationwide. Permitting banks to open branch offices in any state has led to consolidation of banks, the emergence of a few very large national banks, many mergers and acquisitions, and a resulting increase in the efficiency of bank operations.

This decrease in regulation was accompanied by a high degree of financial innovation. Financial innovation refers to the introduction of new financial products, both for depositors and for those seeking debt capital. By introducing variable-rate mortgages, S&Ls were able to transfer some of the risk of rising inflation and rising interest rates to the borrowers of the funds. Computers have significantly reduced the cost of credit and debit card transactions and led to huge growth in these markets. The capacity of large banks to process millions of electronic transactions and checks at low cost with innovative computer systems was also a factor in the wave of mergers and acquisitions. Cost savings were realized when all institutions did not have to provide this capacity individually. The widespread use of ATMs and internet banking are further examples of the financial innovation that has grown out of technological advances.

Some innovation has been specifically adopted to avoid or circumvent regulation. New account types have been introduced to circumvent Regulation Q, which prohibits banks from paying interest on checking account deposits.

LOS 24.c: Explain how banks create money, and calculate the amount of loans a bank can generate, given a certain amount of deposits.

In a **fractional reserve banking** system, such as the Fed system, a bank is only required to hold a fraction of its deposits in reserve. The **required reserve ratio** is used to measure the reserve requirement. Deposits in excess of the required reserve (excess reserves) may be loaned.

When a bank makes a loan, the borrower spends the money. The sellers who received the cash may deposit it in their banks. This action creates additional loanable funds, because only a fractional amount of the deposit is required by law to be held in reserve. This process of lending, spending, and depositing can continue until the amount of excess reserves available for lending is zero. This is referred to as the *multiplier effect*.

The potential **deposit expansion multiplier** is the maximum potential increase in the money supply due to the multiplier effect. The actual deposit expansion multiplier will be less than the potential deposit expansion multiplier if some people decide to hold currency rather than deposit it into the bank, and if banks fail to loan out excess reserves. It is important to note that *money is created only when banks make loans*, and a single bank can only lend out its excess reserves. It is the *banking system* as a whole that expands the money supply. There is also a multiplier effect when the Fed decreases the monetary base through open market sales of Treasury securities. Since this removes reserves from the banking system, the amount of loans must contract by an even greater amount.

To calculate the potential deposit expansion multiplier and the potential increase in the money supply, we use the following formulas:

potential deposit expansion multiplier = 1 / (required reserve ratio)

potential increase in money supply = potential deposit expansion multiplier × increase in excess reserves

For example, assume that the required reserve ratio is 25%, and a bank finds itself with $1,000 in excess reserves. The bank can only lend out its own excess reserves of $1,000. If the borrower of the $1,000 deposits the cash in a second bank, the second bank will be able to lend its excess reserves of (0.75 × $1,000) = $750. Those funds may be deposited in a third bank, which can then lend its excess reserve of (0.75 × $750) = $563. If this lending and depositing continues, the money supply may eventually expand to [(1/0.25) × $1,000] = $4,000. If no other banks took deposits or made loans, there would be no increase in the money supply.

LOS 24.d: Discuss the goals and targets of the U.S. Fed, the balance sheet, and compare and contrast the policy tools.

The goals of the U.S. Federal Reserve are to manage the money supply in such a way as to keep inflation low and at the same time, promote economic growth and full employment. Additionally, the Fed attempts to reduce the magnitude of the expansions and recessions that make up business cycles.

One of the ways the Fed attempts to reach these goals is to target the **federal funds rate**. This is the rate at which banks make short-term (typically overnight) loans of reserves to other banks. The Fed influences the federal funds rate, which is a market-determined rate, through changes in the money supply.

The three **policy tools of the Federal Reserve** are:

1. In the U.S., banks can borrow funds from the Fed if they have temporary shortfalls in reserves. The **discount rate** is the rate at which banks can borrow reserves from the Fed. A lower rate makes reserves less costly to banks, encourages lending, and tends to decrease interest rates. A higher discount rate has the opposite effect, raising interest rates.

2. **Bank reserve requirements** are the percentage of deposits that banks must retain (not loan out). By increasing the percentage of deposits banks are required to retain as reserves, the Fed effectively decreases the funds that are available for lending. This decrease in the amount available for lending will tend to increase interest rates. A decrease in the percentage reserve requirement will increase the funds available for loans, which tends to decrease interest rates. This tool only works well if banks are willing to lend, and customers are willing to borrow, the additional funds made available by reducing the reserve requirement.

3. **Open market operations** are the buying or selling of Treasury securities by the Fed in the open market. When the Fed buys securities, cash replaces securities in investor accounts, banks have excess reserves, more funds are available for lending, and interest rates decrease. Sales of securities by the Fed have the opposite effect, reducing cash balances and funds available for lending, and increasing interest rates. This is the Fed's most commonly used tool and is important in achieving the federal funds target rate.

The Fed's Balance Sheet

The assets of the U.S. Federal Reserve consist of:

- Gold, deposits with other central banks, and special drawing rights at the International Monetary Fund.
- U.S. Treasury bills, notes, and bonds.
- Loans to banks (reserves loaned at the discount rate).

The most important of these is U.S. government securities, which are almost 90% of the Fed's assets.

The great majority (over 90%) of the liabilities of the Federal Reserve are Federal Reserve notes, that is, U.S. currency in circulation. Bank reserve deposits are a small part of the Fed's liabilities.

Coins are issued by the U.S. Treasury and, together with currency and bank deposits at the Fed, make up what is called the **monetary base**.

KEY CONCEPTS

1. The functions of money are as a medium of exchange, a store of value, and a unit of account.
2. Commercial banks, thrift institutions, and money market funds all act as intermediaries in lending the funds of savers to borrowers of various types.
3. A fractional reserve banking system allows banks to loan out a maximum proportion of deposits, and thereby increase the money supply by a multiple equal to the reciprocal of the required reserve ratio.
4. The U.S. Fed has a mandate to manage the money supply in such a way as to produce low inflation, full employment, and economic growth.
5. The U.S. Fed can increase (decrease) the money supply by buying (selling) Treasury securities in the open market, decreasing (increasing) the discount rate, or decreasing (increasing) the required reserve ratio.

CONCEPT CHECKERS: MONEY, BANKS, AND THE FEDERAL RESERVE

1. Which of the following statements is *least accurate*? The existence and use of money:
    A. permits individuals to perform economic calculations.
    B. requires the central bank to control the supply of currency.
    C. increases the efficiency of transactions as against a barter system.
    D. provides a means of preserving the value of labor until it can best be used.

2. Depository institutions include all of the following EXCEPT:
    A. growth funds.
    B. credit unions.
    C. savings banks.
    D. commercial banks.

3. Banks and savings institutions lower the cost of funds for borrowers by saving them the time and expense of finding numerous individuals who are willing to lend to them. This statement *best describes* the depository institutions' function as:
    A. risk poolers.
    B. exchange media.
    C. liquidity creators.
    D. financial intermediaries.

4. Assume the Federal Reserve purchases $1 billion in securities in the open market. What is the maximum amount of money the banking system can create as a result, if the required reserve ratio is 15%?
    A. $66.7 million.
    B. $850 million.
    C. $1 billion.
    D. $6.67 billion.

5. The policy tool the Federal Reserve uses *most often* is:
    A. the discount rate.
    B. issuance of currency.
    C. reserve requirements.
    D. open market operations.

6. The goals and targets of Federal Reserve policy include all of the following EXCEPT:
    A. Promote economic growth and full employment.
    B. Reduce the magnitude of expansions and recessions.
    C. Maintain the balance in the current and capital accounts.
    D. Manage the money supply in such a way as to keep inflation low.

ANSWERS – CONCEPT CHECKERS: MONEY, BANKS, THE FEDERAL RESERVE

1. **B** Money functions as a unit of account, a medium of exchange, and a store of value. Money existed long before central banking was conceived of.

2. **A** The only kind of investment company that would be considered a depository institution is a money market mutual fund.

3. **D** By acting as financial intermediaries, depository institutions lower the cost of funds for borrowers from what they would be if they had to seek out individuals willing to lend.

4. **D** The potential deposit expansion multiplier is $1 / 0.15 = 6.67$, so the banking system can create a maximum of $6.67 billion in new money.

5. **D** Open market operations are the Fed's most commonly used tool.

6. **C** The current and capital accounts apply to foreign trade and are not among the explicit policy goals of the Fed.

The following is a review of the Economics principles designed to address the learning outcome statements set forth by CFA Institute®. This topic is also covered in:

MONEY, INTEREST, REAL GDP, AND THE PRICE LEVEL

EXAM FOCUS

The interest rate here is the equilibrium price (opportunity cost) of holding money instead of interest bearing securities. You need to know the factors that influence money demand and the process by which equilibrium interest rates are reached. Then focus on the short-run and long-run effects of changes in the money supply by the central bank and their effect on real output based on the aggregate supply-aggregate demand model.

LOS 25.a: Discuss the factors determining the demand for money, define the demand for money curve, and the effects of changes in real GDP and financial innovation on the demand for money curve.

There are different definitions of money. For our purposes here, we define it as currency in circulation, checking account deposits, and travelers checks. The **demand for money** is largely determined by interest rates. Think of the interest that could be earned on money deposited in a savings account or money market fund as the opportunity cost of holding money.

The relation between short-term interest rates and the quantity of money that firms and households demand to hold is illustrated in Figure 1, where the downward slope indicates that at lower interest rates, firms and households choose to hold more money. At higher interest rates, the opportunity cost of holding money increases, and firms and households will desire to hold less money and more interest bearing financial assets.

The **supply of money** is determined by the central bank (the Fed in the U.S.) and is independent of the interest rate. This accounts for the vertical (perfectly inelastic) supply curve in Figure 1.

Figure 1: The Supply and Demand for Money

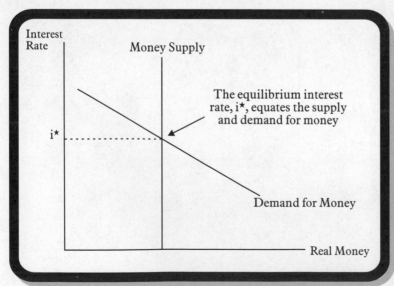

©2007 Schweser

Now if we measure the money supply in nominal currency units, it will be sensitive to the price level. As inflation increases, households and businesses need more money to buy costlier goods and services. If prices doubled, firms and households would need approximately twice the amount of money to fund their purchases and to meet their needs for money in reserve. If we divide the nominal supply of money by the price level (a price index), we have the money supply in real terms. We can think of the real money supply as the money supply in terms of constant purchasing power. The equilibrium interest rate in Figure 1, i*, is the interest rate for which the demand to hold real money balances is just equal to the real money supply.

If real gross domestic product (GDP) rises, more goods and services are bought and sold, and more money is needed to conduct these transactions. Increases in real GDP shift the money demand curve up. Decreases in real GDP shift it down so that less money is demanded at each level of interest rates.

The increased use of credit cards and debit cards, the availability of interest bearing checking accounts, easier transfer of funds from savings to checking, the proliferation of ATMs, and internet banking and bill paying are all financial innovations that have affected the demand for money curve. Overall, financial innovation has reduced the demand for money below what it would have been if only the increase in real GDP was at work. The increased use of credit cards and the proliferation of ATMs have likely been the most important innovations with respect to the demand for money.

LOS 25.b: Explain how interest rates are determined, the influence on the money market equilibrium, and the interaction between interest rate changes and the money supply.

Interest rates are determined by the equilibrium between money supply and money demand. As illustrated in Figure 2, if the interest rate is above the equilibrium rate (i_{high}), there is excess supply of real money. Firms and households are holding more real money balances than they desire to, given the opportunity cost of holding money balances. They will purchase securities to reduce their money balances, which will decrease the interest rate as securities prices are bid up. If interest rates are below equilibrium (i_{low}), there is excess demand for real money balances, as illustrated in Figure 2. Firms and households will sell securities to increase their money holdings to the desired level, decreasing securities prices and increasing the interest rate.

Figure 2: Disequilibrium in the Money Market

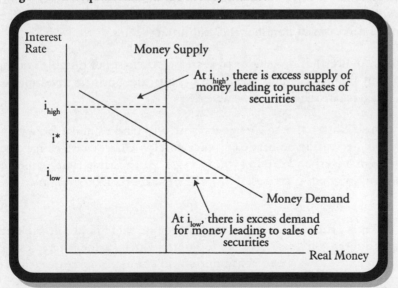

Let's look at how the central bank can affect interest rates by examining the effects of open market operations on the equilibrium interest rate when the money supply is changed. Consider a situation where the central bank wants to decrease short-term interest rates and will do so by buying securities in the open market. The cash paid for the securities increases the real money supply and bank reserves, which leads to a further increase in the real money supply as banks make loans based on the increase in excess reserves. This shifts the real money supply curve to the right as illustrated in Figure 3. At the previous equilibrium interest rate of 5%, there is now excess supply of money balances. To reduce their money holdings, firms and households buy securities, increasing securities prices and decreasing interest rates until the new equilibrium interest rate in Figure 3 (4%) is achieved. Of course, if the central bank sold securities to decrease the money supply, excess demand for real money balances would result in sales of securities and an increase in the interest rate.

Figure 3: An Increase in the Money Supply Lowers the Interest Rate

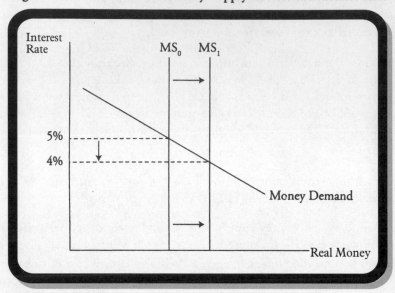

LOS 25.c: Discuss the short-run and long-run effects of money on real GDP.

Now that we have determined the effects of monetary policy changes (changes in the money supply) on nominal interest rates, we turn our attention to the effect on the overall economy. In the short run, the effects of money supply changes on nominal interest rates will be the same for real interest rates. Let's first consider the effects of an increase in the money supply that leads to decreases in nominal and real interest rates.

Lower real rates will cause businesses to invest more and households to increase purchases of durable goods, automobiles, and other items that are typically financed at short-term rates. Thus, the business investment (I) and consumer spending (C) components of aggregate demand both increase.

Lower real interest rates will make investment less attractive to foreigners, who will tend to move money out of the country, selling the domestic currency and decreasing domestic currency/foreign currency exchange rates. This will make exports less expensive to foreign buyers and exports will increase. At the same time, imports will decrease as the domestic currency price of foreign goods increases. Thus, the net exports (X) component of aggregate demand increases.

The effect of the interest rate decrease in the short run will be even stronger because there is a **multiplier effect**. The increase in aggregate demand and expenditures will cause incomes to go up, which further increases consumption and investment. This spending on investment and consumption, in turn, also increases (someone's) income. This process is repeated and, even though not all of each consumer's increase in income is used to increase consumption, the eventual effect on consumption and aggregate demand will be much greater than the initial increase in consumption and aggregate demand.

This increase in aggregate demand will increase real GDP and the price level, as we saw in our analysis of the aggregate supply-aggregate demand model. Action by the central bank to decrease the money supply and increase rates will have the opposite effect. Rising rates will reduce household purchases, business investment, net exports, and aggregate demand, resulting in a decrease in real GDP and the price level.

If the economy is operating at the full-employment level (long-run aggregate supply) when the central bank increases the money supply, the increase in real GDP must be temporary. Recall that when an increase in aggregate demand increases real GDP above full-employment GDP, money wages and the cost of other productive resources will rise, causing a shift to a new short-run aggregate supply curve. Thus, the long-run effect of an increase in the money supply will simply be an increase in the price level (rate of inflation) as the economy returns to full-employment GDP on the long-run aggregate supply curve. This is illustrated in Figure 4. The right-hand side of the figure is the same initial and long-run response to an increase in aggregate demand (from AD_0 to AD_1) that we saw in the review of aggregate supply and aggregate demand. Initially, the price level rises to P_1, and the resulting increase in inflation decreases the real wage so that SAS shifts from SAS_0 to SAS_1. The new long-run equilibrium real GDP is back to potential real GDP (along LAS) and the price level has increased to P_2. Note that when the price level has increased to P_2, the increase in the price level has just offset the increase in the nominal money supply, so the real money supply returns to MS_0. This long-run adjustment is illustrated in panel (a) of Figure 4. As a result of this decrease in the real money supply, the equilibrium interest rate returns to its original equilibrium level of 5% in Figure 4.

Figure 4: An Increase in the Money Supply at Full-Employment GDP

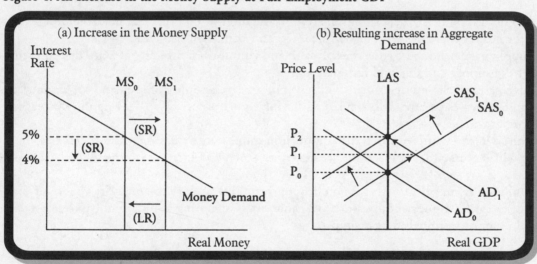

LOS 25.d: Explain the quantity theory of money.

If we break GDP into the price level and its real output component (price × real output), we obtain an identity known as the **equation of exchange**, which is:

money supply × velocity = GDP = price × real output

Velocity is the average number of times per year each dollar is used to buy goods and services (velocity = GDP / money). Therefore, the money supply multiplied by velocity must equal nominal GDP. The equation of exchange must hold with velocity defined in this way. Letting money supply = M, velocity = V, price = P, and real output = Y, the equation of exchange may be symbolically expressed as:

$$MV = PY$$

The **quantity theory of money** states that an increase in the money supply will cause a proportional increase in prices. The original proponents of the quantity theory felt that velocity and output were determined by institutional factors other than the money supply and were thus nearly constant. Therefore, if the money supply increases while velocity and quantities are fixed, prices must rise. Rearranging the equation of exchange, we get:

$$price = \frac{MV}{Y}$$

Since velocity (V) and real output (Y) change very slowly, an increase in the money supply (M) must result in a proportional increase in prices (inflation). If we increase M by 5%, nominal GDP (=PY) will increase 5% as well. Under the assumption that real GDP (Y) changes only very slowly in the short run, the entire increase must be reflected in the price level (P). Monetarists believe, based on this relation, that the money supply (M) should be increased only at the growth rate of real output (Y) so as to maintain price stability.

In the long run the quantity theory of money will describe the results of money supply growth in excess of the growth rate of real output. If real GDP grows at 3% over time and the money supply is increasing at 5%, we can expect long-run inflation of 2% (5% – 3%). This result parallels the result we obtained using the aggregate supply-aggregate demand model.

KEY CONCEPTS

1. The demand to hold money is a decreasing function of the interest rate that can be earned on securities.
2. The demand for money increases with higher incomes, and with the price level.
3. The money supply is determined by the central bank and equilibrium interest rates are determined by the intersection of the supply and demand for money.
4. An increase (decrease) in the money supply will result in an excess supply of (demand for) money, leading individuals and businesses to buy (sell) securities, driving securities prices up (down) and decreasing (increasing) interest rates.
5. In the short run, decreases (increases) in the equilibrium interest rate from increases (decreases) in the money supply will increase (decrease) aggregate demand, which will increase (decrease) real GDP and the price level.
6. In the long run, money supply growth has no effect on real GDP and, as the quantity theory of money suggests, increases in the money supply, when the economy is operating at potential (full-employment) GDP, will lead to a proportional increase in prices.

CONCEPT CHECKERS: MONEY, INTEREST, REAL GDP, AND THE PRICE LEVEL

1. The money demand schedule slopes downward to the right showing that:
   A. an expansion in the money supply increases interest rates.
   B. as the opportunity cost of holding money rises, people want to hold less money.
   C. when the Fed sells securities, bond prices fall.
   D. a reduction in the money supply reduces the interest rate.

2. The money supply schedule is vertical because the:
   A. money supply is dependent upon interest rates.
   B. demand schedule is downward sloping.
   C. money supply is independent of interest rates.
   D. money supply is set by Congress.

3. Which of the following statements is TRUE? Money:
   A. demand rises with nominal interest rates.
   B. demand rises with nominal income.
   C. supply rises with nominal interest rates.
   D. supply rises with nominal income.

4. If money supply and demand are in equilibrium and the central bank sells securities in the open market:
   A. bank reserves will increase.
   B. short-term interest rates will decrease.
   C. the money supply curve shifts to the right.
   D. firms and households will sell securities for cash.

5. The effect of an anticipated increase in the money supply in a full-employment economy is:
   A. lower output.
   B. higher unemployment.
   C. higher prices.
   D. lower unemployment.

6. If the money supply is rising and velocity is falling:
   A. prices will rise.
   B. prices will fall.
   C. real GDP will rise.
   D. the impact on prices and real GDP is uncertain.

7. According to the quantity theory of money:
   A. real output and velocity are independent of the money supply.
   B. real output and velocity increase with the money supply.
   C. an increase in the money stock will decrease prices.
   D. an increase in the money stock will decrease gross domestic product (GDP).

8. According to the quantity theory of money, if nominal GDP is $7.0 trillion and the money supply is $1.0 trillion, then the velocity of the money supply is:
   A. 0.100.
   B. 0.143.
   C. 7.0.
   D. 8.0.

ANSWERS – CONCEPT CHECKERS: MONEY, INTEREST, REAL GDP, AND THE PRICE LEVEL

1. **B** With interest rates on the vertical axis and the quantity of real money on the horizontal axis, the downward slope of the money demand schedule shows that as the opportunity cost of holding money rises, people want to hold less money. People would prefer to invest money in bonds and CDs rather than hold cash when interest rates are high.

2. **C** The money supply schedule is vertical because the money supply is independent of interest rates. The Fed controls the money supply.

3. **B** Money demand rises with nominal income. As income increases, either because of inflation or increases in real output, more money is needed in the economy to conduct transactions.

4. **D** If the central bank sells securities, it is decreasing the money supply. This will reduce bank reserves and shift the money supply curve to the left. Firms and households will have lower cash balances than they wish to hold at equilibrium, so they sell securities, decreasing securities prices and increasing interest rates to their new equilibrium level.

5. **C** The effect of an anticipated increase in the money supply in a full-employment economy will be higher prices. When people expect the money supply to increase, they will expect inflation to result. Therefore, wages and prices will rise. There will be no increase in output or employment, even in the short run.

6. **D** An increase in the money supply is consistent with an increase in nominal GDP. However, a decrease in velocity is consistent with a decrease in nominal GDP. Unless we know the size of the changes in the two variables, there is no way to tell what the net impact is on real GDP and prices.

7. **A** According to the quantity theory of money, real output and velocity are independent of the money supply. As a result, an increase in the money supply increases prices.

8. **C** The equation of exchange is: $MV = PY$

   Here, $GDP = PY$, so that $MV = GDP$

   Therefore, (1.0 trillion)(V) = 7.0 trillion

   $V = \$7.0$ trillion $/\$1.0$ trillion

   $V = 7.0$

INFLATION

EXAM FOCUS

This is all key material. Defining inflation, measuring inflation, and knowing the difference in the effects of anticipated and unanticipated inflation are all important. Take the time to understand the difference between demand-pull and cost-push inflation in the context of the aggregate supply-aggregate demand model. This review ties together earlier material on nominal interest rates, expected inflation, and the rate of growth of the money supply.

LOS 26.a: Discuss the difference between inflation and price-level, and calculate the inflation rate.

Inflation is a persistent increase in the price level over time. Inflation erodes the purchasing power of a currency. If it accelerates unchecked, inflation ultimately can destroy a country's monetary system, forcing individuals and businesses to adopt foreign money or revert to bartering physical goods.

The key word in our definition is "persistent." If the price level increases in a single jump but does not continue rising, the economy is not experiencing inflation. An increase in the price of a single good or in *relative* prices of some goods are not inflation. If inflation is present, the prices of almost all goods and services are increasing.

In Topic Review 22 we introduced the *inflation rate,* which we defined as the percentage change in the price level from a year ago. Using a numeric measure of the price level, such as the consumer price index or the GDP deflator, we can calculate the inflation rate:

$$\text{inflation rate} = \frac{\text{current price level} - \text{year-ago price level}}{\text{year-ago price level}} \times 100$$

LOS 26.b: Distinguish between the factors resulting in demand-pull and cost-push inflation, and the impact on price levels, and aggregate demand and supply.

The two types of inflation are **demand-pull** and **cost-push**. Demand-pull inflation results from an increase in aggregate demand, while cost-push inflation results from a decrease in aggregate supply.

Demand-Pull Inflation

Demand-pull inflation can result from an increase in the money supply, increased government spending, or any other cause that increases aggregate demand. Figure 1 shows the effect on the price level when aggregate demand increases (shifts to the right). In Figure 1, the economy begins at equilibrium with output at GDP_1 and the price level at P_1. The aggregate demand and short-run aggregate supply curves are AD_1 and $SRAS_1$. Real GDP is equal to potential GDP, which is represented by the long-run aggregate supply curve LRAS.

Figure 1: Demand-Pull Inflation

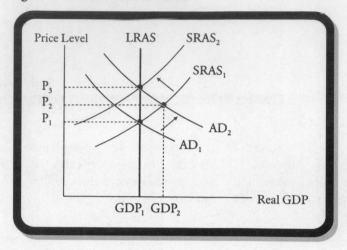

Now suppose the central bank increases the money supply, which increases aggregate demand to AD_2. With no initial change in aggregate supply, output increases to GDP_2 and the price level increases to P_2. Prices rise, and real GDP is above potential (full-employment) GDP.

With real GDP above its full-employment level, the increase in GDP is not sustainable. Unemployment falls below its natural rate, which puts upward pressure on real wages. Rising real wages result in a decrease in short-run aggregate supply (the curve shifts left from $SRAS_1$) until real GDP reverts back to full-employment GDP. The boom turns into a bust as output falls back to GDP_1, and the price level increases further to P_3.

In the absence of other changes, the economy would reach a new equilibrium price level at P_3. But what would happen if the central bank tried to keep GDP above the full employment level with further increases in the money supply? The same results would occur repeatedly. Output could not remain above its potential in the long run, but the induced increase in aggregate demand and the resulting pressure on wages would keep the price level rising ever higher. Demand-pull inflation would persist until the central bank reduced the growth rate of the money supply and allowed the economy to return to full employment equilibrium at a level of real GDP equal to potential GDP.

Cost-Push Inflation

Inflation can also result from an initial decrease in aggregate supply caused by an increase in the real price of an important factor of production, such as wages or energy.

Figure 2 illustrates the effect on output and the price level of a decrease in aggregate supply. The reduction from $SRAS_1$ to $SRAS_2$ increases the price level to P_2 and with no initial change in aggregate demand, reduces output to GDP_2. The impact on output is the key difference between the demand-pull and cost-push effects: the demand-pull effect increases GDP above full-employment GDP, while cost-push inflation from a decrease in aggregate supply initially decreases GDP.

If the decline in GDP brings a policy response that stimulates aggregate demand so output returns to its long-run potential, the result would be a further increase in the price level to P_3.

The increase in the price level would only represent inflation if it persisted. For that to happen, the supply shock that caused SRAS to decrease would have to be repeated, and policy makers would have to keep responding. The oil crisis of the 1970s is an example of a cost-push inflation spiral.

Figure 2: Cost-Push Inflation

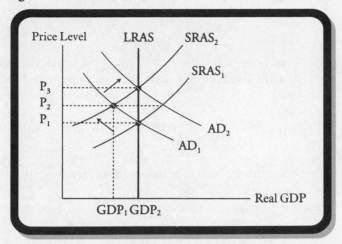

LOS 26.c: Discuss the effects of unanticipated inflation on the labor market and the market for financial capital.

Unanticipated inflation represents an unexpected decrease in the purchasing power of (real value of) currency in the future so that the real present value of a dollar to be received in the future is reduced. Therefore, long-term contracts which entitle their holders to *fixed future payments* decrease in value. Fixed-rate mortgages, fixed-payment annuities, and other fixed-rate loans are examples of such contracts. Individuals and institutions that are obligated to make fixed future payments will gain from unanticipated inflation. Unanticipated increases in inflation decrease the value of a fixed-payment mortgage held by a bank, and benefit borrowers because their future payments will have less real value; that is, borrowers will give up less in real goods in order to make their payments.

Unanticipated inflation causes gains and losses in the labor market as well. When inflation increases unexpectedly, the real value of the wages employees agreed to is less. This represents a gain for employers at the expense of employees as real wage costs decrease. If inflation decreases unexpectedly instead, real wage rates are higher than employers expected to pay, and employees have unexpected gains at the expense of their employers.

LOS 26.d: Distinguish between anticipated and unanticipated inflation, and discuss the adverse effects of anticipated inflation.

In most cases, unanticipated changes have greater impacts on real economic outcomes than anticipated changes. But even when inflation is correctly anticipated, inflation can have adverse effects. While these adverse effects are small when inflation is around its target range of 3% or less, they can be significant when inflation is high.

High anticipated inflation makes currency a poor store of value, since its value decreases rapidly over time. The rational response to this is to spend it as rapidly as possible. **Transaction costs are increased** with high inflation since money functions less well. Potential GDP is reduced (the LRAS curve shifts to the left) and the growth rate of the economy is decreased. Time and effort spent to deal with the effects of high inflation is time and effort not spent in other economically productive activity.

High anticipated inflation also has adverse effects on an economy's output due to **tax effects**. To understand this effect, consider a tax rate of 40% on investment gains. With 2% inflation and a 10% return on an investment, the after-tax return is 10% × (1 - 0.40) = 6%. The real after-tax return after adjusting for inflation is 6% - 2% = 4%. Now consider a situation with 10% inflation and an 18% nominal return on investment. The after-tax return is 18% × (1 - 0.40) = 10.8%. The real after-tax return after adjusting for inflation is 10.8% - 10% = 0.8%. In both examples, the nominal rate of return is 8% higher than the inflation rate, so the real return without taking account of taxes is 8%. Taxes, however, distort real after-tax returns and affect investment and saving decisions as a consequence. Low real after-tax returns will reduce savings, which will further increase interest rates and reduce business investment. The net effect is to reduce both investment and the long-term rate of growth of GDP.

The uncertainty about long-term inflation can be great when rates of inflation are high. This uncertainty makes long-term planning and investment decision making more difficult. This also decreases investment and reduces the long-term growth rate of the economy.

To sum up, high inflation, even when anticipated, reduces economic output and the growth rate of GDP because it:

- Diverts resources from other productive activities to deal with inflation's effects and uncertainty.
- Decreases the value of currency in transactions and as a store of value.
- Distorts returns in the investment and savings market and reduces capital investment in the economy.

Unanticipated increases in inflation have additional adverse effects on economic output and GDP growth, because they effectively transfer wealth from:

- Lenders to borrowers.
- Workers to employers.

LOS 26.e: Discuss the impact of inflation on unemployment, define the short-run and long-run Phillips curve, and discuss changes in the natural rate of unemployment.

Our analysis using the AS-AD model indicated that if expected inflation and actual inflation (based on the increase in aggregate demand) are equal, the economy remains at full-employment GDP and the price level rises. If the increase in aggregate demand is greater than expected, two things happen. The price level increases more than expected (actual inflation is greater than expected inflation), and unemployment decreases to a level below its natural rate. This negative relationship between unexpected inflation and unemployment is depicted in the **short-run Phillips curve** shown in Figure 3. The decrease in unemployment in the short run changes unemployment from its natural rate along the **long-run Phillips curve** to a point like 1. Note that each short-run Phillips curve is constructed holding the expected rate of inflation constant and for a particular natural rate of unemployment.

Figure 3: Long-Run and Short-Run Phillips Curve

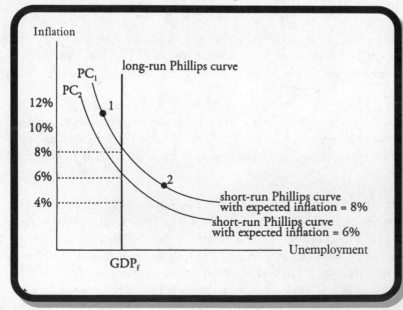

©2007 Schweser

In the long run, expected inflation and actual inflation are equal so the economy is at full employment and the rate of unemployment is equal to its natural rate.

Recall from our previous discussion that when a central bank unexpectedly decreases the rate of money supply growth to reduce inflation, that the initial effect is to decrease aggregate supply as real wages fall and to reduce both GDP and employment. In this case, actual inflation is less than anticipated inflation, and unemployment increases as a result. This situation is represented by a movement along the short-run Phillips curve to a point such as 2.

If the reduced rate of growth of the money supply is maintained, eventually the new lower rate of inflation is correctly anticipated and the decrease in aggregate supply and increase in aggregate demand are such that the economy remains at full-employment GDP. We represent this situation as a shift in the short-run Phillips curve to PC_2. Note that the short-run Phillips curve intersects the long-run Phillips curve at the expected rate of inflation. It is the short-run differences between expected inflation and actual inflation that are driving the relationship between inflation and unemployment in the short run.

Changes in the Natural Rate of Unemployment

Recall that the natural rate of unemployment consists of the frictional and structural unemployment that exists when cyclical unemployment is zero and output is at potential (full-employment) GDP. Changes in the natural rate can come from many sources, including the size and makeup of the labor force, changes that affect labor mobility, and advances in technology that replace some jobs and create new ones. An increase (decrease) in the natural rate would be represented as a shift to the right (left) in the long-run Phillips curve.

LOS 26.f: Explain the impact of inflation on the nominal interest rate, and discuss how this is related to the money supply discussed in the previous reading.

Recall that we previously defined the **nominal risk-free interest rate** as the sum of the real risk-free rate and the expected inflation rate. We now examine why this is necessarily so.

The nominal rate of interest is the equilibrium rate determined in the market for savings and investment. If expected inflation is higher, business will expect greater returns on their investments because they will factor in higher prices for their output in the future. At the same time, savers will require a greater rate of return on their savings because they are considering the trade-off between current consumption and future consumption. Since they are concerned with real consumption, they will require a greater nominal rate of return when the expected rate of inflation is higher, so that the real consumption that they receive in the future in return for not consuming now (saving) is the same. When presented in terms of nominal interest rates, this combination of an increase in demand for financial capital and a decrease in the supply of financial capital (savings) increases the equilibrium nominal rate of interest.

We have also related the actual inflation rate and, eventually, the expected inflation rate to the rate of growth of the money supply. We can conclude that higher rates of growth of the money supply lead to higher rates of inflation, higher rates of expected inflation, and higher nominal interest rates.

KEY CONCEPTS

1. Inflation is a persistent increase in the price level over time.
2. The rate of inflation is calculated as:

$$\text{inflation rate} = \frac{\text{current price level} - \text{year-ago price level}}{\text{year-ago price level}} \times 100$$

3. Demand-pull inflation results from an unexpected increase in aggregate demand that increases the price level and pulls economic output above its potential or full-employment level.
4. Cost-push inflation arises from an unexpected decrease in aggregate supply from equilibrium, usually the result of an increase in the cost of an important factor of production.
5. Unanticipated increases in inflation create losses (gains) for fixed-rate lenders (borrowers) and gains for employers at the expense of their workers, who see their real wages fall.
6. High anticipated inflation reduces the level and growth rate of GDP by reducing real after-tax returns on investment, increasing transaction costs as currency is less valuable, and decreasing productive activity as individuals and businesses devote time and effort to dealing with the effects of and uncertainty caused by inflation.
7. The short-run Phillips curve is constructed holding expected inflation and the natural rate of unemployment constant, and illustrates the negative relationship between unexpected inflation and unemployment.
8. The long-run Phillips curve is vertical at the natural rate of unemployment, which can be affected by the size and makeup of the labor force, changes that affect labor mobility, and advances in technology that replace some jobs and create new ones.
9. A premium for the expected inflation rate is reflected in all nominal interest rates and will depend in the long run on the rate of growth of the money supply.

CONCEPT CHECKERS: INFLATION

1. A price index for the broad economy was at the following year-end levels over a 5-year period:
    Year 1   106.5
    Year 2   114.2
    Year 3   119.9
    Year 4   124.8
    Year 5   128.1

    Which statement *best describes* the behavior of inflation as measured by this index?
    A. Stable
    B. Accelerating
    C. Decelerating
    D. Accelerating then decelerating

2. For a demand-pull effect or a cost-push effect to cause inflation:
    A. the AS curve has to shift in response to a shift of the AD curve.
    B. the AD curve has to shift in response to a shift of the AS curve.
    C. the cause of the shift in AD or AS must be repeated or sustained.
    D. economic equilibrium must be re-established at a higher price level.

3. Which groups are left better off and which groups are left worse off after an unexpected increase in inflation?

	Better off	Worse off
A.	Fixed rate borrowers	Workers
B.	Fixed rate borrowers	Employers
C.	Fixed rate lenders	Workers
D.	Fixed rate lenders	Employers

4. Which of the following statements about anticipated inflation is *least likely* accurate?
    A. High anticipated inflation makes a currency less effective as a store of value.
    B. The rational response to high anticipated inflation is to delay cash purchases until the price level stabilizes.
    C. The actions people take to avoid the anticipated effects of inflation tend to divert them from productive activity.
    D. Anticipated inflation discourages investment by increasing the uncertainty of long-term planning and reducing real after-tax returns on investments.

5. An unexpected change in the rate of inflation causes:
    A. the long-run Phillips curve to shift.
    B. the short-run Phillips curve to shift.
    C. movement along the short-run Phillips curve.
    D. no change in the short-run or long-run Phillips curves.

Use the following data to answer Questions 6 and 7.

The unemployment rate in Fredonia is 7%, which economists estimate to be its natural rate. The inflation rate for the past year was 3%. Fredonia's policy makers believe they can reduce unemployment to a permanently lower rate by continually stimulating aggregate demand.

6.   If Fredonia adopts this policy, what are the *most likely* short-run effects on inflation and unemployment?

     Unemployment rate   Inflation rate

A. Less than 7%   Less than 3%

B. Less than 7%   More than 3%

C. Remains at 7%   Less than 3%

D. Remains at 7%   More than 3%

7.   If Fredonia adopts this policy, what are the *most likely* long-run effects on inflation and unemployment?

     Unemployment rate   Inflation rate

A. Less than 7%   Less than 3%

B. Less than 7%   More than 3%

C. Remains at 7%   Less than 3%

D. Remains at 7%   More than 3%

8.   In year 1 the nominal interest rate was 10% and the expected rate of inflation was 7%. One year later, the nominal interest rate is 8% and inflation expectations are 6%. What has happened to real interest rates between year 1 and year 2? They:

A. increased by 1%.

B. decreased by 1%.

C. increased by 2%.

D. decreased by 2%.

ANSWERS – CONCEPT CHECKERS: INFLATION

1. C   Using the formula for the inflation rate, we can calculate the inflation rate for years 2 to 5.

    Year 2   7.2%
    Year 3   5.0%
    Year 4   4.1%
    Year 5   2.6%

    Inflation was decelerating over this period.

2. C   To cause more than a one-time increase in the price level, whatever caused the AD curve to shift to the right (demand-pull) or the AS curve to shift to the left (cost-push) must be sustained over time.

3. A   Borrowers who pay fixed rates are left better off by unanticipated inflation because they are repaying their loans with cheaper currency than they borrowed. (But note that *anticipated* inflation would have been reflected in the interest rate.) Workers are left worse off because they receive less real compensation for their labor.

4. B   The rational response to high anticipated inflation is to spend cash as rapidly as possible.

5. C   An unexpected change in inflation causes the unemployment rate to move in the opposite direction. This represents movement along the short-run Phillips curve.

6. B   If unemployment is at its natural rate, GDP growth is at its potential rate. Stimulating AD from this level increases output in the short run, which reduces unemployment, but also increases the price level.

7. D   In the long run, unemployment cannot be held below its natural rate. The stimulus to AD will result in wage pressures, forcing the AS curve to the left, reducing output back to its potential rate, increasing unemployment back to its natural rate, and increasing the price level further. As the vertical long-run Phillips curve shows, the higher inflation rate has no beneficial effect on the natural rate of unemployment.

8. B   Because the nominal interest rate was 10% and the expected rate of inflation was 7% in the first year, the real rate of interest was 3% (10% – 7%). One year later with the nominal interest rate at 8% and inflation expectations at 6%, the real rate of interest was 2% (8% – 6%). Therefore, the real interest rate decreased by 1% between year 1 and year 2.

FISCAL POLICY

EXAM FOCUS

This topic review focuses on fiscal policy, which refers to the taxing and spending decisions of the government. Understand well how changes in taxing and government spending affect economic growth through their effect on the consumption and saving decisions of individuals and the investment spending of businesses. Be sure to understand the different multiplier effects and be able to distinguish between discretionary fiscal policy and automatic fiscal policy stabilizers. Understand the lags involved in the implementation and eventual effects of discretionary fiscal policy decisions.

FISCAL POLICY, BUDGET DEFICITS, AND BUDGET SURPLUSES

Fiscal policy refers to the federal government's use of spending and taxation to meet macroeconomic goals. The federal budget is said to be *balanced* when tax revenues equal federal government expenditures. A *budget surplus* occurs when government tax revenues exceed expenditures, and a *budget deficit* occurs when government expenditures exceed tax revenues. The Administration, through action of the President and Congress, enact fiscal policy laws designed to stabilize the economy. Decisions are made to increase taxes or reduce government spending during inflationary periods, and to reduce taxes or increase government spending during recessionary periods.

LOS 27.a: Interpret potential GDP, and the effects of income tax and tax on expenditure on potential GDP.

Gross Domestic Product (GDP) is the standard measure of the size of a national economy. GDP equals the total market value of all goods and services produced in a given country in a given year. Potential (or natural) GDP is the highest level that real GDP output can reach and sustain for long periods of time, given the existing supply of the factors of production (capital, workers, natural resources, technology, etc.). When real GDP equals potential GDP, the economy is said to be at full employment. The economy is in a recession phase if actual real GDP is less than potential GDP. The economy is in an inflationary state if actual real GDP is greater than potential GDP.

Income taxes dampen the incentive to work. An increase in income taxes causes after-tax wages per hour to fall. Consequently, workers will be less likely to work the same number of hours as they did when their after-tax wages per hour were higher. As income taxes rise, the full-employment supply of labor (a key factor of production) falls, which reduces potential GDP. These effects are illustrated in Figure 1.

Figure 1: Taxes and Potential GDP

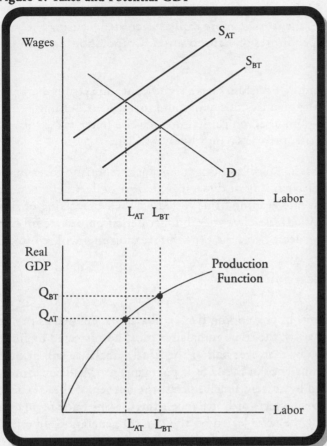

Figure 1 demonstrates that the full-employment quantity of labor hours falls as a result of the tax increase. The tax increase causes the labor supply curve to shift to the left, from the before-tax supply curve S_{BT} to after-tax supply curve S_{AT}, resulting in a drop in the equilibrium (full-employment) quantity of labor from L_{BT} (labor hours before tax) to L_{AT} (labor hours after tax). The figure also shows that potential GDP drops as a result of the decrease in the full-employment quantity of labor hours. The production function in Figure 1 shows real GDP (the output of the economy adjusted for price level changes) as a function of the labor supply. Potential GDP drops from Q_{BT} to Q_{AT} when the labor supply is decreased.

An increase in taxes on consumption expenditures (e.g., sales tax) also causes the supply of labor and potential GDP to drop. Workers "convert" hours of work into purchases of goods and services. An increase in expenditure taxes decreases the amount of goods and services that each hour of labor can buy. This disincentive to work reduces the supply of labor, which causes potential GDP to fall.

LOS 27.b: Discuss the sources of investment sources, and the influence of fiscal policy on capital markets.

Total investment is one of the major components of GDP (the others are consumption, government spending, and net exports). Investment is defined as expenditures for fixed productive assets and inventory. The sources of financing for investment are (1) national savings, (2) borrowing from foreigners, and (3) government savings.

The first two components are private sources of financing. The third source, government savings, equals the difference between government tax revenues and expenditures. Government budget surpluses increase the sources of total investment, but government budget deficits decrease them.

Investment directly affects the growth rate in real GDP. As investment declines, less capital is created, causing the growth rate in real GDP to fall. Conversely, as investment rises, more capital is created, causing the growth rate in real GDP to rise. This is analogous to capital expenditures of a corporation. Corporations invest in capital to increase output.

Fiscal policy decisions (government taxing and spending decisions) have significant impacts on markets for investment capital. Taxes on capital income affect the quantity of savings and investment, leading to changes in real GDP growth. The incentive to save falls as taxes imposed on capital income rise (after-tax earnings on savings fall). Therefore, as taxes on capital income rise, private savings likely will fall.

Fiscal policy also affects the supply of government savings. Just as budget surpluses represent government saving, budget deficits require government borrowing (negative saving or dissaving). Larger budget deficits decrease the quantity of savings, which increases the real interest rate, leading firms to reduce their borrowing of financial capital and their investment in physical capital. This adverse effect of a budget deficit on private investment in capital is referred to as the **crowding out effect**. The decrease in the growth rate of capital will reduce potential GDP.

LOS 27.c: Define the generational effects of fiscal policy.

Generational effects of fiscal policy refer to the effects of postponing fiscal imbalances, defined as the present value of future expected government deficits. Eventually, the fiscal imbalance must be corrected by increasing taxes or decreasing government spending. Studies show that over half of the fiscal imbalance will be paid by future generations. The major source of the fiscal imbalance in the U.S. is payments for Medicare. Since the costs of funding Medicare expenditures are not supported by current federal taxes, the burden of these expenditures will fall on taxpayers in the future. This a generational effect (or imbalance); the present value of government benefits to the current generation is not fully paid by the taxes levied on the current generation. In effect, current policy is to postpone the payment of taxes so the burden of government expenditures (to pay for current promises) falls on a future generation (one that isn't around yet to vote!).

LOS 27.d: Compare and contrast how the government purchases multiplier, the tax multiplier, the balanced budget multiplier, and discretionary fiscal policy can assist in stabilizing the business cycle.

Discretionary fiscal policy refers to the spending and taxing decisions of a national government that are intended to stabilize the economy. During recessions, actions can be taken to increase government spending or decrease taxes. Both decisions strengthen the economy by increasing aggregate demand, putting more money in the hands of corporations and consumers to invest and spend. During inflationary economic booms, actions can be taken to decrease government spending or increase taxes. Both decisions slow the economy by decreasing aggregate demand, taking money out of the hands of corporations and consumers, causing both investment and consumption spending to fall.

Discretionary fiscal policy decisions produce *multiplier* or magnified effects. The **government purchases multiplier** refers to the disproportionate effect of government purchases on aggregate demand. A dollar of government spending causes more than a $1 change in aggregate demand. Initially, aggregate demand increases by a full $1 after the government spends the money. Subsequently, because of the new program, additional workers might be hired. The new workers will use their new wages to consume more, which might induce corporations to hire more workers, who then will use their new wages for additional consumption. The process continues to multiply until all the effects of the original $1 of government spending have been realized.

Similarly, the **tax multiplier** refers to the disproportionate effects of tax policy changes on aggregate demand. An increase in taxes causes a magnified negative effect on aggregate demand, and a decrease in taxes causes a magnified positive effect on aggregate demand. The magnitude of the tax multiplier will be smaller than the government purchases multiplier because not all of the tax cut will be spent. A portion of the tax cut will be saved

©2007 Schweser

(determined by the marginal propensity to save). The remainder will be spent and then magnified though additional rounds of spending by subsequent parties.

The **balanced budget multiplier** refers to the disproportionate effects that a combined government purchase and tax program has on aggregate demand. The combined program has no effect on the budget because the amount of government purchases is equal to the increase in taxes. The increased government purchases have a positive multiplier effect and the increased taxes have a negative multiplier effect. However, as noted above, the government purchase multiplier is stronger than the tax multiplier. Consequently, the multiplier from the combined program is positive.

LOS 27.e: Discuss the limitations of discretionary stabilizers, and distinguish between discretionary fiscal policy and automatic stabilizers.

Discretionary fiscal policy is not an exact science. First, economic forecasts might be wrong, leading to incorrect policy decisions. Second, complications arise in practice that delay the effects of the discretionary stabilizers.

- *Recognition delay.* Discretionary fiscal policy decisions are made by the President and voted on by Congress. The state of the economy is complex and it may take the Administration time to recognize the extent of the economic problems.
- *Administrative or law-making delay.* The Administration and Congress cannot vote and enact decisions overnight. Legal changes are delayed while elected officials debate the issues.
- *Impact delay.* Time passes before the effects of the fiscal policy changes are felt. Delays occur in implementing increases and decreases in government spending and taxing. Moreover, it takes time for corporations and individuals to act on the fiscal policy changes.

In contrast to discretionary fiscal policy stabilizers, **automatic stabilizers** are built-in fiscal devices triggered by the state of the economy. Automatic fiscal stabilizers minimize timing problems encountered by discretionary fiscal policy stabilizers. Automatic fiscal stabilizers fall into two main categories: induced taxes and needs-tested spending.

- *Induced taxes* refer to the amount of taxes collected as a percentage (i.e., income tax rate) of income. Incomes are positively related to GDP. Incomes rise during an economic boom. As incomes rise, the total amount of taxes collected automatically increases. The increase in taxes paid by corporations and individuals slows down the economy. Conversely, incomes fall during a recession. As incomes fall, the total amount of taxes collected automatically falls. The decline in taxes paid by corporations and individuals stimulates the economy.
- *Needs-tested spending* refers to government expenditures for programs that pass a "needs" test, such as unemployment. During a recession, unemployment is high. The government automatically pays out more in unemployment compensation. The increase in unemployment compensation stimulates the economy. During an expansion, unemployment payments automatically drop. The decline in unemployment compensation dampens the economy.

Together, induced taxes and needs-tested spending offer automatic stability to the economy. Both actions are countercyclical: taxes rise and needs-based spending falls during expansions, and taxes fall and needs-based spending rises during recessions.

Professor's Note: The automatic stabilizers mentioned here are based on the U.S. tax law and entitlement programs.

KEY CONCEPTS

1. Potential GDP is the highest sustainable, or full employment, level of real GDP, given the existing supply of the factors of production.

2. An increase in taxes on income and expenditures reduces the incentive to work and the equilibrium quantity of labor falls, reducing potential GDP.

3. The sources of financing for total investment in an economy are national savings, foreign borrowing, and government savings. Government budget surpluses contribute to total investment, but government budget deficits detract from total investment.

4. Tax and spending decisions have significant impacts on capital markets. Budget deficits and increases in taxes on capital cause savings and investment to decline. Taxes on savings make saving less attractive. Budget deficits indicate negative savings by the government. Increased taxes and budget deficits reduce the sources of financing for investment, causing a decrease in the long-run growth rate of real GDP.

5. Generational effects of fiscal policy refer to the effects of postponing fiscal imbalances. Eventually, the fiscal imbalance must be corrected by increased taxes or decreased government spending. Studies show that over half of the fiscal imbalance will be paid by future generations.

6. The government purchases multiplier, tax multiplier, and balanced budget multiplier determine how large an effect different fiscal policy tools will have on aggregate demand.

7. The government purchases multiplier is stronger than the tax multiplier because aggregate demand is affected by the full amount of government expenditure, whereas aggregate demand is affected by only the portion of a tax cut that is spent; the remainder will be saved.

8. Discretionary fiscal policy refers to government spending and taxing decisions designed to stabilize the economy. Automatic fiscal policy refers to built-in fiscal stabilizers that are triggered by the state of the economy. Automatic fiscal stabilizers smooth out economic fluctuations.

9. Discretionary fiscal policy is plagued by delays. A recognition delay occurs in which time passes before the Administration recognizes the extent of the economic problem. A law-making delay occurs during the time needed to enact the legal changes. And an impact delay occurs during the time needed for a change in fiscal policy to be implemented and for its effects on the economy to be felt.

10. Automatic fiscal stabilizers minimize the timing problems encountered by discretionary fiscal policy stabilizers. Two types of automatic fiscal stabilizers are induced taxes and needs-tested spending.

CONCEPT CHECKERS: FISCAL POLICY

1. Which of the following statements is **TRUE** regarding the economic effects of taxes?
    A. An increase in income taxes creates an incentive to work more hours.
    B. A decrease in sales taxes reduces the supply of labor and potential GDP.
    C. Decreasing the income tax rate increases the long-term growth rate of the economy.
    D. Taxing consumption instead of income would eliminate the negative effect of taxes on economic growth.

2. All of the following factors reduce the level of investment **EXCEPT:**
    A. lower savings rates.
    B. fiscal crowding out.
    C. federal budget surpluses.
    D. increased taxes on capital income.

3. Sales in the retail sector have been sluggish and consumer confidence has recently declined, indicating fewer planned purchases. In response, the President sends an expansionary government spending plan to Congress. The plan is submitted on March 30 and Congress refines and approves the terms of the spending plan on June 30. What type of fiscal plan is being considered, and what type of delay did the plan experience between March 30 and June 30?

	Fiscal Plan	Type of Delay
A.	Automatic	Recognition delay
B.	Automatic	Law-making delay
C.	Discretionary	Impact delay
D.	Discretionary	Law-making delay

4. Congress is concerned about delays in the effects of fiscal policy, and is considering requiring the compilation and reporting of economic statistics weekly, rather than quarterly. The new reporting period is intended to decrease:
    A. the impact delay.
    B. the information cost.
    C. the law making delay.
    D. the recognition delay.

5. Congress recently passed an income tax rate hike on all income levels at a time when the economy was at the full employment level. As a result of the tax increase, what are the *most likely* changes in the quantity of labor and potential GDP?

	Quantity of Labor	Potential GDP
A.	Increases	Increases
B.	Increases	Decreases
C.	Decreases	Increases
D.	Decreases	Decreases

6. Congress enacts a program to subsidize farmers in the Midwest with an expansive spending program of $10 billion. At the same time, Congress enacts a $10 billion tax increase. Which of the following *best describes* the impact on the economy?
    A. Lower growth due to the negative tax multiplier.
    B. Higher growth due to the net positive balanced budget multiplier.
    C. Higher growth due to the positive government spending multiplier.
    D. No effect on growth because the tax and spending multiplier effects offset.

7. Recent reports indicate that real GDP growth was negative over the past two quarters. To counter the recent trend, Congress is considering a $10 billion cut in taxes. However, there is also severe pressure to maintain a balanced budget, so Congress decides to create a balanced budget tax cut plan. Which of the following *best describes* whether the plan is likely to succeed in countering the recent economic trend?
    A. Likely, because of the positive multiplier effect.
    B. Unlikely, because of the negative multiplier effect.
    C. Likely, because the plan has no net multiplier effect.
    D. Unlikely, because the plan has no net multiplier effect.

ANSWERS – CONCEPT CHECKERS: FISCAL POLICY

1. C   Income taxes reduce the incentive to work. Decreasing income taxes encourages workers to work more hours, which increases potential GDP. Consumption taxes also create a disincentive to work because they reduce the amount of goods and services an hour of labor is worth.

2. C   Federal budget surpluses represent government savings, a source from which investment can increase.

3. D   The expansionary plan initiated by the President and approved by Congress is an example of discretionary fiscal policy. The lag from the time of the submission (March 30) through time of the vote (June 30) is known as law-making delay. It took Congress three months to write and pass the necessary laws.

4. D   More frequent and current economic data would make it easier for authorities to monitor the economy and to recognize problems. The reduction in the time lag between economic reports would reduce the recognition delay.

5. D   The increase in income taxes shifts the labor supply curve to the left, resulting in a lower equilibrium quantity of labor. Labor is one of the input factors of production for the economy. Therefore, the lower quantity of labor causes potential GDP to fall.

6. B   The amount of the spending program exactly offsets the amount of the tax increase, leaving the budget unaffected. The multiplier effect is stronger for government spending than for the tax increase. Therefore, the multiplier will be positive. All of the government spending enters the economy as increased expenditure, whereas only a portion of the tax increase results in lessened expenditure.

7. B   The economy is in recession as indicated by the weak GDP growth. The balanced budget program is unlikely to end the recession because the multiplier will be negative. The multiplier effect is stronger for government spending versus the tax increase. Only a portion of the tax increase will be spent, but all of the decrease in government expenditure will be taken out of the economy. Both changes will then be magnified through their multiplier effects.

The following is a review of the Economics principles designed to address the learning outcome statements set forth by CFA Institute®. This topic is also covered in:

MONETARY POLICY

EXAM FOCUS

Monetary policy refers to attempts by a central bank to influence inflation and the growth rate of the economy through changes in the money supply and interest rates. Understand how changes in monetary policy affect inflation and economic growth in the context of the aggregate supply-aggregate demand model. Know the differences among fixed-rule, feedback-rule, and discretionary approaches to monetary policy and the difference between the new Monetarist feedback rule and the new Keynesian feedback rule. Be able to explain the difference between the effects of announced, credible monetary policy changes and the effects of surprise monetary policy changes on inflation and real output and how these differences are related to the short-run Phillips curve.

LOS 28.a: Distinguish between price level stability, and sustainable real GDP growth.

The primary objective of the Federal Reserve is to maintain *price level stability*, defined as a stable inflation rate between zero and three percent. By maintaining a stable inflation rate, the Fed reduces uncertainty in the marketplace, which is important for many reasons. In particular, consumers and lenders can plan more appropriately and efficiently if there are few inflation surprises. The more stable the inflation rate becomes, the closer real interest rates and real wages are to their expected values.

Price level stability also creates an environment with incentives to save and invest, which strengthens the economy. For example, consider a period of price instability in which inflation rises higher than expected. During this period of price instability, consumers likely will not exchange consumption for saving because the real interest rate earned on savings will fall. Therefore, by keeping the inflation rate stable, the Federal Reserve encourages savings. That, in turn, improves long-run economic growth, which brings us to the next major point.

The broader outcome of price level stability desired by the Fed is to maintain the long-term strength of the economy. Perhaps the most popular measure of the performance of the economy is the growth rate in real GDP. As discussed in a previous topic review, an increase in savings and investment causes an increase in *sustainable real GDP growth*, defined as the growth rate in real GDP that is sustainable over the long term, given the state of technology, natural resources, and the propensity to save and invest. Recent technological advances and the resulting productivity gains have increased the sustainable annual growth rate in real GDP in the U.S. to over 3%. Sustainable real GDP growth is achieved when real GDP equals potential GDP. Therefore, while the Fed's primary goal is to achieve price level stability, the broader objective is to create and maintain a strong and growing economy.

LOS 28.b: Compare and contrast the policies that can be implemented to achieve price level stability.

The Federal Reserve can pursue various monetary policies designed to achieve price level stability. These policies fall into three categories:

- *Fixed-rule policies* refer to actions of the Fed that are taken regardless of the health of the economy. Examples include rules ensuring stable money supply growth. Nobel laureate economist Milton Friedman is a well-known proponent of increasing the money supply only at a constant rate equal to the long-term growth rate in real GDP. Fixed rules are often recommended because of lags and credibility problems associated with more active monetary policy.

- *Feedback-rule policies* refer to a set of rules dictating actions to be taken by the Federal Reserve in response to the changing health of the economy. Examples include actions to increase the money supply or decrease interest rates if the unemployment rate rises above the natural rate (full employment rate) or if real GDP growth is less than potential real GDP growth for a particular span of time.

- *Discretionary policies* are similar to feedback policies in that they also refer to actions taken in response to changes in the economy, but they do not follow a strict set of rules, but rather use subjective judgment to treat each situation in a unique manner. In practice, most policy changes are discretionary in nature.

LOS 28.c: Discuss policy credibility in relation to aggregate demand and aggregate supply, and the Phillips curve.

Macroeconomists often examine theories related to *policy credibility*, which refers to whether decision makers in the economy (individuals and businesses) believe announced monetary policy changes will actually be implemented as claimed. We will illustrate the difference in effects between an announced, credible policy change and a policy change that comes as a surprise, either because it was not announced or because it was announced but it was not credible (believed by decision makers).

Our scenario here involves an economy with relatively high expected and actual inflation. Consider that the central bank wants to reduce this inflation rate and will do so by reducing the growth rate of the money supply. The current (inflationary) situation is illustrated in Figure 1 by the aggregate demand and short-run aggregate supply curve pairs, $AD_1 - SRAS_1$ and $AD_2 - SRAS_2$.

Figure 1: AD – AS Curves: No Change in Policy

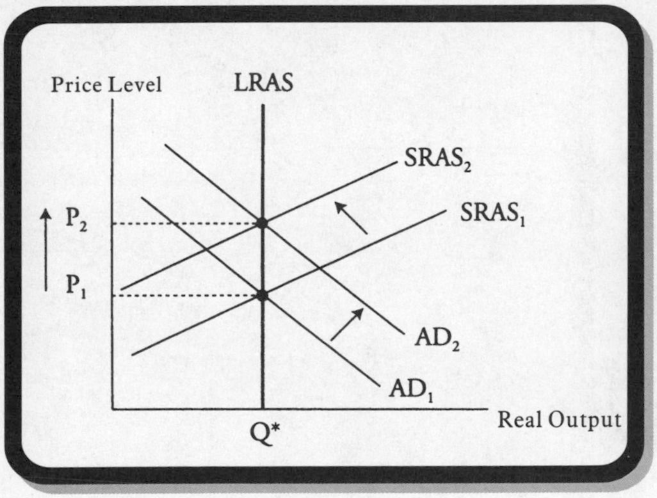

The current situation is represented by AD_1 and $SRAS_1$ which intersect at a real output level of Q^*, which is full employment GDP and is therefore on the LRAS curve as shown. With the money supply growing at its current rate, over time inflation will increase the price level from its current level of P_1 to P_2. If current inflation expectations are correct and inflation increases the price level from P_1 to P_2, aggregate demand a year from now will be at AD_2 as incomes and the components of aggregate demand (consumption, government expenditures, investment, and net exports) all increase because of inflation. Real aggregate demand is actually the same in the future, but the price level is higher.

Aggregate supply depends importantly on the real wage rate and the amount of labor supplied. If increases in nominal (money) wages do not keep pace with inflation in the prices of goods and services, the real wage falls, and less labor will be supplied. In our current situation, workers require nominal wage increases (wage inflation) that correspond to the same increase as that of the price level of goods and services, from P_1 to P_2. If the expectations for wage and goods inflation are met over the next year, the new equilibrium is at the intersection of AD_2 and $SRAS_2$, at the new price level P_2, and at the same (full employment level) Q^*. So that's the initial situation for our example inflation will be just as expected over the next year, raising the price level from P to P_2, and aggregate demand and aggregate supply will both shift so that equilibrium output is still at the full employment level.

Now we want to look at a change in monetary policy, a decrease in the growth rate of the money supply, designed to reduce the inflation rate. The point we will illustrate is that the outcome will be different if the policy change is announced and credible, than it will be if the policy change is a surprise (unannounced) or is announced but is not believed (not credible).

Figure 2 illustrates the new equilibrium if the policy change is announced and credible. In response to an announcement that the central bank will slow the growth of the money supply, which will increase interest rates and slow aggregate demand growth, decision makers revise their inflation expectations downward. Based on the new (lower) expected rate of inflation, workers require smaller nominal wage increases so that aggregate supply does not decrease as much over the next year, it falls only to $SRAS_2'$. Because of the decrease in the rate of growth of the money supply, aggregate demand increases only to AD_2'. Because the policy change was announced and credible, inflation is less than it would have been, and the policy change has been a success. The increase in the price level (inflation) has been reduced and the economy is still at full employment equilibrium along the LRAS curve.

Figure 2: AD–AS Curves: Credible Policy Change

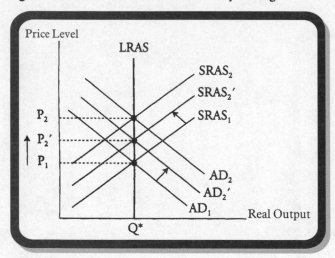

In contrast, let's now consider what happens if the monetary policy change is not clear or credible. Figure 3 illustrates these effects. If the central bank institutes the same reduction in the growth rate of the money supply as in the previous example, aggregate demand will increase to AD_2', just as it did when the policy change was announced and credible. Because workers either do not know or do not believe that the central bank will slow the growth rate of the money supply, required wages will be based on the old (unchanged) expectations of inflation. Thus the SRAS curve shifts just as it would with no policy change, from $SRAS_1$ to $SRAS_2$. The smaller increase in aggregate demand combined with the large drop in aggregate supply causes the economy to fall into recession, in which real GDP is less than potential GDP ($Q^{**} < Q^*$), as represented by the intersection of AD_2' and $SRAS_2$. Moreover, the new price level (P_2'') exceeds the price level one would expect from a credible policy change (P_2'). When the central bank policy change is unannounced or not credible, it has the unintended effect of reducing output below full-employment output, and the reduction in the inflation rate is less than when the policy change was announced and credible.

Figure 3: AD–AS Curves: Policy Change Lacking Credibility

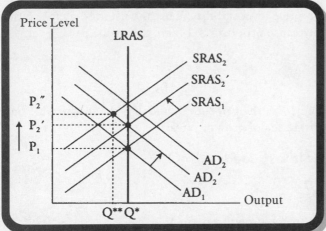

The effects of Fed policy changes also can be demonstrated using the Phillips curve, which is a graph of the (historically observed) negative short-run relationship between the inflation rate and the unemployment rate.

Figure 4: Phillips Curve

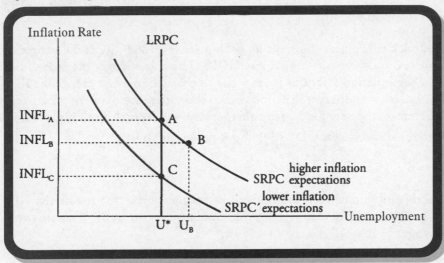

Because the Fed policy change is unexpected or lacks credibility, individuals will continue to have high inflation expectations, as represented by the intersection of the higher short-run Phillips curve (SRPC) with the long-run Phillips curve (LRPC). But the Fed policy actually causes the inflation rate to be less than expected (INFL$_B$ rather than originally expected INFL$_A$). The effect on the economy is illustrated as a movement along the SRPC from point A to point B. Point B represents lower inflation, but comes at a cost of a higher unemployment rate (increase in the unemployment rate from the full-employment rate, U*, to U$_B$). Therefore, the unexpected change in Fed policy causes the unemployment rate to increase.

On the other hand, if the policy change is clearly understood and credible, individuals will revise their inflation expectations downward and the short-run Phillips curve will shift down to SRPC. The inflation rate will drop all the way to INFL$_C$ and the unemployment rate will remain at the full-employment level. Therefore, the clear and credible tightened Fed policy causes the inflation rate to drop, and does so without increasing the unemployment rate (without decreasing employment and output).

LOS 28.d: Compare and contrast the new Monetarist and new Keynesian feedback rules.

The **new Monetarist feedback rule** places emphasis on price level stability. The rule uses the quantity theory of money, which states that increases in the money supply cause proportional increases in the price level. The quantity theory of money equation is:

$$MV = PY$$

where M is the money supply, V is the velocity of money, P is the price level, and Y is the quantity of output (goods and services). The equation often is rewritten in terms of growth rates:

growth rate in M + growth rate in V = growth rate in P + growth rate in Y

Solving for the money supply growth rate:

growth rate in M = growth rate in P + growth rate in Y – growth rate in V

Based on this equation, the new Monetarist feedback rule sets the money supply growth rate equal to the target inflation rate plus the 10-year moving average real GDP growth rate minus the 4-year moving average velocity growth rate. Therefore, money supply growth is triggered by changes in the target inflation rate and changes in the moving average growth rates in real GDP and money supply velocity. Notice that the new Monetarist feedback rule adjusts rather slowly to changes in the business cycle since it is based on longer-term moving averages of the growth rates of real GDP and velocity.

In contrast, the **new Keynesian feedback rule** places emphasis on both price level stability and business cycle stability (i.e., reducing deviations of real GDP from potential real GDP). The rule changes the federal funds target rate in response to changes in the inflation rate, and in response to changes in other premiums associated with the differences between actual inflation and target inflation and to the difference between actual real GDP and full-employment real GDP. Therefore, the new Keynesian rule increases the federal funds target rate as inflation and inflation indicators increase and as real GDP rises above potential GDP.

The main differences between the two rules are:

- The new Keynesian rule is directly and immediately affected by the business cycle. Gaps between GDP and potential GDP bring quick action under the new Keynesian rule. In contrast, the new Monetarist rule produces a slow response to changes in real GDP.
- The new Keynesian rule uses the federal funds target rate as the policy variable, whereas the new Monetarist rule uses the growth rate of the money supply as the policy variable.

The Fed's actions have more closely followed the new Keynesian rule over the past two decades.

KEY CONCEPTS

1. The Fed defines price level stability as a stable inflation rate between zero and three percent.

2. Sustainable real GDP growth is defined as the growth rate in real GDP that is sustainable over the long term, given the state of technology, natural resources, and propensity to save and invest.

3. While the Fed's primary goal is to achieve price level stability, its broader objective is to create and maintain a strong and vibrant economy.

4. The Fed can pursue various monetary policies designed to achieve price level stability. Fixed-rule policies refer to actions of the Fed that are taken regardless of the health of the economy. Feedback-rule policies refer to a set of rules dictating actions to be taken in response to the changing health of the economy. Discretionary policies are similar to feedback policies, but rather than follow a strict set of rules, they use subjective judgment to treat each situation in a unique manner.

5. Monetary policy may fail as a result of a lack of credibility. If policy changes are not credible, individuals will not revise expectations correctly. Consequently, Fed policy can produce unwanted results. Fed policy designed to slow the inflation rate may throw the economy into recession (as demonstrated by the aggregate demand and supply curves) and high levels of unemployment (as demonstrated by the Phillips curve).

6. The new Monetarist feedback rule sets the growth rate in money supply as a function of the target inflation rate and of the moving average growth rates in GDP and money velocity.

7. The new Keynesian feedback rule sets the federal funds target rate as a function of the inflation rate and the differences between actual and target inflation and actual and potential real GDP.

8. The new Keynesian rule is directly and immediately affected by the business cycle, whereas the new Monetarist rule reacts slowly to changes in real GDP. The new Keynesian rule uses the federal funds target rate as the decision variable, while the new Monetarist rule uses growth in the money supply.

CONCEPT CHECKERS: MONETARY POLICY

1. The Federal Reserve's primary objective is to:
    A. reduce the inflation rate to zero in the long run.
    B. encourage savings by increasing nominal interest rates.
    C. prevent economic growth from falling below its sustainable rate.
    D. maintain price level stability and thereby improve the long-term strength of the economy.

2. The Federal Reserve is debating two alternative policies. Policy 1 maintains the same growth rate in the money supply during inflationary periods and during recession periods. Policy 2 increases the money supply growth rate during recession periods and decreases the money supply growth rate during inflationary periods. Indicate which policy is an example of a feedback rule policy and indicate which policy, if implemented correctly, is likely to shorten the duration of a recession.

	Feedback rule policy	Shortened recession
A.	Policy 1	Policy 1
B.	Policy 1	Policy 2
C.	Policy 2	Policy 1
D.	Policy 2	Policy 2

3. The business cycle is experiencing a recession, and monetary authorities are considering taking action to counter the downtrend. Proper discretionary policy actions taken by the Federal Reserve should have the following effects on the aggregate demand curve and on the price level:

	Aggregate demand	Price level
A.	Increase	Increase
B.	Increase	Decrease
C.	Decrease	Increase
D.	Decrease	Decrease

4. With the economy at full employment, the Federal Reserve unexpectedly decides to decrease the money supply and increase interest rates. The *most likely* effects of the Fed policy change on the economy and on the unemployment rate are:

	Economy	Unemployment
A.	Real GDP < potential real GDP	Unemployment rate > natural rate
B.	Real GDP < potential real GDP	Unemployment rate < natural rate
C.	Real GDP > potential real GDP	Unemployment rate > natural rate
D.	Real GDP > potential real GDP	Unemployment rate < natural rate

5. In the past two quarters, real GDP dropped below potential GDP. Two competing policy rules have been proposed to counter adverse movements in price levels and real GDP: the new Monetarist feedback rule and the new Keynesian feedback rule. Indicate which rule places more emphasis on the supply of money, and which policy is better equipped to address the GDP gap.

	Emphasis on supply of money	Emphasis on GDP gap
A.	New Monetarist	New Monetarist
B.	New Monetarist	New Keynesian
C.	New Keynesian	New Monetarist
D.	New Keynesian	New Keynesian

ANSWERS – CONCEPT CHECKERS: MONETARY POLICY

1. **D**   The Fed's primary objective is to maintain price stability, which it defines as an inflation rate between zero and three percent. Keeping the inflation rate low and stable encourages savings, which improves long-run economic growth.

2. **D**   Policy 2 is a monetary policy change made based on the state of the economy, which is the definition of a feedback rule policy. In contrast, a fixed rule policy refers to action that does not depend on the state of the economy. If implemented well, the feedback policy is expected to stabilize the economy. It is designed to increase aggregate demand during recessions and to decrease aggregate demand during inflationary periods.

3. **A**   Discretionary policy refers to actions taken by the Fed that address each economic situation in a unique manner. To counter the recession, the Fed likely will increase the money supply and decrease interest rates. If implemented properly, the action is expected to stimulate the economy by increasing the aggregate demand curve. The increase in aggregate demand will cause the price level to rise.

4. **A**   With the economy at full employment, real GDP equals potential real GDP and the unemployment rate equals the natural (full employment) rate. The unexpected decrease in the money supply causes aggregate demand to drop. Because the action was unexpected, individuals have not renegotiated their wage rates, so aggregate supply remains unaffected. The drop in aggregate demand with no change in aggregate supply causes a recession, implying that real GDP will drop below potential GDP and that the unemployment rate will increase above the natural rate.

5. **B**   The new Monetarist feedback rule is based on the quantity theory of money. Under this rule, the Federal Reserve changes the growth rate of the money supply only slowly, based on the target inflation rate, the moving average growth rate of real GDP, and the moving average growth rate of the velocity of money. In contrast, the new Keynesian feedback rule changes the federal funds target rate in response to the gap between actual inflation and target inflation and the gap between actual real GDP and potential real GDP. The new Keynesian feedback rule produces more and quicker responses to changes in inflation and real GDP.

TRADING WITH THE WORLD

EXAM FOCUS

You should understand the principle of comparative advantage as that is the basis of the case for free trade. Make sure you understand the difference between the effects of tariffs and the effects of quotas, and how restrictions on trade in general decrease the wealth of a country. Know who gains and who loses from trade restrictions and that trade restrictions are considered to be primarily driven by the political activity of those who stand to gain from specific trade restrictions.

LOS 29.a: Discuss opportunity cost associated with trade, how countries can gain from international trade, how countries determine whether to import, export or produce goods and services, and explain the gains of trade for all parties.

Comparative advantage refers to the lowest *opportunity cost* to produce a product.

The **law of comparative advantage** holds that *trading partners can be made better off if they specialize* in the production of goods for which they are the low-opportunity-cost producer (have a comparative advantage) and trade for those goods for which they are the high-opportunity-cost producer. A country gains (i.e., it realizes expanded consumption possibilities) from international trade when it *exports* those goods for which it has a comparative advantage and *imports* those goods for which it does *not*.

An example will illustrate the gains from trade in terms of expanded consumption opportunities for two countries. Figures 1 and 2 show the production possibility frontiers (PPF) for two countries, Alton and Borton, for two generic goods, food and machinery.

Figure 1: Production Possibility Frontier for Alton

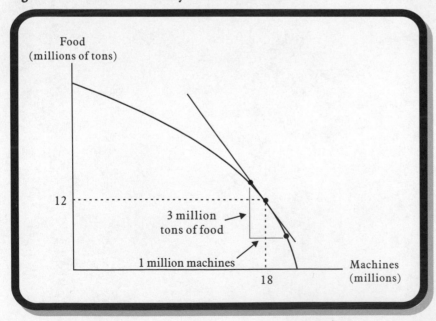

©2007 Schweser

Figure 2: Production Possibility Frontier for Borton

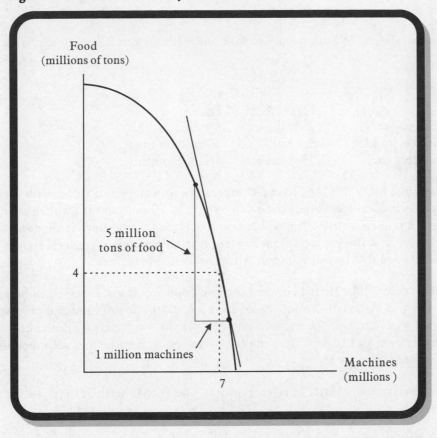

Without trade, Alton chooses to produce 12 million tons of food and 18 million units of machinery, while Borton chooses to produce 4 million tons of food and 7 million machines. The slope of the each country's PPF at its chosen production point represents the opportunity cost of food in terms of machinery. Given their possible production levels of the two goods, the opportunity cost of producing a unit of one good can be expressed in terms of how many units of the other good they must give up to produce it.

For Alton, the opportunity cost of producing another million units of machinery is 3 million tons of food, while for Borton, the opportunity cost of producing another million units of machinery is 5 million tons of food. The opportunity costs of food are simply the reciprocals of these amounts. For Alton, the opportunity cost of producing another million tons of food is 1/3 million units of machinery, and for Borton, the opportunity cost of producing another million tons of food is 1/5 million units of machinery. We say that Alton has a comparative advantage in the production of (the lowest opportunity cost of producing) machinery and that Borton has a comparative advantage in the production of food. If one country has a lower opportunity cost of producing one good, the other country must have a comparative advantage in the production of the other good in our simple example. Next we will show that, as long as their opportunity costs of production differ, trade will allow both countries to consume more than they can without trade.

Since Alton has a comparative advantage in the production of machinery, it will be advantageous for Alton to produce more machinery and to trade with Borton for food. For example, Alton could produce 2 million more units of machinery and 6 million tons less food. Borton could produce 6 million more tons of food and, given that their opportunity cost of a ton of food is 1/5 of a million units of machinery, produce 1.2 million fewer units of machinery.

Professor's Note: I realize these are not realistic trade-offs because the PPFs are curved and we're using the approximate slope (trade-off) at a point. The results would be qualitatively the same if we used 6 tons of food and 1.2 units of machinery in our examples. Using these smaller amounts, the curvature of the PPF would not be significant, and the slope would be an accurate estimate of the actual trade-off in production.

The table in Figure 3 illustrates the total output of both countries with and without specialization and trade.

Figure 3: Gain From Trade

| | Without Trade | | With Trade | |
	Machinery	Food	Machinery	Food
Alton	18 million	12 million tons	20 million	6 million tons
Borton	7 million	4 million tons	5.8 million	10 million tons
Total	25 million	16 million tons	25.8 million	16 million tons

When each country specializes in the good for which they have a comparative advantage and trades with the other, there are clear gains in our example. Total food production can remain at 20 million tons while the total output of machinery is increased by 0.8 million units. Alton will export machinery, since they are the low (opportunity) cost producer of machinery, and import food from Borton. Borton has a comparative advantage in the production of food, and will export food to Alton and import Alton-produced machinery.

How the gains from specialization and trade will be shared between the two countries is not determined here, but clearly there is a possible exchange that will allow both countries to enjoy a combination of food and machinery that they could not reach on their own without trade. In terms of our PPF graphs, each country can consume at a point *outside* its PPF through specialization and trade. That's the important point here, as long as opportunity costs differ, two countries can both benefit from trade.

LOS 29.b: Compare and contrast tariffs, non-tariff barriers, quotas and VERs with respect to international trade.

Although the gains from trade are very apparent, countries erect barriers to trade, including tariffs and quotas, and sometimes impose voluntary export restraints (VER).

Tariffs

A *tariff* is a tax imposed on imported goods while a *quota* is a limitation on the quantity of goods imported.

Tariffs benefit domestic producers because the level of imports will be reduced due to an effective increase in the price of the good. For example, if the world price of semiconductors is $40, and domestic producers can only profitably meet domestic semiconductor demand at a price of $45, foreign producers have a comparative advantage. Hence, domestic producers will not be able to compete in their own domestic semiconductor market. However, if the government places a $10 tariff on imported semiconductors, domestic producers will become competitive with foreign producers in the domestic market, and domestic semiconductor production will rise compared to the level of production without tariffs. Tariffs will also benefit the government, because it will collect the $10 tax (tariff) on all foreign semiconductors sold in the domestic market. Even though the government collects tariffs and supposedly uses these funds to increase the welfare of its citizens, domestic consumers still lose. Because the demand curve is downward sloping, the loss in consumer surplus cannot be fully recovered by tax revenue.

Figure 4 shows that if the world price prevails, domestic producers will offer a quantity of Q_{DNT} to the market. At this same price, the total quantity demanded will be relatively high at Q_{NT}. Upon the imposition of a tariff, the quantity supplied to the market by domestic suppliers rises to Q_{DT}, but total quantity demanded falls to Q_T. The amount of goods imported into the domestic economy *prior* to the imposition of the tariff was $Q_{NT} - Q_{DNT}$, but the import quantity shrinks to $Q_T - Q_{DT}$ after the tariff is in place. Since domestic producers are *high-cost suppliers* of this good, we shift domestic production toward goods for which we are the high-cost producer and away from goods for which we have a comparative advantage. This is one of the key drawbacks of imposing a tariff.

Domestic producers gain by the increase in their producer surplus from A to A + B. The government collects tariff revenue equal to area *C*. However, consumers lose the entire area A + B + C + D due to higher prices and a reduction in consumer surplus. Area *D* can also be thought of as *deadweight loss* or the *efficiency loss* of tariff imposition.

Figure 4: The Impact of Tariffs

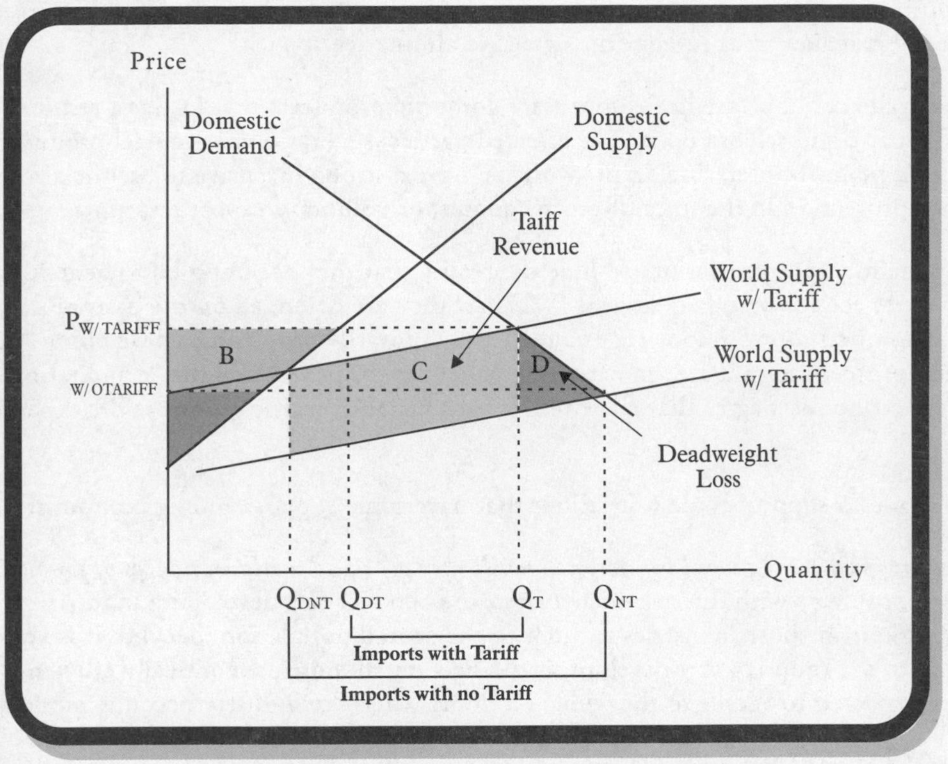

Quotas

A quota has an effect very similar to that of a tariff. Under a quota system, importers in the domestic country are given licenses to import specific amounts of a foreign-produced good. The supply of imported goods is reduced, and a lower supply means a higher price domestically. In Figure 4, the imposition of a quota equal to $Q_T - Q_{DT}$ would produce the same equilibrium domestic price and quantity, but with no government tariff revenue. Rather, the area labeled "tariff revenue" will be shared by the importers who are granted portions of the quota amount, because they are allowed to sell their goods at the higher price that results from the imposition of the quota. Clearly, domestic producers also benefit from the quota because competition from foreign producers is limited. The bottom line is that *quotas can be more harmful than tariffs* because the government does not receive any funds from the imposition of quotas; it is the importers who receive the revenue transfer (due to higher prices received for all goods sold under the import license).

Voluntary export restraints (VER) are agreements by exporting countries to voluntarily limit the quantity of goods they will export to an importing country. The primary difference between VERs and quotas is that the gains that accrue to those with import licenses under a quota system are received by the firms in the exporting countries that hold export permits under a VER system. It is probably common that the foreign government officials who determine which exporters get permits find ways to receive some of the value of these licenses.

LOS 29.c: Discuss the advantages and disadvantages of protection for each party, and explain the main reasons for trade restriction.

It is reasonable at this point to ask why trade restrictions are as common as they are, given that free trade appears to offer societal gains to all countries. While trade restrictions have fallen over recent decades, they are still prevalent and significant in such products as sugar, textiles, footwear, meat, and metals, among others.

The primary forces underlying trade restrictions are twofold. Governments like tariff revenue, and domestic producers affected by lower-cost imports use political means to gain protection from foreign competition. In developing countries, the ability to collect income tax revenue is restricted by both the lack of financial records and problems of compliance. This makes tariff revenue an attractive alternative.

In theory, the benefits of free trade could be used to compensate domestic producers that lose as a result of free trade. This, however, is problematic and seldom done. The affected parties, such as domestic steel producers and steel workers or domestic textile manufacturers and textile workers, have a strong incentive to use their votes and political contributions to gain protection in the form of tariffs, quotas, or voluntary export restraints.

A variety of arguments are made for trade restrictions to hide the reality that they are imposed to benefit one group at the expense of the entire economy and its citizens. Whether they are defended on the basis of saving jobs, protecting workers from competition with low-wage countries, temporarily protecting a developing "infant" industry, lower environmental protection standards in exporting countries, or preventing the "exploitation" of less-developed countries, most economists agree that trade restrictions benefit specific groups at the expense of the whole economy.

Some arguments commonly made to support trade restrictions that have some support among economists are:

- *Developing industries (infant industries) should be protected while they get up to world standards of productivity and quality.* There are two problems with this argument. First, the benefits of a developing industry mainly accrue to the firms and workers in those industries and not to the overall population. Second, it is argued that a government subsidy to the industry as it develops would be a much more economically efficient way to gain any benefits that are expected to accrue to the whole economy when the industry becomes globally competitive.
- *Exporters should be prohibited from selling goods abroad at less than production cost (anti-dumping argument).* It is difficult to estimate production costs, and just the fact that a foreign firm sells at a lower price in the export market than in its own domestic market is not evidence of dumping as it is usually defined. Even if a foreign firm managed to drive domestic firms out of business, there could still be foreign competition from other countries, and domestic firms could re-enter the business if the foreign firm subsequently raised prices.
- *Industries associated with national defense should be protected by trade restrictions so they will exist domestically in case of war.* One problem with this argument is that it is hard to find an industry that does not contribute, or cannot potentially contribute, to national defense. From an economic efficiency perspective, it is better for the government to subsidize strategic industries judged essential to national defense directly, rather than impose costs on all domestic consumers by imposing trade restrictions.

Other arguments for trade restrictions that have very little support among economists are:

- *Trade barriers protect jobs.* Part of the popularity of trade restrictions stems from their ability to protect easily identifiable jobs and the high wage levels in these jobs. However, in the long run, trade restrictions cannot protect the *net* number of jobs in the country. The number of jobs protected by import restrictions will be offset by jobs lost in other industries in general (that would sell less because more is spent on higher-priced imported goods) and in the import/export industry. Import/export firms will be unable to sell the overpriced domestic product abroad or import and sell the lower-priced, restricted foreign-made product.
- *Trade restrictions create jobs.* In the short run maybe, but in the long run, no. First of all, trade restrictions prevent your trading partners from developing the purchasing power needed to buy import goods from you,

thus depressing your own export industry. Secondly, the higher price of the protected domestic goods dampens domestic aggregate purchasing power, taking sales away from other domestic products. Finally, the jobs that would have been created in the import industry are never created.

- *Trade with low-wage countries depresses wage rates in high-wage countries.* The belief that trading with low-wage countries depresses wages is based on a misunderstanding of the law of comparative advantage. A high hourly wage does not necessarily mean high per-unit labor costs. Labor productivity must be considered. The worker's skill level, the amount of invested capital, and production methods may produce labor costs per unit of output below those found in low-wage countries. Consider the law of comparative advantage. When each country produces goods for which it has a comparative advantage, both countries will benefit. High-wage countries will have an advantage in high-tech manufacturing, and low-wage countries will have an advantage in labor-intensive goods. When both produce the goods in which they have an advantage, total output and the availability of goods will increase.

In summary, tariffs benefit domestic producers, industry workers, and governments, at the expense of domestic consumers and workers outside the protected industry. Quotas benefit domestic producers, industry workers, and those with import licenses at the expense of domestic consumers and workers outside the protected industry. VERs benefit domestic producers, industry workers, and those with export licenses or the power to grant them at the expense of domestic consumers and workers outside the protected industry.

KEY CONCEPTS

1. If two countries have different opportunity costs of producing goods, each will have a comparative advantage in some goods, and trade will increase the total production and consumption possibilities in both countries, improving economic welfare.
2. International trade will tend to increase domestic supply as imports are available and increase domestic demand because exports will be possible.
3. Tariffs are taxes on imports. Quotas restrict physical amounts of imports by granting import licenses. Voluntary export restraints are agreements by exporting countries to limit exports to an importing country. An exporting country gives export licenses for specific quantities to its exporting firms.
4. Trade barriers reduce the possible consumption for a country's citizens.
5. Tariffs benefit domestic producers, industry workers, and government workers at the expense of domestic consumers.
6. Quotas benefit domestic producers, industry workers, and import license holders at the expense of domestic consumers.
7. Voluntary export restraints benefit domestic producers, industry workers, and export license holders at the expense of domestic consumers.
8. In general, trade restrictions arise from a desire by government for tariff revenue and from economically motivated political activity by the domestic groups who will gain from protection from foreign competition.
9. Of the reasons commonly used to support trade restrictions, national defense arguments and infant industry arguments may have some validity, but the goals of maintaining these industries are likely reached in a more economically efficient manner by direct government subsidy than by imposing costs on all domestic consumers and the entire economy.
10. Other arguments for trade restrictions are not supported by economic theory.

CONCEPT CHECKERS: TRADING WITH THE WORLD

1. Which of the following statements about international trade is *least accurate*? If two countries have different opportunity costs of production for two goods, by engaging in trade:
   A. both countries can increase their total consumption.
   B. each country gains by importing the good for which it has a comparative advantage.
   C. each country can achieve a level of consumption outside its domestic production possibility frontier.
   D. the low opportunity cost producer of each good will export to the high opportunity cost producer of that good.

2. The *least likely* result of import quotas and voluntary export restraints is:
   A. increased revenue for the government.
   B. a decrease in the quantity of imports of the product.
   C. an increase in the domestic price of the product.
   D. a shift in production toward higher-cost suppliers.

3. Which of the following statements about the imposition of trade restrictions has the *most support* among economists?
   A. Trade restrictions are needed to ensure the existence of industries needed for national defense and to protect developing industries until they grow to a competitive size.
   B. Developing industries should be protected until they become competitive and trade restrictions will prevent trade with low-wage countries from depressing the wages of high-wage trading partners.
   C. Restrictions are necessary because trade with low-wage countries depresses wage rates in high-wage countries and to protect industries involved in national defense.
   D. Trade restrictions are necessary to prevent exporters from "dumping" goods abroad at less than their domestic production costs and because developing industries need protection while they get to the point where they can compete on a world scale.

4. Which of the following groups would be *most harmed* by the imposition of a tariff on steel imports?
   A. Domestic steel producers.
   B. The national government.
   C. Workers in the domestic auto industry.
   D. Workers in the domestic steel industry.

ANSWERS – CONCEPT CHECKERS: TRADING WITH THE WORLD

1. **B**   Each country gains by *exporting* the good for which it has a comparative advantage.

2. **A**   Import quotas and voluntary export restraints, unlike tariffs, do not generate tax revenue. The other choices describe effects that result from all trade restrictions, including tariffs, quotas, and VERs.

3. **A**   The case for trade restrictions to ensure the existence of industries producing goods important to national defense and the temporary protection of developing industries have more relative merit than other arguments put forward as reasons for restricting trade. It can be argued, however, that direct subsidies to such industries would be a more efficient way to achieve these ends than restricting trade in these products.

4. **C**   Imposing a tariff on steel imports benefits domestic steel producers and workers by increasing the domestic price of steel, and benefits the national government by increasing tax (tariff) revenue. However, the increase in the domestic price of steel would increase costs in industries that use significant amounts of steel, such as the automobile industry. The resulting increase in the price of automobiles reduces the quantity of automobiles demanded and ultimately reduces employment in that industry.

The following is a review of the Economics principles designed to address the learning outcome statements set forth by CFA Institute®. This topic is also covered in:

INTERNATIONAL FINANCE

EXAM FOCUS

You need to know the basics of the balance of payments accounts and to understand the factors that can shift the demand for one currency in terms of another. Focus on the fact that an exchange rate is the equilibrium "price" of a currency, why exchange rates can be volatile even with little change in trading volume, and how this volatility can be reduced by central bank intervention. Don't worry too much about purchasing power and interest rate parity here, they are covered in more detail in the two topic reviews that follow.

LOS 30.a: Explain the different components of the Balance of Payments Accounts, the transactions recorded for import and export on the different accounts, and how the three sector balances are related.

Balance-of-payments (BOP) accounting is a method used to keep track of transactions between a country and its international trading partners. It includes government transactions, consumer transactions, and business transactions. The balance-of-payments accounts reflect all payments and liabilities to foreigners and all payments and liabilities from foreigners. The BOP equation is:

current account + capital account + official reserve account = 0

The **current account** measures the exchange of merchandise goods, services, investment income, and unilateral transfers (gifts to and from other nations). The *current account balance* is the net exchange of goods and services, investment income, and unilateral transfers.

The **capital (or financial) account** measures the flow of funds for the principal value of investment into a country from abroad and out of a country due to investment by its citizens in foreign assets. This includes investment in real assets as well as purchases of financial securities. When a country runs a current account deficit (imports more than it exports), one way to make up the difference is to borrow from foreign countries, which leads to a capital account surplus.

The **official settlements account** is where changes in official reserves are recorded. **Official reserves** are funds held by a government in foreign currencies. In 1997, the U.S. ran a current account deficit and a smaller surplus in its capital account. As a result, the U.S. ran a surplus in the reserve account to balance the BOP accounts. A surplus in the official reserve account means that the U.S. traded dollars for foreign currency. These reserve balances are used by the Fed to *intervene* in the foreign exchange markets in an attempt to loosely control exchange rates.

The impact of borrowing to finance a deficit in the current account over time depends on whether the country is borrowing to finance investment or borrowing to finance consumption. If the deficit is the result of borrowing primarily to finance consumption, consumption in the future must be reduced to repay the borrowings. If, on the other hand, the borrowing is primarily to finance investment, then future growth in the economy will provide the means to repay the borrowings without an equal decrease in consumption.

LOS 30.b: Explain the law of demand and the law of supply for foreign exchange, and how changes in demand and supply occur.

Consider the demand for U.S. dollars and for euros. The reason there is a demand by foreigners for U.S. dollars is to purchase U.S. goods or to buy U.S. financial assets (securities) or U.S. real assets (e.g. real estate or factories). We can construct a demand curve for U.S. dollars in terms of euros. As shown in Figure 1, the demand for a country's currency is downward sloping, as it is for any good. The price of dollars expressed in euros is an exchange rate. From the graph in Figure 1, we can see that the quantity of dollars demanded is greater at an exchange rate (price) of 0.85 euros per U.S. dollar than the quantity demanded at an exchange rate of 0.90. At a lower exchange rate in terms of euros per dollar, U.S. goods and assets are relatively cheaper to euro-based consumers and investors, and they will demand a greater quantity of both, leading to an increase in the quantity of dollars demanded to fund these purchases.

Two factors are important determinants of the demand for a currency: the interest rate for deposits in that currency, and expected future exchange rates. Changes in these factors can either increase or decrease the demand for currency as illustrated in Figure 1.

Figure 1: Demand for U.S. Dollars

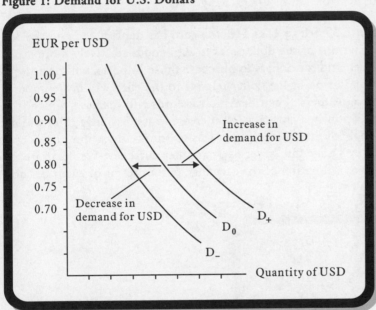

Investors make investment decisions based on interest rate differentials, the difference between what they can earn on investments in their own currency and what they can earn in other currencies. If the euro rate of interest rises relative to the U.S. dollar rate of interest, U.S. dollar-based investors will find euro investments more attractive, and demand for euros will increase. When a country's interest rates fall relative to those of other countries, demand for that country's currency will fall because the demand for investments denominated in that currency will decrease.

When the exchange rate for a country's currency in terms of another currency rises, we say that the country's currency has *appreciated*. If the price of euros in terms of yen rises from 140 yen per euro (140 ¥/€) to 145 ¥/€, we say that the euro has appreciated relative to the yen. Each euro will now purchase more yen and, in that sense, has become more valuable. When the exchange rate falls, from 140 to 135 ¥/€ for example, we say that the euro has *depreciated* relative to the yen.

The second factor that influences demand for a currency is its expected future exchange rate. Other things equal, if a currency is expected to appreciate over time, it is more attractive. Consider a current (spot) exchange rate quote of 0.80 €/$ and an initial expectation that the dollar will appreciate so that the exchange rate in one year will be 0.81 €/$. If the expected future exchange rate rises to 0.83 €/$, the expected appreciation in the dollar has increased, and demand for dollars will increase. From the standpoint of a euro-based investor, an investment in U.S. assets is now more attractive because the expected return in euros is not only the expected U.S. interest, but also additional expected gains when dollar investments are converted back to euros at the end of one year. Rather than receiving 0.81 euros for each dollar, investors now expect to receive 0.83 euros for each dollar, making the expected euro return from an investment in dollars almost 2.5% greater than when the expected exchange rate was 0.81 €/$. So, an increase in the expected future exchange rate for a country's currency will increase demand for that currency, and a decrease in the expected future exchange rate will decrease the demand for the currency.

Supply of Foreign Exchange

Typically in microeconomics, the factors that affect the supply of a good (e.g. input costs) are separate from those that affect demand (e.g. tastes, price of substitute goods). In foreign exchange markets this is not the case. When a U.S. dollar-based investor's demand for euros increases, he wants to buy euros, but this also means selling dollars. For this reason, the supply of a currency in foreign exchange markets is driven by the same factors that affect demand: interest rate differentials and the expected future exchange rate.

If the U.S. dollar/euro exchange rate falls from 1.25 $/€ to 1.23 $/€, the euro has depreciated and the dollar has appreciated. This increase in the value (appreciation) of the dollar makes U.S. goods relatively more expensive. Demand for imports from the U.S., and the demand for dollars to purchase those imports, will decrease as we have seen. At the same time, however, the appreciation of the dollar relative to the euro will make imports from the euro zone more attractive to dollar-based consumers. Their demand for euros will increase, which is an increase in the supply of dollars. So an appreciation in a currency (an increase in its exchange rate) will decrease demand for that currency and increase the supply of that currency. For this reason we draw the supply curve for a currency as an upward sloping function of its exchange rate in terms of another currency. We illustrate this in Figure 2, where the supply of dollars is shown as a function of the exchange rate in terms of euros per dollar.

Figure 2: Supply of U.S. Dollars

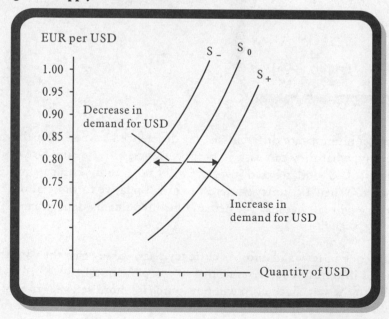

The same factors that cause shifts in the demand for a currency, interest rate differentials and expected future exchange rates, can also increase or decrease the supply of that currency. These shifts are illustrated in Figure 2. However, the effects are opposite to those on demand. An increase in the U.S. dollar interest rate relative to the euro interest rate or an increase in the expected future euro-dollar exchange rate will decrease the supply of dollars. A decrease in the U.S. dollar interest rate relative to the euro interest rate or a decrease in the expected future euro-dollar exchange rate will increase the supply of dollars.

Professor's Note: These supply and demand effects get a bit confusing sometimes. I think you should focus on understanding the effects on demand curves of interest rate differentials and expected future exchange rates. Then, just remember that the effects are all opposite for supply curves.

LOS 30.c: Discuss the influence of supply and demand on the exchange rate, and why exchange rates can be volatile.

In our typical analysis of supply and demand equilibrium, supply and demand are considered independently, as noted previously. Other things equal, an increase (decrease) in demand leads to an increase (decrease) in equilibrium price and an increase (decrease) in equilibrium quantity. An increase or decrease in supply has the opposite effect on equilibrium price and quantity.

Since supply and demand curves for foreign exchange are both affected by the same factors, the adjustment is different. Figure 3 shows the demand and supply for dollars as functions of the euro-dollar exchange rate. Initially, the equilibrium price of a dollar is 0.80 euros, at the intersection of S_0 and D_0. If the exchange rate is lower than this, there is excess demand for dollars and the exchange rate will rise toward equilibrium. If the exchange rate is greater than 0.80 €/$, then there is an excess supply of dollars, and the exchange rate will fall toward the equilibrium rate.

Figure 3: Demand and Supply Shifts in the Foreign Exchange Market

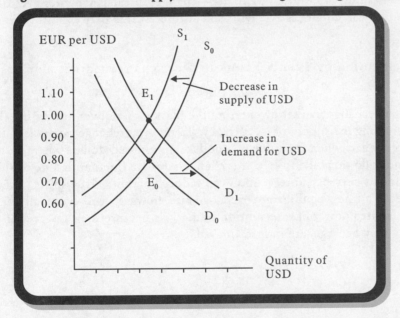

The curves S_1 and D_1 represent the increased demand for and decreased supply of dollars that would result from either an increase in the U.S. dollar interest rate or an increase in the expected future euro-dollar exchange rate. Note that while the new equilibrium euro-dollar exchange rate is higher from both the increase in demand and the decrease in supply, the equilibrium quantity of trading may be very close to the quantity traded prior to the shifts in supply and demand. For this reason, exchange rates may be quite volatile (more so than if supply and demand were independent), even though the quantity of currencies actually exchanged is not.

LOS 30.d: Distinguish between purchasing power and interest rate parity.

The concept of purchasing power parity is based loosely on the idea that the same goods should cost the same in different countries, once we have factored in the current exchange rate. If a barrel of oil costs $70 in the U.S. and the yen/dollar exchange rate is 125, a barrel of oil should cost ¥8,750 (= 125 × 70) in Japan. While differences in transportation costs and some other factors may mean that such a relation need not hold exactly, purchasing power parity is based on the idea that changes in the price levels in the two countries should be reflected in changes in the exchange rate. Consider an example where inflation in the U.S. is greater than inflation in Japan. Since U.S. goods have increased more in price than Japanese goods, they are less attractive at the existing exchange rate. Purchasing power parity requires that the exchange rate adjust (dollar depreciate relative to the yen) so that exchange-rate adjusted goods prices return to the same relation that existed before the changes in the Japanese and U.S. price levels. Another way to state this is that exchange rates will change to reflect differences in inflation between countries. We will have more to say about purchasing power parity later in this study session.

Interest rate parity is the idea that exchange rates must change so that the return on investments with identical risk will be the same in any currency. Another way to say this is that differences in interest rates are equal to differences in expected changes in exchange rates. If the U.S. interest rate is 6% and the U.K interest rate (on British pounds) is 4%, we might think that all U.K. investors would want to convert their pounds to dollars so that they could earn 2% more. The key here is expected future exchange rates. If the dollar is expected to depreciate 2% relative to the pound over the next year, there is no expected gain from investing in dollars rather than pounds. At the end of one year, a U.K.-based investor could have 6% more dollars, but would have to exchange them for pounds at an exchange rate 2% below the current rate. So, rather than having 6% more pounds at the end of one year, a U.K. investor would have 4% more pounds, just as they would have investing in pounds rather than in dollars. This is the meaning of interest rate parity—changes in exchange rates over time should just offset interest rate differences between countries. We will look at interest rate parity in more detail in another topic review as well.

LOS 30.e: Discuss how and why intervention by a central bank in the exchange market may be required.

A central bank can intervene in the foreign exchange market by entering the market as a buyer, increasing the demand for its currency, or as a seller, increasing the supply of its currency. To reduce exchange rate volatility, for example, the U.S. Federal Reserve can buy dollars when the value of a dollar falls and sell dollars when the value of a dollar rises. While a central bank cannot do this indefinitely, if exchange rates are fluctuating due to short-term changes in the supply and demand for its currency, intervention can reduce volatility. True shifts in the supply and demand for a currency that lead to a new equilibrium exchange rate, however, will eventually have their expected effect. Central banks have limited power of intervention in markets because their reserves of both domestic and foreign currency, while they may be large, are in fact, limited.

KEY CONCEPTS

1. The balance of payments relation states that
    current account + capital account + official reserve account = 0.
2. The current account includes international payments for goods and services (net exports), the net income from asset ownership, and net gifts.
3. The capital account includes international payments for the purchase and sales of debt and equity securities and real assets.
4. Official reserve accounts consist of the foreign currencies held by governments.
5. The demand for a country's currency is a downward-sloping function of its exchange rate and is increased by increases in the country's interest rate and by increases in the expected future value of the currency.
6. The supply of a country's currency is an upward-sloping function of its exchange rate and is decreased by increases in the country's interest rate and by increases in the expected future value of the currency.
7. Since the same factors shift currency supply and demand curves, exchange rates can be quite volatile even with relatively stable trading volume.
8. Purchasing power parity refers to the relation between differences between countries' inflation rates and changes in the exchange rates for their currencies.
9. Interest rate parity refers to how differences in interest rates for two currencies are related to changes in their exchange rate over time.
10. Central bank intervention in currency markets (buying or selling their country's currency) can reduce short-term exchange rate volatility but cannot prevent real long-term changes in equilibrium exchange rates.

CONCEPT CHECKERS: INTERNATIONAL FINANCE

1. The current account includes all of the following components EXCEPT:
    A. unilateral transfers.
    B. flow of funds for investment.
    C. payments for goods and services.
    D. investment income.

2. Which of the following equations is CORRECT?
    A. Balance of payments = current account + capital account.
    B. Official settlements account = current account + capital account.
    C. Current account = goods and service balance + official reserves.
    D. Current account + capital account + official settlements account = 0.

3. The Fredonian currency (the fredo) is currently valued at 2.50 per U.S. dollar. Fredo deposit rates are 1% above U.S. dollar deposit rates. All other things equal, which of the following scenarios would decrease demand for the fredo on the foreign exchange markets?

	Fredonia interest rate - U.S. interest rate differential	Expected dollar-per-fredo exchange rate in one year
A.	Increases	Decreases
B.	Increases	Increases
C.	Decreases	Decreases
D.	Decreases	Increases

4. Which of these statements is *most accurate?* Exchange rates can be especially volatile because:
    A. the quantities of currencies traded are volatile.
    B. interest rate differentials determine the demand for currencies.
    C. supply and demand for currencies are affected by the same factors.
    D. the supply of a currency is a function of expected future exchange rates.

5. The theory of interest rate parity suggests that:
    A. exchange rates will change to reflect differences in inflation between countries.
    B. changes in the price levels in two countries should be reflected in changes in the exchange rate.
    C. the same combinations of goods should cost the same in different countries, once we have factored in the current exchange rates.
    D. exchange rates will change so that the return on investments with identical risk will be the same in any currency.

6. A central bank's primary goal when intervening in the foreign exchange markets is typically to:
    A. reduce exchange rate volatility.
    B. increase its foreign currency holdings.
    C. prevent long-term currency depreciation.
    D. offset structural shifts in the demand for the domestic currency.

ANSWERS – CONCEPT CHECKERS: INTERNATIONAL FINANCE

1. **B**   The flow of funds for investment in debt and equity is recorded in the capital account. Exchange of investment income, such as interest payments, is a component of the current account, along with goods and services trade and unilateral transfers.

2. **D**   The three balance of payments accounts must sum to zero.

3. **C**   A decrease in fredo interest rates minus U.S. rates and a decrease in the expected future exchange rate would both decrease demand for the fredo. When a country's interest rates fall relative to those of other countries, demand for that country's currency decreases because demand for investments denominated in that currency will decrease. A decrease in the expected future exchange rate also decreases the demand for a currency.

4. **C**   Because shifts in supply and demand are affected by the same factors, exchange rates may be quite volatile even though the quantity of currencies actually exchanged is not.

5. **D**   The other three choices describe the concept of purchasing power parity.

6. **A**   Central banks can reduce exchange rate volatility in the short term through intervention in the foreign exchange market. Longer-term shifts in supply and demand, however, will eventually have their expected effects on exchange rates. Intervention can increase or reduce the central bank's foreign currency holdings, but that would rarely be the central bank's primary objective.

The following is a review of the Economics principles designed to address the learning outcome statements set forth by CFA Institute®. This topic is also covered in:

FOREIGN EXCHANGE

EXAM FOCUS

No fluff here; you need it all. Take it slow and get a good understanding of direct and indirect quotes, spot rates and spreads, forward rates, forward discounts and premiums, currency cross rates, interest rate parity, and covered interest arbitrage. The probability of this material being tested is very high—approaching certainty.

EXCHANGE RATES AND THE FOREIGN EXCHANGE MARKET

An **exchange rate** is a ratio that describes how many units of one currency you can buy per unit of another currency. Note that an exchange rate is quoted relative to another currency. You *cannot* quote three exchange rates (three currencies) with one ratio.

Professor's Note: As you work through the two foreign exchange material reviews, you will notice that the notation for currency rates is not consistent. For example, for the Japanese yen, you may see the currency symbol, such as ¥, or the three-letter notation, JPY. The U.S. dollar may be shown as USD, $, or U.S. dollar. Be prepared to see various notations on the exam.

Example: Exchange rates

If the Australian dollar (AUD) is trading at 0.60 U.S. dollars ($0.60), each AUD will buy 60 U.S. cents. Remember the following: AUD = $0.60 = 0.60 dollars per AUD. Whatever currency in which the *quote* is made (in this case, $U.S.) belongs in the numerator while the denominator is always *one* unit of the currency you are interested in (in this case the AUD). For instance, $/AUD = 0.60.

Exchange rates between countries are the *inverse* of one another. Thus the U.S. dollar quote in terms of AUD is:

U.S. dollar = 1/0.60 = 1.67 AUD per U.S. dollar

Therefore, if you are given dollars per AUD, you can easily get AUD per dollar by taking the inverse of the original quote.

Example: Transactions with exchange rates

Suppose that you want to buy some Australian beer. The Australian distributor tells you the beer sells for 25 AUD per case. How many U.S. dollars will it cost you to buy one case, given that the AUD exchange rate is $0.60?

Answer:

- You know that the beer is quoted in AUD per case. So the numerator is AUD and the denominator is a case (AUD/case).
- You know that your exchange rate has $ in the numerator and AUD in the denominator ($/AUD).
- You want $ in the numerator and cases in the denominator, so multiply the two together:

$$\left(\frac{25\,\text{AUD}}{\text{case}} \right) \times \left(\frac{0.60\,\$}{\text{AUD}} \right) = \frac{\$15}{\text{case}}$$

The AUDs cancel and you are left with $15 in the numerator and case in the denominator, so the beer costs $15 per case.

Example: Exchange rate appreciation and depreciation

If the AUD moves from $0.60 to $0.70, has the AUD depreciated or appreciated?

Answer:

The AUD has *appreciated*—previously each AUD would only buy 60 cents, whereas now each AUD buys 70 cents. What has the U.S. dollar done in this example? To find out, invert each quote so that you get the U.S. dollar moving from 1/$0.6 = AUD1.67 to 1/$0.7 = AUD1.43. The dollar has *depreciated* in value. It used to buy 1.67 AUD but only buys 1.43 AUD today. Again, always remember what is in the *denominator*.

It is important to note that the *appreciation* of a currency makes that country's goods more *expensive* to residents of other countries while *depreciation* makes a country's goods more *attractive* to foreign buyers. In our Australian beer example above, if we let the AUD depreciate against the U.S. dollar, the U.S. dollar price of the beer will fall.

You must know how to determine whether a currency has depreciated or appreciated over time. As a straightforward example, if the Swiss franc goes from 1.7799 CHF/USD to 1.8100 CHF/USD, the Swiss franc has depreciated relative to the dollar. Why? It is worth less—it now takes more Swiss francs to buy a dollar. This example could have been worded, "If the CHF to USD exchange rate increases from 1.7799 to 1.8100, the Swiss franc has depreciated relative to the U.S. dollar." Don't be confused by the word "increases"—the CHF still depreciated. Focus on the numbers and the logic.

Foreign Exchange Markets

The trading of currencies takes place in foreign exchange markets, which have the primary function of facilitating international trade and investment. Knowledge of the operation and mechanics of these markets is important for a fundamental understanding of international financial management.

The foreign exchange market permits the transfer of purchasing power denominated in one currency for that of another currency. This market is not a physical place but rather an electronically linked network of banks, foreign exchange brokers, and dealers whose function it is to bring together buyers and sellers of foreign exchange. Transactions occur over the phone, telex, or the SWIFT system (Society for Worldwide Interbank Financial Telecommunications).

Participants in the foreign exchange (interbank) market are large commercial banks, foreign exchange brokers, major multinational corporate customers, and central banks. Most of the trading in the U.S. goes through foreign exchange brokers, who match buyers and sellers for a small commission (1/32 of 1%).

Foreign-exchange brokers provide *information*, participant *anonymity*, and *reduced time and effort* (meaning a bank need only deal with one broker rather than contracting several other banks) in trading.

The typical small client gets foreign exchange from a local bank. The local bank in turn gets the exchange from its major correspondent bank, and the major bank gets the exchange from a foreign exchange broker.

The *interbank market* is the wholesale market where the major banks trade with one another. Most currency transactions occur here. The interbank market is generally referred to as the foreign exchange market and is segmented into three separate markets: (1) the spot market, (2) the forward market, and (3) the currency swap market.

LOS 31.a: Define direct and indirect methods of foreign exchange quotations and convert direct (indirect) foreign exchange quotations into indirect (direct) foreign exchange quotations.

Local *nonbank public customer* quotes can be stated as:

- **Direct quotes** are expressed in domestic currency units per foreign currency unit: DC/FC. For example, a direct quote to a U.S. investor for euros might be 1.21 $/€. This represents an exchange rate of $1.21 per euro.
- **Indirect quotes** are expressed as foreign currency unit per domestic currency unit: FC/DC.

To convert a direct quote to an indirect quote, or vice versa, you simply take the reciprocal of the one that you are given. For example, in Japan, a direct quote of 125 ¥/$ is equivalent to an indirect quote of

$$\left(\frac{1}{125 \text{ ¥/\$}}\right) = 0.0080 \text{ \$/¥}.$$ Just use the 1/x key on your calculator to turn the indirect quote 125 ¥/$ into the direct quote of 0.0080 $/¥.

LOS 31.b: Calculate and interpret the spread on a foreign currency quotation and explain how spreads on foreign currency quotations can differ as a result of market conditions, bank/dealer positions, and trading volume.

Banks and other dealers generally do not charge commissions on foreign currency transactions. Instead, they make their profit from the *bid-ask spread*.

- The *bid price* is always listed first. It is the price the *dealer will pay* for FC.
- The *ask price* is always listed second. It is the price at which the *dealer will sell* FC.
- The bid is less than the ask for direct quotes.

Example: Bid-ask spread

Consider the following quotations: The bid of $1.6625\dfrac{USD}{GBP}$ and the ask of $1.6635\dfrac{USD}{GBP}$ are listed as USD1.6625 – 35. Calculate the bid-ask spread as a direct quote from the perspective of a British banker.

Answer:

Note that this quote is a direct quote in the U.S. To switch the bid-ask spread to a direct quote from the British perspective $\left(\dfrac{GBP}{USD}\right)$, which is an indirect quote to a U.S. investor, take the reciprocal of each number.

$$\frac{1}{1.6625\dfrac{USD}{GBP}} = 0.60150\frac{GBP}{USD}$$

$$\frac{1}{1.6635\dfrac{USD}{GBP}} = 0.60114\frac{GBP}{USD}$$

Note that buying Currency 1 in terms of units of Currency 2 is equivalent to selling Currency 2 for units of Currency 1. A bid-ask dealer quote using direct exchange rates can be converted to indirect terms by taking the reciprocals, but the ask and the bid are reversed. A direct Canadian dealer quote of

$1.25 - 1.26 \left(\frac{CDN}{USD} \right)$ for the U.S dollar is equivalent to an indirect Canadian dealer quote of

$USD \left(\frac{1}{1.26} \right)$ bid and $USD \left(\frac{1}{1.25} \right)$ ask or USD0.7937 bid and USD0.8000 ask for Canadian dollars, which will be a direct quote for a U.S. dealer.

Spreads are often expressed as a percentage of the ask. For the direct U.S. quote, we get a percentage spread as:

$$\frac{0.80 - 0.7937}{0.80} = 0.0079 = 0.79\%$$

How Spreads Differ as a Result of Market Conditions, Bank/Dealer Positions, and Trading Volume

Market conditions affect currency spreads because the bid-ask spread on foreign currency quotations increases as exchange rate volatility (uncertainty) increases. Larger spreads compensate dealers for the higher risk of dealing in more volatile currencies.

Bank and currency dealer positions do not directly affect the size of foreign currency spreads. If a dealer wants to reduce her holdings, she will usually adjust the midpoint of the spread rather than the absolute size of the spread.

Greater trading volume leads to narrower spreads (and vice versa), just as with equities trading.

LOS 31.c: Calculate and interpret currency cross rates, given two spot exchange quotations involving three currencies.

The **cross rate** is the rate of exchange between two countries, computed from the exchange rates between each of these two countries and a third country. Cross exchange rate calculations are necessary because each currency is quoted against the dollar in the interbank market but currencies are quoted using the direct method against other currencies in local nonbank markets.

As a simple example of calculating a cross rate, consider that spot rates are 0.00833 $/¥ and 148 ¥/€, and we wish to calculate the dollar/euro cross rate. When we multiply $/¥ by 148¥/€, the yen term drops out and we have 0.00833 × 148 = 1.2328 $/€. If the quotes are not given in a form that yields a simple solution for the cross rate to be calculated, the easiest way to proceed is to convert the rates using reciprocals as needed. Consider the following example.

Example: Currency cross rate calculation

If spot rates are 120 ¥/$ and 148 ¥/€, what is the cross rate expressed as €/$?

Answer:

We want our answer expressed as EUR/USD, so we can multiply ¥/$ times €/¥ since $\frac{JPY}{USD} \times \frac{EUR}{JPY} = \frac{EUR}{USD}$.

We take the reciprocal of 148 ¥/€ and get 0.006757 €/¥. We can then multiply 120 × 0.006757 to get 0.8108 €/$.

Since multiplying by the reciprocal of a fraction is equivalent to dividing by the fraction we could also get our answer by taking 120/148 = 0.8108 €/$. The spot rates given show that one euro is worth more yen (148) than one U.S. dollar (120). This tells us that one euro is worth more than one dollar and that our EUR/USD quote of less than one is to be expected.

One more example will further illustrate the technique.

Example: 3-currency cross rate calculation

The spot exchange rate between the Swiss franc (CHF) and the USD is 1.7799 CHF/USD, and the spot exchange rate between the New Zealand dollar (NZD) and the U.S. dollar is 2.2529 NZD/USD. Calculate the CHF/NZD spot rate.

Answer:

In Switzerland, the direct exchange rate is:

$$\frac{1.7799 \dfrac{CHF}{USD}}{2.2529 \dfrac{NZD}{USD}} = 0.79005 \frac{CHF}{NZD}$$

Professor's Note: Make sure you can do the calculations described above. Since the LOS says "...cross rates, given two spot exchange quotations..." it is possible that you may have to calculate a cross rate quotation as a bid-ask from bid-ask quotes. Although I believe this is unlikely at Level 1, the following illustrates an intuitive approach you can use if such a problem comes up.

When given two bid-ask spot exchange quotations involving three currencies, we can get the cross rate bid and ask quotations by working through the actual purchase/sale transactions involved. The following example illustrates this.

Example: Bid-ask cross rates

A London dealer gives a spot quotation of 0.583 bid/0.588 ask $\left(\frac{£}{\$}\right)$ for the U.S. dollar. An Australian dealer quotes British pounds at 1.90 bid/1.91 ask $\left(\frac{AUD}{£}\right)$. Calculate the $\frac{AUD}{\$}$ bid and ask from the perspective of an Australian dealer.

Answer:

The $\frac{AUD}{\$}$ ask is based on buying pounds with AUD and buying USD with pounds. We would buy pounds at the $\frac{AUD}{£}$ ask of $\frac{AUD1.91}{£}$ and each pound would buy one USD at the ask of 0.588. The cost of one USD acquired through these transaction is 1.91 × 0.588 = AUD1.1231, which is the $\frac{AUD}{\$}$ ask cross rate.

The $\frac{AUD}{\$}$ bid cross rate is the rate at which an Australian dealer would purchase $U.S. We can construct it by selling $U.S. for pounds at the $\frac{£}{\$}$ bid of 0.583 and selling the 0.583 pounds at the $\frac{AUD}{£}$ bid of 1.90, which would result in 0.583 × 1.90 = AUD1.1077.

Our bid-ask cross rate quotation is 1.1077 – 1.1231 $AUD/\$$, the rate at which an Australian dealer would buy and sell USD.

Here's another approach to this same example that involves two steps.

1. State the bid-ask quote for the currency you want in the numerator (of your answer) as a direct quote in that currency, and the bid-ask quote for the currency you want in the denominator as an indirect quote.

2. Multiply the (direct) quote for the currency you want in the numerator by the (indirect) quote for the currency you want in the denominator, in such a way as to give the widest bid-ask spread.

For the above problem we have:

	Bid	Ask
AUD/£	1.90	1.91
£/$	0.583	0.588

We now just need to multiply AUD/£ quote times the £/$ quote to get AUD/$.

To get the widest possible quote, we multiply the bids to get the bid and the asks to get the ask, and have:

AUD/$ bid = 1.90 × 0.583 = 1.1077 and AUD/$ ask = 1.91 × 0.588 = 1.1231

LOS 31.d: Distinguish between the spot and forward markets for foreign exchange.

Spot markets refer to transactions that call for immediate delivery of the currency. In practice, the settlement period is two business days after the trade date.

Forward markets are for an exchange of currencies that will occur in the future. Both parties to the transaction agree to exchange one currency for another at a specific future date. Forward contracts are typically for transactions 30, 60, or 90 days in the future, although the contracts can be written for any period. There is no option involved in the contract; both parties to a forward currency contract are obligated to execute the specified transaction in the future.

A firm that has a foreign-currency-denominated obligation in 60 days can remove any uncertainty about the cost of the obligation in its home currency by entering into a forward contract to buy the required amount of foreign currency 60 days from now (at the 60-day forward rate). The forward exchange rate in the contract will reflect the expected movement of exchange rates over the next 60 days so that the forward rate may be greater than or less than the current spot rate. Note that the current spot rate is not locked in by entering a forward contract, unless the expectation is that the exchange rate will be the same 60 days from now so that the forward and spot rates are the same.

Example: Foreign currency forward transactions

A U.S. firm is obligated to make a future payment of CHF100,000 in 60 days. To manage its exchange rate risk, the firm contracts to buy the Swiss franc 60 days in the future at 1.7530 CHF/USD. The current exchange rate is 1.7799 CHF/USD. (Note this is the indirect method of quoting exchange rates.)

Part 1: How much would the U.S. firm gain or lose on its commitment if, at the time of payment, the exchange rate fell below the 1.7530 Swiss francs to the dollar forward rate to 1.6556 Swiss francs to the dollar? What is the net impact on the firm?

Answer:

Without the forward contract, the firm *would have lost* (100,000 / 1.7530 – 100,000 / 1.6556) = – USD3,356.00 on its commitment. Fortunately, the firm gets to buy the Swiss franc at 1.7530 CHF/USD rather than at the 1.6556 rate in effect at the time the payment must be made. The actual loss on the commitment is exactly offset by the gain on the forward contract. The forward contract has locked in the price (in $) that the firm will pay for CHF in the future. Fluctuations in the actual spot rate in 60 days do not affect the (net) cost of CHF at contract expiration.

Part 2: Keeping in mind the information from Part 1 of this example, how much would the U.S. firm gain or lose on its commitment if at the time of payment the exchange rate had risen to 1.8250 CHF, and what is the net impact on the firm?

Answer:

Without the forward contract, the firm *would have gained* (100,000 / 1.7530 – 100,000 / 1.8250) = +USD2,250.55 by being able to pay off its commitment with cheap Swiss francs. Unfortunately, the firm must buy the Swiss francs at 1.7530 CHF/USD. Thus the gain on the commitment is exactly offset by the loss on the forward contract.

You should learn three things from this example:

- The gain or loss on the forward contract is unrelated to the current spot rate, 1.7799 CHF/USD.
- The gain or loss on the forward contract exactly offsets the loss or gain on the dollar cost of the original commitment. Note that gains and losses are measured *relative to the forward contract rate*, not the initial spot rate.
- The forward contract is not an option contract. Both parties (the firm and the bank) must perform on the agreed contract.

LOS 31.e: Calculate and interpret the spread on a forward foreign currency quotation and explain how spreads on forward foreign currency quotations can differ as a result of market conditions, bank/dealer positions, trading volume, and maturity/length of contract.

Consider a 6-month forward exchange rate quote from a U.S. currency dealer of 1.63843 – 1.64073 USD/GBP. This means that the dealer will commit today to buy pounds for 1.63843 dollars in six months or sell pounds in six months for 1.64073 dollars.

As with spot rates, the forward foreign currency spread is the difference between the bid and the ask quotes.

Example: Forward bid-ask spread

Assume that the USD/GBP 6-month forward rate is quoted at a bid of 1.63843 and an ask of 1.64073. From a U.S. dealer's perspective, calculate the bid-ask spread.

Answer:

In this case, the spread is simply 0.0023 USD/GBP = 1.64073 – 1.63843.

Forward Spreads and Market Conditions, Bank/Dealer Positions, Trading Volume, and Maturity/Length of Contract

Just as with spot market foreign currency spreads, spreads in the forward foreign currency market increase with greater exchange rate volatility and decrease when trading volume is higher. Spreads tend to increase with the term of the forward contract, and forward currency spreads are typically greater than spot currency spreads.

LOS 31.f: Calculate and interpret a forward discount or premium and express it as an annualized rate.

Professor's Note: Your life will be a lot easier on the exam if you make sure all of your quotes are in domestic currency over foreign currency (DC/FC) when using these formulas. If you work in FC/DC, a premium is a negative number, and your confusion factor will rise significantly!

A foreign currency is at a **forward discount** if the forward rate *expressed in domestic currency units* is less than the spot rate. Foreign currency units will be *cheaper* in the future.

> forward discount = forward rate – spot rate = negative number

A foreign currency is at a **forward premium** if the forward rate *expressed in domestic currency units* is greater than the spot rate. Foreign currency units will be more expensive in the future.

> forward premium = forward rate – spot rate = positive number

The **forward premium or discount** is frequently stated as an annualized percentage using the following formula:

$$\left(\begin{array}{c} \text{forward premium} \\ \text{or discount} \end{array} \right) = \left(\frac{\text{forward rate} - \text{spot rate}}{\text{spot rate}} \right) \left(\frac{360}{\text{number of forward contract days}} \right)$$

Example: Annualized forward rate premium and discount

Assume the 90-day forward rate for the NZD is USD0.4439 and the spot rate is USD0.4315. Determine if the NZD is trading at a premium or discount to the USD. Calculate the annualized premium or discount.

Answer:

Since it takes more dollars to buy the NZD in the forward market relative to the spot, the NZD is trading at a *premium* to the dollar.

$$(\text{forward premium}) = \left(\frac{0.4439 - 0.4315}{0.4315} \right) \left(\frac{360}{90} \right) = 0.1149 \text{ or } 11.49\%$$

- *Note:* Later in this topic review, the term [(forward rate – spot rate) / spot rate] will be called the *forward differential*. This is just the forward premium stated as a percentage of the spot rate.
- *Another note:* The forward and spot rates in this equation are direct quotes, DC/FC.
- *Yet another note:* The bid-ask spread on forward contracts will *widen* with increases in currency volatility or contract maturity.

LOS 31.g: Explain interest rate parity and illustrate covered interest arbitrage.

The only difference between exchanging currencies in the spot market and exchanging currencies in the forward market is the timing of the transaction, where time is represented by interest rates. Covered interest rate parity, or simply **interest rate parity** (IRP), shows that there is a relationship between the spot and forward exchange rates and the domestic (r_D) and foreign (r_F) interest rates in the countries represented. Covered interest rate parity holds because investors will take advantage of interest rate differentials to move funds between countries where spot and forward exchange rates are not in balance. Covered means that the currency exposure in the foreign investment is hedged or "covered" by a forward contract.

IRP is approximated by equating the difference between the domestic interest rate and the foreign interest rate to the forward premium or discount. That is:

interest differential $\approx$ forward differential

Restating this relationship in more familiar terms gives:

$$(r_D - r_F) \approx \left(\frac{\text{forward exchange rate} - \text{spot exchange rate}}{\text{spot exchange rate}} \right)$$

where the forward and spot exchange rates are expressed as DC/FC.

When the above condition prevails, equilibrium exists in the international money markets.

You should also know that the exact IRP equation using direct quotes is:

$$\frac{\text{forward}}{\text{spot}} = \left(\frac{1 + r_D}{1 + r_F} \right)$$

Professor's Note: If this equity does not hold, an arbitrage opportunity exists. To remember this formula, note that when the forward and spot rates are expressed as direct quotes (DC/FC), right-hand side of the equation also has the domestic (interest rate) in the numerator and the foreign (interest rate) in the denominator. If we expressed the forward and spot rates as indirect quotes (FC/DC), then the right-hand side of the equation would have the foreign (interest rate) in the numerator and the domestic (interest rate) in the denominator. So it's either domestic over foreign for everything, or foreign over domestic for everything.

IRP ensures that the return on a hedged (covered) foreign investment will just equal the domestic interest rate of investments of identical risk. When this happens, there are no arbitrage possibilities, and the difference between the domestic interest rate and the hedged foreign rate (called the covered interest differential) is zero.

Example: Covered interest rate parity

Suppose you can invest in NZD at 5.127%, or you can invest in Swiss francs at 5.5%. You are a resident of New Zealand, and the current spot rate is 0.79005 NZD/CHF. Calculate the 1-year forward rate expressed in NZD/CHF.

Answer:

$$\text{forward (DC/FC)} = \text{spot (DC/FC)} \left(\frac{1 + r_D}{1 + r_F} \right) = 0.79005 \left(\frac{1.05127}{1.05500} \right) = 0.78726$$

Covered Interest Arbitrage

Covered interest arbitrage is a trading strategy that exploits currency positions when the interest rate parity equation is not satisfied. You can check for an arbitrage opportunity by using the *covered interest differential*. The covered interest differential says that the domestic interest rate should be the same as the hedged foreign interest rate. More specifically, the difference between the domestic interest rate and the hedged foreign rate should be *zero*. The covered interest differential can be viewed by rewriting IRP in the following way:

$$1 + r_D = \frac{(1 + r_F)(\text{forward rate})}{\text{spot rate}}$$

The left-hand side of the equation is the domestic interest rate, while the right-hand side is the hedged foreign rate (the foreign rate expressed in domestic terms). Arbitrage will prevent this relationship from getting out of line. To preclude arbitrage, the left-hand side minus the right-hand side should equal zero. Hence, the *covered interest differential* can be written as:

$$(1 + r_D) - \left(\frac{(1 + r_F)(\text{forward rate})}{\text{spot rate}} \right) = \text{covered interest differential}$$

For example, if the domestic interest rate is less than the hedged foreign interest rate, an arbitrageur will borrow in the domestic cash market, buy foreign currency at the spot rate, and enter into a forward contract, granting him the ability to convert the foreign funds back to domestic funds at some future date. The foreign funds are invested at the foreign interest rate until the forward contract expires, at which time the arbitrageur will convert the proceeds from the foreign investment back into the domestic currency via the forward contract. This results in an arbitrage (riskless) profit with no net investment.

Professor's Note: This parity relationship can seem complex but you must learn it; this important concept will come up in other contexts at Level 1 and subsequent levels. Consider an extreme example: the U.S. interest rate is 5% and the Mexican interest rate is 25%. Why can't a U.S. investor make a 25% return by investing in pesos at the Mexican risk-free rate?

The intuition here is that he can't because the Mexican peso will depreciate; he can have 25% more pesos at the end of one year but (if interest rate parity holds) he will be able to exchange these pesos for only 5% more dollars than he started with. The peso must depreciate. The exact calculation is $\frac{1 + r_d}{1 + r_f} - 1 = \frac{1.05}{1.25} - 1 = -16\%$. For interest rate parity to hold, the forward exchange rate for the peso (quoted in USD/peso) must be 16% less than the spot exchange rate. The peso is expected to depreciate 16% relative to the dollar over the next year. If a dollar currently buys 10 pesos (1 peso = 0.10 USD), he has 12.5 pesos at the end of the year. The peso value in USD falls to $0.10 \times 0.84 = 0.084$ (a depreciation of 16%), the ending value is $12.5 \times 0.084 = 1.05$ USD, the same ending result as if he had invested the $1 at the U.S. interest rate of 5%. The parity relation is: $\frac{1.05}{1.25} = \frac{0.084}{0.10}$; if the forward peso rate is greater than 0.084 USD, a dollar-based investor can earn more than 5% by investing in pesos; if the forward peso rate is less than 0.084 USD, a peso-based investor can earn more than 25% by investing in dollars. When you can create an example like this with different numbers and work through it, you have mastered interest rate parity and covered interest arbitrage.

Example: Identifying covered interest arbitrage opportunities

Assume you are a New Zealand investor and have 1,000 NZD. You can invest in NZD at 5.127%, or invest in Swiss francs at 5.5%. The current spot rate is 0.79005 NZD/CHF, and the forward rate is 0.78726 NZD/CHF.

Determine if there are any arbitrage opportunities.

Answer:

Let's insert the numbers and see if interest rate parity holds.

$$\frac{0.78726}{0.79005} = \frac{1.05127}{1.05500}$$

No arbitrage is available.

To verify this, work through the following steps:

- Convert your 1,000 NZD to Swiss francs at the spot rate.

$$\left(\frac{1,000 \text{ NZD}}{0.79005 \dfrac{\text{NZD}}{\text{CHF}}} \right) = 1,265.74 \text{ CHF}$$

- Invest your Swiss francs at 5.5% in Switzerland. At year-end you will have:

$$1,265.74 \text{ CHF} \times 1.055 = 1,335.36 \text{ CHF}$$

- Simultaneously enter into a 1-year forward contract to convert Swiss francs back to NZD at the forward rate of 0.78726 NZD/CHF.
- When the Swiss franc investment matures, collect the interest and principal (1,335.36 CHF) and convert it back to NZD:

$$1,335.36 \text{ CHF} \times \left(0.78726 \frac{\text{NZD}}{\text{CHF}} \right) = 1,051.28 \text{ NZD}$$

- If you had invested the NZD directly in New Zealand, you would have at year-end:

$$1,000 \text{ NZD} \times 1.05127 = 1,051.27 \text{ NZD}$$

- While there is a modest rounding error, there is no arbitrage opportunity here.

So here's the deal: The interest rate is 5.127% in New Zealand and 5.5% in Switzerland. To prevent arbitrage, the forward discount *should be* approximately 5.127% – 5.5% = –0.373%. (Remember that the *interest differential* is *approximately* equal to the forward premium.) You can invest NZD in New Zealand at 5.127%; *or* you can take those NZD, convert them into Swiss francs at the current spot rate, invest them in Switzerland at 5.5% and simultaneously enter into a forward contract to sell Swiss francs for NZD at today's forward rate. The hedged return from investing in Switzerland is the 5.5% return from your investment minus the 0.373% loss on your currency hedge (this is the 0.373% Swiss franc forward discount—it takes more Swiss francs to buy a NZD in the forward market than in the spot market). This is the same as the 5.127% return you can earn in New Zealand.

Example: Covered interest arbitrage opportunities

The forward rate between GBP and U.S. dollars is 0.7327 GBP/USD, and the current spot rate is 0.7045 GBP/USD. The U.K. interest rate is 6.056%, and the U.S. rate is 5.95%. Assume you can borrow GBP1,000 or the equivalent in USD and that you live in the U.K. Is there an arbitrage opportunity? If so, how would you take advantage of it?

Answer:

First check to see if arbitrage is possible.

$$\frac{0.7327}{0.7045} > \frac{1.06056}{1.0595}$$

So an arbitrage opportunity exists because the interest rate parity condition is not met.

Second, determine whether to borrow domestically or in the foreign market.

Since the left-hand side is "too high," we know that the forward exchange rate is greater than the forward exchange rate for parity. This means the forward price of USD is too high in GBP. We know from this that we do not want to hold GBP and buy (overpriced) USD in the future. The profitable arbitrage must be based on holding USD.

To arbitrage:

- Borrow GBP1,000 at 6.056%. At year-end you must pay back:

    $$1,000 \text{ GBP} \times 1.06056 = \text{GBP}1,060.56$$

- Convert the borrowed pounds to dollars:

    $$\left(\frac{1,000 \text{ GBP}}{0.7045 \dfrac{\text{GBP}}{\text{USD}}} \right) = 1,419.45 \text{ USD}$$

- Lend out the USD1,419.45 in the U.S. at 5.95%. At year-end you will have:

    $$1,419.45 \text{ USD} \times 1.0595 = 1,503.91 \text{ USD}$$

- Simultaneously, enter into a 1-year forward contract to convert USD back to GBP at the forward rate of 0.7327 GBP/USD.

- When the USD investment matures, collect the interest and principal (1,503.91 USD) and convert it back to GBP:

    $$1,503.91 \text{ USD} \times \left(0.7327 \frac{\text{GBP}}{\text{USD}} \right) = 1,101.91 \text{ GBP}$$

- After you pay off your GBP1,000 loan and interest for GBP1,060.56, you will have GBP41.35 left over.

So it is profitable to borrow money in the U.K. and make a hedged loan in the U.S. You will continue to do this until the money markets (interest rates) and exchange rates adjust and interest rate parity holds.

Example (continued): Another perspective on covered interest arbitrage

Let's do this example again, looking at things from a slightly different perspective. Recall that the purpose of interest rate parity is to keep the hedged foreign interest rate (the foreign rate expressed in domestic terms) equal to the domestic interest rate. Since this *must* be the case, recall that we rewrote IRP by setting the domestic rate equal to the hedged foreign rate:

$$1{,}503.91 \text{ USD} \times \left(0.7327 \, \frac{\text{GBP}}{\text{USD}} \right) = 1{,}101.91 \text{ GBP}$$

If we put the data from the previous example into this relationship, we get the following:

$$1.06056 \neq 1.0595 \text{USD} \left(\frac{0.7327 \text{GBP}}{0.7045 \text{USD}} \right) = 1.1019 \text{GBP}$$

We find that the domestic rate is 6.056%, whereas the hedged foreign rate is 10.19% (multiplying the foreign interest rate by F/S serves to *lock-in* the foreign rate in domestic terms). Your goal here is to *borrow at the low rate* and *lend at the high rate*. Hence, your arbitrage procedure is to borrow pounds, convert these pounds into dollars at today's spot rate, lend these dollars in the U.S., and simultaneously enter into a forward contract to sell dollars for pounds. Through this procedure, you will have an arbitrage profit.

KEY CONCEPTS

1. Direct foreign exchange quotations are in domestic currency per unit (or 100 units) of foreign currency and indirect quotations are in the foreign currency per unit of the domestic currency.

2. The difference between the bid and ask prices for foreign currency is the spread, sometimes expressed as a percentage of the ask price.

3. Foreign currency spreads increase with exchange rate volatility and decrease with increased trading volume, but the size of the spread is not dependent on dealer positions in the market.

4. The reciprocals of the bid and ask as a direct quote are an indirect quote, but viewed from the foreign country the bid and ask are reversed.

5. The exchange rates of two countries with a third can be used to obtain a cross rate (of exchange) between the two countries.

6. Forward foreign exchange rates are for currency to be exchanged at a future date while spot rates are for immediate delivery.

7. Forward foreign exchange rates have a bid-ask spread calculated as for spot rates.

8. The forward contract price is said to be at a forward premium (discount) for a currency if the direct quote of the forward rate is higher (lower) than the spot rate.

9. A forward premium or discount is often stated as an annualized percentage of the spot rate as:

$$\left(\frac{\text{forward rate}}{\text{spot rate}}-1\right)\left(\frac{360}{\text{term in days}}\right)$$

10. Interest rate parity equates forward premiums or discounts to interest rate differentials between countries

by the relation: $\dfrac{\text{forward}\left(\dfrac{DC}{FC}\right)}{\text{spot}\left(\dfrac{DC}{FC}\right)}=\dfrac{1+r_{\text{domestic}}}{1+r_{\text{foreign}}}$

11. When interest rate parity does not hold, there is a profitable arbitrage either from lending a currency that has a forward rate above the parity value or borrowing a currency that has a forward rate below the parity value.

CONCEPT CHECKERS: FOREIGN EXCHANGE

1. The spot and 30-day forward rates for the Australian dollar (AUD) are USD0.3075 and USD0.3120, respectively. The AUD is selling at a forward:
   A. discount of USD0.0045.
   B. premium of USD0.0045.
   C. rate of USD0.3075.
   D. neither a premium nor a discount.

2. Suppose that the quote for British pounds (GBP) in New York is 1.3110 USD/GBP. What is the quote for U.S. dollars (USD) in London (GBP/USD)?
   A. 1.3110.
   B. 0.3110.
   C. 0.7628.
   D. 0.2372.

3. The interest rates in the U.S. (USD) and Sweden (SEK) are 4% and 7% per year, respectively. If the current spot rate is 9.5238 SEK/USD, then the 1-year forward rate in SEK/USD from the perspective of a U.S. investor is:
   A. 9.2568 SEK/USD.
   B. 10.2884 SEK/USD.
   C. 10.1905 SEK/USD.
   D. 9.7985 SEK/USD.

4. Interest rates are 10% in the U.S. and 4% in Switzerland (CHF), respectively, and the 1-year forward rate is USD0.80/CHF. If interest rate parity holds, today's spot rate:
   A. cannot be determined using the above information.
   B. must be 0.8462 USD/CHF.
   C. must be 0.7564 USD/CHF.
   D. must be 0.8888 USD/CHF.

5. The spot rate on the New Zealand dollar (NZD) is 1.4286 NZD/USD, and the 180-day forward rate is 1.3889 NZD/USD. This difference means:
   A. interest rates must be lower in the U.S. than in New Zealand.
   B. interest rates must be higher in the U.S. than in New Zealand.
   C. the NZD is expected to depreciate.
   D. the dollar is expected to appreciate.

6. Today's spot rate for the Indonesian rupiah (IDR) is 2,400 IDR/USD, and the New Zealand dollar trades at 1.60 NZD/USD. The NZD/IDR cross rate is:
   A. 0.00067 NZD/IDR.
   B. 1,492.53 NZD/IDR.
   C. 3,840 NZD/IDR.
   D. 0.00015 NZD/IDR.

7. An American wants to buy six cases of champagne. Each case costs 390 SEK. If the SEK/USD exchange rate is 6.90, what is the USD cost of the champagne?
   A. USD2,340.00.
   B. USD56.52.
   C. USD241.50.
   D. USD339.13.

8. Today's spot USD/NZD ask exchange rate is 0.6010, and the bid is 0.6000. The percentage spread on the USD is:
A. 0.6600%.
B. 0.1664%.
C. 6.0010%.
D. 1.5151%.

9. Suppose that the spot rate for the dollar is 0.7102 USD/CHF. Swiss and U.S. interest rates are 7.6% and 5.2%, respectively. If the 1-year forward rate is 0.7200 USD/CHF, a U.S. investor could earn an arbitrage profit per dollar invested of:
A. USD0.0000.
B. USD0.7200.
C. USD1.0908.
D. USD0.0388.

10. The NZD is trading at 0.3500 USD/NZD and the SEK is trading at 0.3100 NZD/SEK. The USD/SEK exchange rate is:
A. 0.1129 USD/SEK.
B. 9.2166 USD/SEK.
C. 0.1085 USD/SEK.
D. 0.1050 USD/SEK.

11. Suppose that the quote for GBP in New York is 1.7574–84 USD/GBP. The equivalent quote for U.S. dollars in London would be:
A. 0.5687–90 GBP/USD.
B. 0.5690–87 GBP/USD.
C. 1.7574+09 GBP/USD.
D. 1.7584–09 GBP/USD.

12. Assuming no transaction costs, if a U.S. investor can make risk-free profits by borrowing the Japanese yen, then:
A. the hedged Japanese interest rate is low relative to the U.S. interest rate.

B. $1 + r_D < \dfrac{(1 + r_F)(\text{forward rate})}{\text{spot rate}}$.

C. the U.S. interest rate is low relative to the hedged Japanese interest rate.
D. the interest rate differential is approximately equal to the forward premium.

13. Assume the Philippine peso is at a 1-year forward discount of 1.25% to the Thai baht and that Thailand's 1-year interest rate is at 3.00%. If a Thai investor has no arbitrage opportunities, the Philippine interest rate is *closest* to:
A. 3.10%.
B. 4.25%.
C. 1.76%.
D. 1.25%.

14.   The bid-ask quote for yen (JPY) in London $\left(\frac{£}{JPY}\right)$ is 0.0050 – 0.00504. In New York, the bid-ask quote

for British pounds $\left(\frac{\$}{£}\right)$ is 1.671 – 1.678. What is the $\left(\frac{USD}{JPY}\right)$ ask as a cross rate?

A. 0.008390.
B. 0.008457.
C. 0.008422.
D. 0.008355.

ANSWERS – CONCEPT CHECKERS: FOREIGN EXCHANGE

1. **B**   USD0.3120 – USD0.3075 = USD0.0045 premium.

2. **C**   0.7628 = 1/1.311

3. **D**   The formula is as follows: forward (DC/FC) = spot (DC/FC)$\left(\dfrac{1+r_{domestic}}{1+r_{foreign}}\right)$. Since our quotes are in foreign/domestic

instead of domestic over foreign, it may be easier for us to express interest rate parity in FC/DC terms as

follows: forward (FC/DC) = spot (FC/DC)$\left(\dfrac{1+r_{foreign}}{1+r_{domestic}}\right)$. Hence, the forward rate in SEK/USD is

$9.7985 = 9.5238\left(\dfrac{1.07}{1.04}\right)$. Since it takes more SEK to buy a USD in the forward market, the forward SEK is

depreciating relative to the USD. The forward SEK must be depreciating because the Swedish interest rate exceeds
the U.S. rate, and the purpose of interest rate parity is to keep the hedged foreign rate equal to the domestic rate.
You can either invest in the U.S. at 4% or in Sweden at 7%. When you lock in your Swedish lendings by selling
SEK forward, you *must* face a loss of 3% on this forward currency trade.

4. **C**   We can solve interest rate parity for the spot rate as follows:

$$\text{spot (DC/FC)} = \text{forward (DC/FC)}\left(\frac{1+r_{foreign}}{1+r_{domestic}}\right)$$

Hence, spot is $0.7564 = 0.80\left(\dfrac{1.04}{1.10}\right)$. Since the interest rate is higher in the U.S., it should take fewer USD to buy

CHF in the spot market. In other words, the forward USD must be depreciating relative to the spot.

5. **B**   Interest rates are higher in the U.S. than in New Zealand. It should take fewer NZD to buy a USD in the forward
market as the forward NZD appreciates.

6. **A**   (1.60 NZD/USD) / (2,400 IDR/USD) = 0.00067 NZD/IDR

7. **D**   Total SEK cost = 390 × 6 = 2,340 SEK. Invert the quote = 1 / 6.9 = 0.1449 USD/SEK.

Total dollar cost = 0.1449 USD/SEK × 2,340 SEK = USD339.13.

8. **B**   The USD percent spread = $\dfrac{0.6010-0.6000}{0.6010}(100) = 0.1664\%$.

9. **D**   To determine any arbitrage opportunities, you should first examine the interest rate parity relationship:

$$(1 + r_D) < \frac{(1+r_F)(\text{forward rate})}{\text{spot rate}}$$

$$1.052 < \frac{(1.076)(0.72)}{0.7102} = 1.0908$$

By viewing this relation, we find that the investor will want to borrow in the U.S. and lend in Switzerland.

Today:
- Borrow USD1 at 5.2%. (You will owe $1 \times 1.052 = \$1.052$ at the end of the year.)
- Exchange $1 borrowed and buy CHF = $1/0.7102 = 1.408$ CHF at spot rate.
- Lend the purchased CHF at the Swiss rate (you will receive 1.408 CHF $\times 1.076 = 1.5150$ in one year).
- Purchase a forward contract to sell the 1.5150 CHF and buy $1.098 USD (1.5150 CHF $\times$ 0.7200 USD/CHF = 1.0908 USD) to pay off the loan.

In one year:
- Close the Swiss savings account. Proceeds: $(1.408)(1.076) = 1.5150$ CHF.
- Use the proceeds of the savings account to purchase USD1.0908 at the prespecified forward rate (1.515 CHF $\times$ 0.72 USD/CHF).
- Pay off the loan. Money needed = USD1 $\times 1.052 =$ USD1.052.
- Riskless profit = USD1.0908 – USD1.052 = USD0.0388.

10. **C**   0.3500 USD/NZD $\times$ 0.3100 NZD/SEK = 0.1085 USD/SEK. Notice that the NZD cancels in the multiplication.

11. **A**   Invert the quotes: $1/1.7574 = 0.5690$ and $1/1.7584 = 0.5687$. Remember, when you invert a quote, the ask becomes the bid for the other currency and vice versa. So the quote is 0.5687–90 GBP/USD in London.

12. **A**   Stating that an investor can make risk-free profits is just another way of saying that arbitrage opportunities exist. This choice is equivalent to saying that the domestic (U.S.) rate is high relative to the hedged foreign rate, or

$1 + r_D > \dfrac{(1+r_F)(\text{forward rate})}{\text{spot rate}}$. The other statements are false (note that choices B and C are the same). If the U.S.

interest rate is low relative to the Japanese hedged interest rate, a U.S. investor could earn risk-free profits by borrowing domestic. When the interest rate differential is approximately equal to the forward premium, interest rate parity holds, and there are *no* arbitrage profits.

13. **B**   If there are no arbitrage opportunities, IRP holds, and the interest rate differential is equal to the forward differential, or $r_d - r_f = -0.0125$, $0.030 - r_f = -0.0125$, $r_f = 0.0425 = 4.25\%$.

14. **B**   To buy a JPY with USD, we buy a pound at the New York ask of $1.678. We can use that pound to buy

$\dfrac{1}{0.00504} = 198.41$ JPY in London. The cost of each JPY in USD is $\dfrac{1.678}{198.41} = 0.008457$.

The following is a review of the Economics principles designed to address the learning outcome statements set forth by CFA Institute®. This topic is also covered in:

FOREIGN EXCHANGE PARITY RELATIONS

EXAM FOCUS

This review focuses on the balance-of-payments accounts and the factors that influence exchange rates between countries. Concentrate your efforts on understanding the components of the current account and the financial account. If a country's imports exceed exports (current account deficit), then the difference must be made up by investment by foreigners in the physical or financial assets of the country. You should be able to explain both absolute and relative purchasing power parity and how fixed and pegged exchange rate systems differ. Finally, understand the effects of monetary and fiscal policy on the current account and financial account. Try to grasp the analytical arguments about how monetary and fiscal policy affect the balance-of-payments accounts through their effects on inflation, incomes, and real interest rates.

Professor's Note: A previous review referred to the capital account, which is also called the financial account. The terms are interchangeable.

LOS 32.a: Explain how exchange rates are determined in a flexible or floating exchange rate system.

Exchange rates are determined by supply and demand in a flexible exchange rate system (also called a floating exchange rate system). If there is an excess demand for U.S. dollars by Australians at the current exchange rate, they will sell AUD and buy U.S. dollars. This will cause the U.S. dollar to appreciate relative to the AUD. Intuitively, when might this happen? Australians would create an excess demand for U.S. dollars if they desired to increase their *imports* of U.S. goods. In order to buy U.S. goods, Australians need U.S. dollars. Hence, the value of the U.S. dollar rises relative to the AUD.

LOS 32.b: Explain the role of each component of the balance-of-payments accounts.

Balance-of-payments (BOP) accounting is a method used to keep track of transactions between a country and its international trading partners. It includes government transactions, consumer transactions, and business transactions. The balance-of-payments accounts reflect all payments and liabilities to foreigners and all payments and obligations received from foreigners. The BOP equation is:

current account + financial account + official reserve account = 0

The **current account** measures the exchange of merchandise goods, the exchange of services, the exchange of investment income, and unilateral transfers (gifts to and from other nations). The *balance on current account* summarizes the balance on goods and services, the exchange of investment income, and unilateral transfers. All other factors constant, a deficit balance on a country's current account implies that there is an excess supply of its currency in foreign exchange markets. Hence, its currency should depreciate (decline in value).

The **financial (capital) account** measures the flow of funds for debt and equity investment into and out of the country. All other factors constant, a surplus balance in a country's financial account implies that there is an excess demand for assets denominated in its currency. Hence, its currency should appreciate.

Official reserve account transactions are funds held at the *International Monetary Fund* (IMF) in the form of gold, other foreign currencies, and special drawing rights at the IMF. In 1997, the U.S. ran a current account deficit and a smaller surplus in its capital account. As a result, the U.S. ran a surplus in the reserve account to

---

balance the BOP account. These reserve balances are used by the Fed to *intervene* in the foreign-exchange markets in an attempt to loosely control exchange rates.

Professor's Note: For the exam, assume that the official reserve account is equal to zero (or fixed). Then, if you are given (or you determine) a change in the current account, say a decrease, you know that the financial account must change in the opposite direction, or increase. The current account measures exports minus imports, while the financial account measures the flow of capital transactions. If a country imports more than it exports, the difference must be made up by foreign investment (i.e., an increase in the financial account).

LOS 32.c: Explain how current account deficits or surpluses and financial account deficits or surpluses affect an economy.

Is a nation's current account balance a good measure of its economic health? No, there is no law, economic or political, which states that the current account must be positive to indicate economic health. Unlike running a *budget deficit* in which a person or institution spends more than it makes, running a deficit in the current account balance simply means a country imports more than it exports, and a country can do this for a long time. Also, countries that run current account deficits tend to run financial account surpluses so that they offset each other. Is an inflow of capital bad? No, if the capital is being invested in such a way as to enhance the productive capacity of the country. Is a current account surplus and financial account deficit an indication of economic strength? No, particularly if this occurs because there are few good investment opportunities in the country to attract investment and there are more attractive investment opportunities abroad.

LOS 32.d: Describe the factors that cause a nation's currency to appreciate or depreciate.

There are *three major factors* that cause a country's currency to appreciate or depreciate relative to another's.

- **Differences in income growth** among nations will cause nations with the highest income growth to demand more imported goods. The heightened demand for imports will increase demand for foreign currencies, appreciating the foreign currencies relative to the domestic currency.
- **Differences in inflation rates** will cause the residents of the country with the highest inflation rate to demand more imported (cheaper) goods. For example, if prices in the U.S. are rising twice as fast as in Australia, U.S. citizens will increase their demand for Australian goods (because Australian goods are now cheaper relative to domestic goods). If a country's inflation rate is higher than its trading partners', the demand for the country's currency will be low, and the currency will depreciate.
- **Differences in real interest rates** will cause a flow of capital into those countries with the highest available *real* rates of interest. Therefore, there will be an increased demand for those currencies, and they will appreciate relative to the currencies of countries whose available real rate of return is low.

Figure 1 summarizes the factors that cause a nation's currency to appreciate or depreciate.

Figure 1: Factors That Affect Currency Movements

Factors*	Lower	Higher
Income growth rate	Appreciation	Depreciation
Inflation rate	Appreciation	Depreciation
Domestic real interest rate	Depreciation	Appreciation

* relative to trading partners.

LOS 32.e: Explain how monetary and fiscal policies affect the exchange rate and balance-of-payments components.

Exchange rate effects. Since monetary and fiscal policies affect income growth, inflation, and real interest rates, they will also influence exchange rates. The monetary and fiscal policy effects on exchange rates discussed below are only relevant in a system of flexible (floating) exchange rates.

An unanticipated shift to an expansionary monetary policy will lead to more rapid economic growth, an accelerated inflation rate, and lower real interest rates. The rapid economic growth stimulates imports, the higher inflation rate makes domestic products more expensive, which reduces exports, and the low real interest rate reduces foreign investment. Each of these factors increases the demand for foreign currencies relative to the domestic currency, causing the domestic currency to *depreciate*. Given an unanticipated shift to a restrictive monetary policy, the opposite occurs.

An unanticipated shift to a more restrictive fiscal policy will result in budget surpluses. The reduced aggregate demand causes an economic slowdown and lower inflation. These factors discourage imports and encourage exports, resulting in appreciation of the domestic currency. However, budget surpluses suggest that government borrowing declines, which reduces real rates and causes investment funds to flow out of the country. As a result, the domestic currency tends to depreciate. Thus, the results are conflicting. However, since financial capital is mobile, the effect of the interest rate change generally dominates in the short run, leading to short-run depreciation. Given an unanticipated shift to an expansionary fiscal policy, appreciation occurs.

BOP component effects. Monetary and fiscal policy can also affect the current and financial accounts through their impact on income, inflation, and real interest rates.

An unanticipated shift to an expansionary monetary policy will lead to higher income, an accelerated inflation rate, and lower real interest rates. The higher income and higher domestic prices stimulate imports and discourage exports, causing the current account balance to move toward deficit. The lower real interest rate discourages foreign and domestic investment at home, moving the financial account toward deficit. At the same time, the value of the domestic currency declines because of the earlier shift to imports. Now, however, the depreciation in the domestic currency encourages exports and discourages imports. This more than offsets the movement toward deficit in the current account. Thus, the impact of an unanticipated shift to an expansionary monetary policy will be a shift toward a deficit in the financial account and a shift toward surplus in the current account. An unanticipated shift to a more restrictive monetary policy produces opposite effects.

An expansionary change in fiscal policy (to a larger budget deficit) will cause an increase in aggregate demand and an increase in domestic interest rates (due to crowding out). The increased aggregate demand encourages imports, which moves the current account toward deficit. Meanwhile, the higher interest rates attract foreign investment and discourage domestic investment from leaving the country. Thus, the financial account will move toward surplus. An unanticipated shift to a budget surplus would produce opposite results.

Figure 2 summarizes the impacts of expansionary monetary and fiscal policy on currency rates, the current account, and the financial account. The impacts of restrictive policy are the reverse.

Figure 2: Impacts of Expansionary Monetary and Fiscal Policy

Policy	Currency	Current Account	Financial Account
Monetary policy	Depreciation	Surplus	Deficit
Fiscal policy	Appreciation	Deficit	Surplus

Professor's Note: Here's where the "trick" about assuming that the BOP official reserve account is fixed comes in handy. As long as you know the impact on the current account, you know the impact on the financial account is the opposite.

LOS 32.f: Describe a fixed exchange rate and a pegged exchange rate system.

Up until now, we have been dealing with flexible exchange rate systems. There are two other exchange rate systems that may also occur: a fixed exchange rate system and a pegged exchange rate system.

A **fixed exchange rate system** has a set rate of exchange and is supported by giving up discretion in monetary policy. Some countries fix their exchange rates to other currencies, such as the U.S. dollar, and sacrifice independent monetary policy. For example, Panama, Hong Kong, and the U.S. have a unified currency. The non-U.S. countries accomplish this through the use of a *currency board*, which has the power to create domestic currency only in exchange for a specific quantity of U.S. dollars they hold in bonds and other liquid assets. The currency board promises to redeem the domestic currency at the fixed exchange rate into dollars.

The EU has a similar system with the 11 countries that have joined the system using the euro as the unified currency. The distinguishing characteristic of a fixed-rate, unified currency system is the existence of only one central bank that can increase or decrease the money supply. A country that imports more than it exports under this system will find a net decrease in the money supply, which should lead to downward pressure on prices. Lower prices should reverse the export-import relationship until the country's exports begin to exceed its imports.

A **pegged exchange rate system** involves a commitment of a country to use fiscal and monetary policy to maintain the country's exchange rate within a narrow band relative to another (stronger) currency or to a bundle of currencies. This type of system requires a country to use its monetary policy to maintain the desired exchange rate.

LOS 32.g: Discuss absolute purchasing power parity and relative purchasing power parity.

The *law of one price* states that identical goods should have the same price in all locations. For instance, a pair of designer jeans should cost the same in New York and London after adjusting for the exchange rate. The potential for arbitrage profits is the basis for the law of one price. If widgets cost less in New York than in Paris, an enterprising individual will buy widgets in New York and sell them in Paris until the price differential disappears. The law of one price does not hold in practice due to the effects of tariffs and transportation costs.

Instead of focusing on individual products, **absolute PPP** compares the average price of goods between countries. Absolute PPP only requires that the law of one price is correct *on average*.

So, according to absolute PPP, the ratio of the weighted average of the prices of all goods in two economies should equal the exchange rate. In practice, such weighted averages are never calculated and, even if the law of one price held for every good in the two economies, absolute PPP might not hold. This could be the case, since the weights of the various goods in the two economies may not be the same. Absolute PPP is not used in practice to predict exchange rate movements, and the weighted-average price of all goods in an economy is not calculated in any event.

Relative PPP

The practical measure of the change in a country's price level is a price index, such as the CPI or the GDP deflator. Either can be used to calculate the inflation rate based on a particular "basket" of goods and services. **Relative purchasing power parity** is based on a relation between exchange rate movements and differences in inflation rates between two countries. Simply put, if (over a 1-year period) Country A has a 6% inflation rate and Country B has a 4% inflation rate, then Country A's currency should *depreciate* by approximately 2% relative to Country B's currency over the period. Relative PPP states that changes in exchange rates should exactly offset any inflation differential between the two countries.

We can express the relative PPP relationship (over one period) as:

$$\frac{\text{expected exchange rate at time 1}}{\text{spot exchange rate at time 0}} = \frac{1 + \text{domestic inflation}}{1 + \text{foreign inflation}}$$

where the spot exchange rates are expressed as direct quotes (DC/FC). Note that if the exchange rates are quoted as indirect rates (FC/DC) then the right-hand side of the equation must be inverted with foreign inflation in the numerator.

Professor's Note: To remember this formula, note that if the exchange rates are expressed as DC/FC, then the right-hand side of relative PPP is domestic/foreign as well, and vice versa! This is essentially the same formula we had for IRP, with interest rates replaced by inflation rates and the forward exchange rate replaced by the expected future spot rate.

Let's do the calculation for our 6% and 4% inflation rates example. Assume domestic inflation is 4%, foreign inflation is 6%, and initially each foreign currency unit is priced at 2 domestic currency units. We want to find the expected future spot exchange rate consistent with relative PPP.

Recall that the country with the higher inflation rate will see its currency depreciate. We expect the foreign currency to depreciate by 6 − 4 = 2%, relative to the domestic currency. This means that the price of a foreign currency unit (expressed in domestic currency units) will *decrease* by approximately 2%. It will decrease from 2 to $2 \times 0.98 = 1.96$ DC/FC.

Now let's use the exact relation to get the expected future spot rate under relative PPP based on these assumptions. Rearranging the relative PPP relation, we get:

$$\text{expected exchange rate at time 1} = \text{exchange rate at time 0} \times \left[\frac{1 + \text{domestic inflation}}{1 + \text{foreign inflation}} \right]$$

and we can solve for the expected exchange rate at time 1 as:

$$2 \times \frac{1.04}{1.06} = 1.9623 \text{ DC/FC}$$

Since we know that the currency with the higher inflation rate is expected to depreciate, we can see that we have applied the relation correctly because the value of a foreign currency unit is expected to decrease from 2 to 1.9623 domestic currency units. Given an indirect quote of 0.5 foreign currency units per domestic currency unit, we could calculate the expected future spot exchange rate as $0.5 \times \frac{1.06}{1.04} = 0.5096$ (more FC per DC unit indicates a depreciation of the FC).

Relative PPP is a theory, and while it tends to hold in the long run, violations of the relative PPP relation in the short run are common in real markets. With covered interest rate parity, we noted that arbitrage will move forward exchange rates to levels consistent with our parity relation. There is no arbitrage available to force the PPP relation to hold; the question is whether the relation can be used to predict future exchange rate movements (how well the relation predicts future spot rates).

The following example illustrates using the relative PPP relation to calculate the expected spot exchange rate more than one period in the future.

Example: Relative PPP

Suppose that the current spot quote for the Australian dollar is 0.20 USD/AUD. Also, annual Australian inflation is expected to be 10%, while annual U.S. inflation is expected to be 5%. Calculate the expected future spot rate in two years under relative PPP.

Answer:

$$\text{expected future exchange rate}_2 = 0.20 \left[\frac{1.05}{1.10}\right]^2 = 0.1822 \, USD/AUD$$

This example illustrates that to keep the relative cost of goods and services the same across borders, countries with higher rates of expected inflation should see their currencies depreciate. This is precisely what has happened in this example. Today it takes USD0.20 to buy each AUD. However, since prices are expected to rise faster in Australia relative to the U.S., it should only take USD0.1822 to buy each AUD two years from now. In a relative PPP world, the relative cost of Australian widgets to a U.S. purchaser will be constant after adjusting for exchange rates.

Closing Remarks on Purchasing Power Parity

Empirical evidence suggests that purchasing power parity does not hold, at least in the short run. That means exchange rates tend to change by amounts that differ from those implied by the inflation differentials. For example, suppose annual inflation for 2004 is 4% in the U.S. and 1% in Japan. Relative PPP would predict that the USD should have *depreciated* by 3% during the year. However, suppose that the USD actually *appreciates* by 2%. We would conclude that the USD is overvalued in relation to relative PPP. In other words, the USD is above its "fundamental" value.

Empirical research also suggests that relative PPP *does* tend to hold more closely over the longer term. Currencies that become overvalued or undervalued in relation to PPP over time tend to eventually revert to the long-term level predicted by relative PPP. That means relative PPP is somewhat useful in exchange rate determination in the short run because currencies that are overvalued relative to their PPP-determined fundamental value will tend to depreciate, while undervalued currencies will tend to appreciate. However, the adjustment period can sometimes be quite long (i.e., several years).

Professor's Note: It appears that we've made two contradictory statements: relative PPP doesn't hold in the short run, but it is useful in exchange rate determination. The key to understanding this LOS is to recognize that because relative PPP tends to hold in the long run, exchange rates that deviate from fundamental value in the short run tend to revert to the level predicted by relative PPP in the long run. We can use this fact to make short-run predictions: overvalued currencies will depreciate over time, while undervalued currencies will appreciate.

Absolute purchasing power parity is of little use in determining exchange rates. In order to directly compare the prices of goods and services between two countries, we would need to have identical individual goods and services to establish the validity of the law of one price. However, goods consumed are rarely identical between various countries. In reality, differences in taxes, transportation and labor costs, rents, and government controls (e.g., tariffs) between countries provide complexities that prevent direct comparison. Therefore, it's difficult (if not impossible) to confirm absolute PPP and to determine whether the exchange rates are under- or overvalued according to the theory of absolute PPP.

KEY CONCEPTS

1. Supply and demand determine the exchange rates in flexible (or floating) exchange rate systems; there is supply of and demand for every currency in the foreign exchange market.

2. The balance of payments is given by the equation:
current account balance + financial account balance + official reserve account balance = 0.
The current account includes the exchange of goods, services, and investment income, while the financial account includes payments for securities, direct investment, and bank deposits.

3. A current account deficit simply means that a country imports more than it exports and if offset by a surplus in the financial account, a deficit in the current account can continue for a long period with no apparent problem.

4. Three major factors cause a country's currency to appreciate or depreciate:
   • The growth rate of income relative to trading partners (high growth → depreciation).
   • The rate of inflation relative to trading partners (high inflation → depreciation).
   • Domestic real interest rates relative to those of other countries (high real rates → appreciation).

5. An unanticipated shift to an expansionary monetary policy causes higher income, accelerated inflation, and lower real interest rates, leading to currency depreciation, a current account surplus, and a financial account deficit, while restrictive monetary policy has the opposite effect.

6. An unanticipated shift to expansionary fiscal policy (a larger budget deficit) causes currency appreciation, a current account deficit, and a financial account surplus, while restrictive fiscal policy has the opposite effect.

7. A fixed exchange rate system exists when a country fixes its exchange rate to the currency of another country; a pegged exchange rate system involves a commitment to use fiscal and monetary policy to maintain the country's exchange rate within a narrow band relative to another currency.

8. Under absolute PPP, the average price of all goods should be the same across borders after adjustment has been made for exchange rates.

9. Relative PPP depends on the inflation rates in two countries:

$$\text{expected future exchange rate}_t = \text{spot rate} \times \left[\frac{1 + \text{inflation}_{\text{domestic}}}{1 + \text{inflation}_{\text{foreign}}} \right]^t$$

where the spot and expected exchange rates are direct quotes (DC/FC).

CONCEPT CHECKERS: FOREIGN EXCHANGE PARITY RELATIONS

1. If the U.S. dollar was quoted at AUD1.73 yesterday and today the U.S. dollar is trading at AUD1.80, the U.S. dollar has:
    A. appreciated, and will purchase less Australian goods.
    B. depreciated, and will purchase less Australian goods.
    C. appreciated, and will purchase more Australian goods.
    D. depreciated, and will purchase more Australian goods.

2. A country's currency will *appreciate* when its:
    A. imports rise in relation to its exports.
    B. current account moves from surplus to deficit.
    C. exports rise in relation to its imports.
    D. capital account is in surplus but not changing.

3. A country's currency will *depreciate* after:
    A. its income is growing slowly relative to the rest of the world.
    B. its inflation rate is lower than that of its trading partners.
    C. the real interest rate is lower than real rates in other countries.
    D. the monetary policy of the country becomes more restrictive.

4. If there were an unexpected decline in the growth rate of the money supply:
    A. real interest rates, output, and prices would fall, causing the dollar to depreciate.
    B. real interest rates would rise, causing an appreciation of the dollar.
    C. nothing would happen to exchange rates in the short run.
    D. real interest rates, output, and prices would rise, causing the dollar to appreciate.

5. The current account balance reflects the exchange of:
    A. merchandise only.
    B. goods and services only.
    C. goods, services, and investment income.
    D. goods, services, investment income, and unilateral transfers.

6. If the current account is in surplus, the *sum* of the financial account and official reserve transactions must be:
    A. in deficit.
    B. in surplus.
    C. equal to zero.
    D. non-negative.

7. In a flexible exchange rate system, the value of a currency is determined by the:
    A. amount of gold held in reserve.
    B. country's currency board.
    C. supply and demand for the country's currency in the foreign exchange markets.
    D. World Bank at its weekly executive-committee meeting.

8. Which of the following would be the *most likely* negative consequence for a country that ran a current account deficit for ten consecutive years?
    A. Hyperinflation.
    B. Rapid economic growth.
    C. High real interest rates.
    D. There would be no negative consequences.

9. Relative purchasing power parity:
    A. does not hold in the short run or the long run.
    B. tends to hold in both the short run and long run.
    C. tends to hold in the short run but not the long run.
    D. tends to hold in the long run but not the short run.

10. Assume that the current spot rate of exchange between the U.S. dollar (USD) and the euro (EUR) is EUR1.2500 per USD. The U.S inflation rate is expected to be 5% and the inflation rate in Europe is expected to be 4%. If relative purchasing power parity holds, the expected exchange rate three years from today is *closest* to:
    A. EUR1.0000.
    B. EUR1.2146.
    C. EUR1.2381.
    D. EUR1.2864.

ANSWERS – CONCEPT CHECKERS: FOREIGN EXCHANGE PARITY RELATIONS

1. C   If it took AUD1.73 to buy one U.S. dollar yesterday and today it takes AUD1.80 to buy one U.S. dollar, the dollar has appreciated and will purchase more Australian goods.

2. C   A country's currency will appreciate after its exports rise in relation to its imports. An increase in exports means that other countries are buying the country's currency, which increases its value.

3. C   A country's currency will depreciate when the real interest rate is lower than real rates in other countries. With a lower real interest rate, foreign investors will not buy the country's currency to invest.

4. B   If there were an unexpected decline in the growth rate of the money supply, real interest rates would rise, causing an appreciation of the dollar.

5. D   The current account balance reflects the exchange of merchandise, services, investment income, and unilateral transfers.

6. A   The balance-of-payments equation is:

    current account + financial account + official reserve account = 0

    So, if the current account balance is in surplus, the sum of the other two accounts must reflect a deficit in order for the sum of all three to be zero.

7. C   In a flexible exchange rate system, currency value is determined by the supply of and demand for the country's currency. Anything that affects the supply of or demand for the country's currency will affect the exchange rate.

8. D   A current account deficit simply means that a country imports more than it exports. There is no reason that this should have a negative effect on the country's economy. If it persists, it is an indication that the country's financial assets have been willingly purchased to maintain the balance of payments.

9. D   Relative PPP is a poor predictor of short-run exchange rate movements. However, purchasing power tends to converge to parity and relative PPP tends to hold in the long run.

10. B $EUR1.2500 \times \left[\dfrac{1.04}{1.05}\right]^3 = EUR1.2146$

    The higher expected rate of inflation in the U.S. should cause the USD to depreciate over the 3-year period. According to relative PPP, the expected depreciation is that which would make the relative cost of goods and services between the U.S. and Euroland the same at the end of the period after adjusting for inflation.

FORMULAS

price elasticity of demand = $\dfrac{\text{percent change in quantity demanded}}{\text{percent change in price}} = \dfrac{\%\Delta Q}{\%\Delta P}$

where: percent change = $\dfrac{\text{change in value}}{\text{average value}} = \dfrac{\text{ending value} - \text{beginning value}}{\left(\dfrac{\text{ending value} + \text{beginning value}}{2}\right)}$

cross elasticity of demand = $\dfrac{\text{percent change in quantity demanded}}{\text{percent change in price of substitute or complement}}$

income elasticity of demand = $\dfrac{\text{percent change in quantity demanded}}{\text{percent change in income}}$

price elasticity of supply = $\dfrac{\text{percent change in quantity supplied}}{\text{percent change in price}} = \dfrac{\%\Delta Q}{\%\Delta P}$

total cost = total fixed cost + total variable cost

marginal cost = $\dfrac{\text{change in total cost}}{\text{change in output}}$, or $MC = \dfrac{\Delta TC}{\Delta Q}$

average fixed cost = TFC / Q

average variable cost = TVC / Q

average total cost = AFC + AVC

unemployment rate = $\dfrac{\text{number of unemployed}}{\text{labor force}} \times 100$

labor force participation rate = $\dfrac{\text{labor force}}{\text{working-age population}} \times 100$

employment-to-population ratio = $\dfrac{\text{number of employed}}{\text{working-age population}} \times 100$

CPI = $\dfrac{\text{cost of basket at current prices}}{\text{cost of basket at base period prices}} \times 100$

$$\text{inflation rate} = \frac{\text{current price level} - \text{year-ago price level}}{\text{year-ago price level}} \times 100$$

aggregate demand = consumption + investment + government spending + net exports

potential deposit expansion multiplier = 1 / (required reserve ratio)

potential increase in money supply = potential deposit expansion multiplier × increase in excess reserves

equation of exchange:

money supply × velocity = GDP = price × real output

quantity theory of money:

$$\text{price} = \frac{MV}{Y}$$

balance of payments:

current account + capital account + official reserve account = 0

$$\begin{pmatrix} \text{forward premium} \\ \text{or discount} \end{pmatrix} = \left(\frac{\text{forward rate} - \text{spot rate}}{\text{spot rate}} \right) \left(\frac{360}{\text{number of forward contract days}} \right)$$

interest rate parity using direct quotes:

$$\frac{\text{forward}}{\text{spot}} = \left(\frac{1 + r_D}{1 + r_F} \right)$$

covered interest differential $= (1 + r_D) - \left(\dfrac{(1 + r_F)(\text{forward rate})}{\text{spot rate}} \right)$

purchasing power parity:

expected exchange rate at time 1 = exchange rate at time $0 \times \left[\dfrac{1 + \text{domestic inflation}}{1 + \text{foreign inflation}} \right]$

INDEX

Notes

Notes

Notes

Notes

Notes

Notes